THE LITERARY
COMPANION
TO CATS

THE LITERARY COMPANION TO CATS

An anthology of prose and poetry

collected by

Clare Boylan

SINCLAIR-STEVENSON

To Nora Lever
and all those who work to relieve
the suffering of animals

First published in Great Britain in 1994
by Sinclair-Stevenson
an imprint of Reed Consumer Books Ltd
Michelin House, 81 Fulham Road, London SW3 6RB
and Auckland, Melbourne, Singapore and Toronto

A CIP catalogue record for this book
is available at the British Library
ISBN 1 85619 394 2

Typeset by Falcon Graphic Art Ltd
Printed and bound in Great Britain
by Mackays of Chatham plc, Chatham, Kent

CONTENTS

LIST OF ILLUSTRATIONS

Elinor Glyn and friends; reproduced courtesy of the National Portrait Gallery, London

Colette and company; reproduced courtesy of the Hulton Deutsch Collection Ltd

Brigid Brophy; photograph by Jerry Bauer

Doris Lessing in 1956; photograph by Mark Gerson

Mervyn Peake with his wife Maeve Gilmore, and cat; reproduced courtesy of the Hulton Deutsch Collection Ltd

Ernest Hemingway with his cat Christopher Columbus at Finca Vigia; (photograph EH 3157 P) reproduced courtesy of the John F. Kennedy Library

Mark Twain and kitten, Connecticut; reproduced courtesy of the Mark Twain Memorial, Hartford, Connecticut

Barbara Pym; photograph by Mark Gerson

Antonia White; photograph by Norman Gold Photography

Dora Carrington with Tiger in 1929; reproduced courtesy of the Tate Gallery Archive, London

David Garnett; photograph courtesy of Macmillan London Ltd

Edith Sitwell with Leo in 1962; photograph by Mark Gerson

For that which befalleth the sons of men befalleth beasts; even one thing befalleth them: as the one dieth, so dieth the other; yea, they have all one breath; so that a man hath no preeminence above a beast: for all is vanity.

All go unto one place; all are of the dust, and all turn to dust again.

Who knoweth the spirit of man that goeth upward, and the spirit of the beast that goeth downward to the earth?

Ecclesiastes 3:19–22

INTRODUCTION

My only rule of thumb when compiling this volume was that the word "puss" should not be admitted, except in irony. This has excluded a good many poems by eminent poets of the eighteenth and nineteenth centuries but the particular works are included in most other anthologies and those who like that sort of thing will know them by heart already. I have compromised my policy only to admit Gertrude Jekyll's bizarre account of a pussies' tea party, simply because it would have delighted me so intensely when I was a child. Mawkish attitudes to cats strike me in the same way as sentimental attitudes to children: insensitive and unimaginative. Throughout history, *felis catus* has earned a good many sobriquets – Grimalkin, Musion, Luchtigern (the ancient Irish name for a cat, meaning 'Lord of the Mice'). "And he is called a catte of Greeks," John Boswell instructed us in *The Workes of Armorie* (1576), "because he is slye and wittie". Tradition has chosen not to condescend the cat and nor shall we.

There are more obvious omissions and these are for the reason of cost. Fashionable authors, dead or alive, tend to carry formidable price tags and with regret I have had to remove endearing, eccentric and well-loved extracts because their reproduction would have cost more than the author is likely to have earned in the year in which they were written. All of these are still in my original manuscript and if an ailurophile archive would like them, the Unexpurgated Cat may be viewed at some future date.

In the earlier centuries, items are in order of date. Nineteenth-century entries have been grouped roughly by theme and in the twentieth century, which is the weightiest part of the book, I have separated the mass with headings. There are additional sections for sayings, short stories, and one for wild cats. These are purely for pleasure.

Readers of this anthology may feel that it has slightly more bite than purr, and they will be correct. It is perfectly all right to be maudlin about dogs, which were created as companion for man and as a J-cloth for emotional spills. Man, on the other hand, was made as a valet for the cat, and the cat knows it and doles out his affections rather as a man of the world dispenses largesse upon his lackeys. Some cats are generous tippers and some are skinflints.

Either way, we are always flattered by their attention. Even relative ailurophobes such as Charles Dickens could be cajoled by the attentions of a particular cat.

My own experience is that cats are serendipitous in novels. On the one occasion when I excluded one, I got bad reviews. Around the house, cats are a presence, a comfort to the idle hand, a stillness for the restless mind and a reminder of the fulfilment of merely being. Cats, as Charles Baudelaire exquisitely expressed, "are the friends of learning and of sexual bliss".

A part of the attraction of cats is their aloofness, the sense that however playful and docile they may be they have other business to attend to, and that when the time comes to see to it they will be off. Every cat lover knows that moment when the blinking, amatory expression on a pet's face is suddenly replaced by one of icy disaffection. This 'other business' includes, but is not limited to, the prolonged and impersonal persecution of rodents and songbirds. When travelling incognito in the shrubbery, my cat often pretends she does not recognise me. I have seen a group of cats sit in a perfect circle in a field at dawn. This unknowable element of cats has caused men, throughout history, both to worship cats and to loathe them. The Egyptians revered them as gods (curiously, no Egyptian writings seem to exist on the theme, except for tomb inscriptions), but Herodotus reveals that the killing of a cat in Egypt, even by accident, carried a capital punishment. Cats failed to permeate the households or literature of ancient Romans (although Pliny praised them for their medical properties) but a thousand years later, Leonardo da Vinci was to declare: "The smallest feline is a work of art". In many places cats were associated with the devil. In ancient Ireland, live cats were bricked up into the walls of new houses so that their howls would deter evil spirits; others believed they *were* evil spirits. No animal in the world has attracted such extremes of deliberate cruelty and unquestioning adulation. For both cat haters and cat lovers it is precisely their independence that is the spur.

Stevie Smith speculated, "Why should such an animal provoke our love? It was the indifference of course, the beastly, truly beastly – that is, as appertaining to beasts." Stevie Smith also delightfully described cats as "a blank page on which to scrawl the hieroglyphics of our own grievance, bad temper and unhappiness, and scrawl also, of course, the desired sweet responses to these uncomfortable feelings". Interestingly, in the twentieth century they have become more than anything a cypher for our griefs. If I have a favourite part of this volume it is the twentieth-century section relating to the death of cats. These unsentimental tributes are written with the austerity of real grief. It is as if the emotional reticence of contemporary human relations leaves us only our little cats through which to express the full measure of love and loss. I find it impossible truly to grieve over cats. My best-loved cats have always come back in dreams. These are mad, galloping dreams in which the particular cat comes flying along the garden, delighted to see me. And I cannot but feel that the lamented and demented Mrs Monster (a bad-tempered female stray who came to have her kittens in our airing cupboard) conspired in the black comedy that was her demise. We were going on holiday, and I had commissioned a minder to look after Mrs Monster and to prepare a nice dinner for my husband's birthday, which coincided with our return. Menus for cat and mate were written out, with a request to cut hydrangeas from the garden for the festive table. We arrived home to a distinctly unfestive note: "Cat is in bin. P.S. What is hydrangeas?" I squeamishly parted parcels of refuse until I came to one filled with mouldering fluff. I buried it swiftly and deeply. When next I saw the good woman I determined the nature of the animal's passing (an encounter with a motor car) and the nature of her shroud (a supermarket bag). Slow and horrible realisation dawned. I had interred the carrier of a fashion store. The cat was still in the bin. But what was in the other bag? "Oh, that," said my home helper, "is where I emptied the hoover."

My most unwomaning feline sentiments have been reserved for old tom cats. Old females have very loud voices and are given to singing come-all-ye's of past wrongs (an unending tale of sexual harassment and multiple childbirth) to anyone who will listen. Old toms are humble and apologetic about their rake-hell pasts. They roll about in odd corners looking like burst cushions, for the sheer happiness of nothing in particular being amiss, and invest any remaining testosterone into a purr like a Harley-Davidson's. True cat lovers, such as Colette and T. S. Eliot and Stevie Smith and Baudelaire, loved cats for their jungle nature, their comic inconsequentiality, their beauty and perhaps above all for what still remains when these most beguiling gifts have been withdrawn. In over a year of trawling the library shelves and the mind-boggling quantity of cat anthologies that have been published, and in over twenty-five centuries of cat literature and reference, the following lines by Francis Scarfe remain for me the essential cat poem.

> *Those who love cats which do not even purr,*
> *Or which are thin and tired and very old,*
> *Bend down to them in the street and stroke their fur*
> *And rub their ears and smooth their breast, and hold*
> *Their paws, and gaze into their eyes of gold.*

1

THE
ANCIENT
WORLD

I might describe the utility of the ichneumon, the crocodile and the cat, but I
do not wish to be tedious.

Cicero, *De Natura Deorum Academica*

Venus and the Cat

In ancient times there lived a beautiful cat who fell in love with a young man. Naturally, the young man did not return the cat's affections, so she besought Venus, the goddess of love and beauty, for help. The goddess, taking compassion on her plight, changed her into a fair damsel.

No sooner had the young man set eyes on the maiden than he became enamoured of her beauty and in due time led her home as his bride. One evening a short time later, as the young couple were sitting in their chamber, the notion came to Venus to discover whether in changing the cat's form she had also changed her nature. So she set down a mouse before the beautiful damsel. The girl, reverting completely to her former character, started from her seat and pounced upon the mouse as if she would eat it on the spot, while her husband watched her in dismay.

The goddess, provoked by such clear evidence that the girl had revealed her true nature, turned her into a cat again.

> *Application*: WHAT IS BRED IN THE BONE WILL
> NEVER BE ABSENT IN THE FLESH.

> Aesop

Cat's Eye

The eyes of animals that see at night in the dark, cats, for instance, are shining and radiant, so much so that it is impossible to look upon them.

> From the *Natural History* by Pliny

A Sharp Tongue

In lions, pards, and all other animals of that class, and in cats as well, the tongue is covered with asperities, which overlap each other, and bear a strong resemblance to a rasp. Such being its formation, if the animal licks a man's skin, it will wear it away by making it thinner and thinner; for which reason it is that the saliva of even a perfectly tame animal, being thus introduced to the close vicinity of the blood, is apt to bring on madness.

From the *Natural History* by Pliny

Doctor's Ordures

When a pointed or other substance has stuck in the throat, by rubbing it externally with cat's dung, the substance, they say, will either come up again or pass downwards into the stomach.

For quartan fever, the magicians recommend cat's dung to be attached to the body, with the toe of a horned owl, and, that the fever may not be recurrent, not to be removed until the seventh paroxysm is passed. Who, pray, could have ever made such a discovery as this? And what, too, can be the meaning of this combination? Why, of all things in the world, was the toe of a horned owl made choice of? Other adepts in this art, who are more moderate in their suggestions, recommend for quartan fever, the salted liver of a cat that has been killed while the moon was on the wane, to be taken in wine just before the paroxysms come on.

Thorns and similar foreign substances are extracted from the body by using cats' dung, or that of she-goats, with wine.

Calf's marrow, boiled in wine and water with the suet, and applied as a pessary, is good for ulcerations of the uterus; the same, too, with foxes' fat and cats' dung, the last applied with resin and oil of roses.

Veal suet, pounded with salt and applied to the ulcers of the head, is a very useful remedy; the fat, too, of the fox is highly spoken of, but the greatest value is set upon cats' dung, applied in a similar manner with mustard.

From the *Natural History* by Pliny

Very Lascivious Females

Those animals in which there is a distinction of the sexes use sexual intercourse, but the mode of this intercourse is not the same in all, for all the males of sanguineous animals with feet have an appropriate organ, but they do not all approach the female in the same manner, but those which are retromingent, as the lion, the hare, and the lynx, unite backwards, and the female hare often mounts upon the male; in almost all the rest the mode is the same, for most animals perform the act of intercourse in the same way, the male mounting upon the female; and birds perform it in this way only . . . Cats do not approach each other backwards, but the male stands erect, and the female places herself beneath him. The females are very lascivious, and invite the male, and make a noise during the intercourse.

From *The History of Animals* by Aristotle

What Happens to Cats

There are many household animals; and there would be many more, were it not for what happens to the cats. When the females have kittened they will not consort with the males; and these seek them but cannot get their will of them; so their device is to steal and carry off and kill the kittens (but they do not eat what they have killed). The mothers, deprived of their young and desiring to have more will then consort with the males; for they are creatures that love offspring. And when a fire breaks out very strange things happen to the cats. The Egyptians stand round in a broken line, thinking more of the cats than of quenching the burning; but the cats slip through or leap over the men and spring into the fire. When this happens, there is great mourning in Egypt. Dwellers in a house where a cat has died a natural death shave their eyebrows and no more; where a dog has so died, the head and the whole body are shaven.

Dead cats are taken away into sacred buildings, where they are embalmed and buried, in the town of Bubastis; bitches are buried in sacred coffins by the townsmen, in their several towns; and the like is done with ichneumons. Shrewmice and hawks are taken away to Buto, ibises to the city of Hermes. There are but few bears, and the wolves are little bigger than foxes; both these are buried wherever they are found lying.

Herodotus

A Capital Offence

When one of these animals dies they wrap it in fine linen and then, wailing and beating their breasts, carry it off to be embalmed; and after it has been treated with cedar oil and such spices as have the quality of imparting a pleasant odour and of preserving the body for a long time, they lay it away in a consecrated tomb. And whoever intentionally kills one of these animals is put to death, unless it be a cat or an ibis that he kills; but if he kills one of these, whether intentionally or unintentionally, he is certainly put to death, for the common people gather in crowds and deal with the perpetrator most cruelly, sometimes doing this without waiting for a trial. And because of their fear of such a punishment any who have caught sight of one of these animals lying dead withdraw to a great distance and shout with lamentations and protestations that they found the animal already dead. So deeply implanted also in the hearts of the common people is their superstitious regard for these animals and so unalterable are the emotions cherished by every man regarding the honour due to them that once, at the time when Ptolemy their king had not as yet been given by the Romans the appellation of 'friend' and the people were exercising all zeal in courting the favour of the embassy from Italy which was then visiting Egypt and, in their fear, were intent upon giving no cause for complaint or war, when one of the Romans killed a cat and the multitude rushed in a crowd to his house, neither the officials sent by the king to beg the man off nor the fear of Rome which all the people felt were enough to save the man from punishment, even though his act had been an accident. And this incident we relate, not from hearsay, but we saw it with our own eyes on the occasion of the visit we made to Egypt.

But if what has been said seems to many incredible and like a fanciful tale, what is to follow will appear far more extraordinary. Once, they say, when the inhabitants of Egypt were being hard pressed by a famine, many in their need laid hands upon their fellows, yet not a single man was even accused of having partaken of the sacred animals. Furthermore, whenever a dog is found dead in any house, every inmate of it shaves his entire body and goes into mourning, and what is more astonishing than this, if any wine or grain or any other thing necessary to life happens to be stored in the building where one of these animals has expired, they would never think of using it thereafter for any purpose. And if they happen to be making a military expedition in another country, they ransom the captive cats and hawks and bring them back to Egypt, and this they do sometimes even when their supply of money for the journey is running short. As for the ceremonies connected with the Apis of Memphis, the Mnevis of Heliopolis and the goat of Mendes, as well as with the crocodile of the Lake of Moeris, the lion kept in the City of Lions (Leontopolis), as it is called, and many other ceremonies like them, they could easily be described, but the writer would scarcely be believed by any who had not actually witnessed them. For these animals are kept in sacred enclosures and are cared for by many men of distinction who offer them the most expensive fare; for they provide, with unfailing regularity, the finest wheaten flour or wheat-groats seethed in milk, every kind of sweetmeat made with honey, and the meat of ducks, either boiled or baked, while for the carnivorous animals birds are caught and thrown to them in abundance, and, in general, great care is given that they have an expensive fare. They are continually bathing the animals in warm water, anointing them with the most precious ointments, and burning before them every kind of fragrant incense; they furnish them with the most expensive coverlets and with splendid jewellery, and exercise the greatest care that they shall enjoy sexual intercourse according to the demands of nature; furthermore, with every animal they keep the most beautiful females of the same genus, which they call his concubines and attend to at the cost of heavy expense and assiduous service. When any animal dies they mourn for it as deeply as do those who have lost a beloved child, and bury it in a manner not in keeping with their ability but going far beyond the value of their estates. For instance, after the death of Alexander and just subsequently to the taking over of Egypt by Ptolemy the son of Lagus, it happened that the Apis in Memphis died of old age; and the man who was charged with the care of him spent on his burial not only the whole of the very large sum which had been provided for the animal's maintenance, but also borrowed in addition fifty talents of silver from Ptolemy. And even in our own day some of the keepers of these animals have spent on their burial not less than one hundred talents.

Diodorus of Sicily

Slyly They Will Sit

Cats too, with what silent stealthiness, with what light steps do they creep towards a bird! How slyly they will sit and watch, then dart out upon a mouse.

From *Natural History* by Pliny

Blaming the Cat

Both this and the following extract reveal that the cat's domestic reputation was just as poor in ancient Greece as it is today. Here Echion confesses to Agamemnon a heinous deceit concerning his son.

He's a bright lad with his head screwed on the right way, though a perfect terror for pet birds. I slaughtered three goldfinches the other day and told him it was the cat. He consoled himself with other pets and now he has taken up painting.

From *Leader of Fashion* by Petronius, transl. Mitchell

Blaming the Cat Again

Procleon complains to Leader of his imprisonment.

Ah, yes, but things were different then. I was a young man, quick-footed and light-fingered; at the height of my powers. And I wasn't under guard: I could get away quite safely. But this place is besieged: there's a whole battalion of heavy infantry right across my line of retreat. There are two of them down by the door, watching every move I make. Anyone'd think I was the cat, trying to make off with tomorrow's joint. They're the ones that have got the spits.

From *The Wasps* by Aristophanes

The Cat and the Mice

A cat, grown feeble with age, and no longer able to hunt for mice as she was wont to do, sat in the sun and bethought herself how she might entice them within reach of her paws.

The idea came to her that if she would suspend herself by the hind legs from a peg in the closet wall, the mice, believing her to be dead, no longer would be afraid of her. So, at great pains and with the assistance of a torn pillow case she was able to carry out her plan.

But before the mice could approach within range of the innocent-looking paws a wise old gaffer-mouse whispered to his friends: 'Keep your distance, my friends. Many a bag have I seen in my day, but never one with a cat's head at the bottom of it.'

Then turning to the uncomfortable feline, he said: 'Hang there, good madam, as long as you please, but I would not trust myself within reach of you though you were stuffed with straw.'

Application: HE WHO IS ONCE DECEIVED IS DOUBLY CAUTIOUS.

Aesop

2

WILD CATS

Beautiful death
Who puts on a spotted robe
When he goes to his victim

'The Leopard' (Yoruba poem)

The Greater Cats

The greater cats with golden eyes
Stare out between the bars.
Deserts are there, and different skies,
And night with different stars.
They prowl the aromatic hill,
And mate as fiercely as they kill,
And hold the freedom of their will
To roam, to live, to drink their fill;
But this beyond their wit know I:
Man loves a little, and for long shall die.

Their kind across the desert range
Where tulips spring from stones,
Not knowing they will suffer change
Or vultures pick their bones.
Their strength's eternal in their sight,
They rule the terror of the night,
They overtake the deer in flight,
And in their arrogance they smite;
But I am sage, if they are strong:
Man's love is transient as his death is long.

Yet oh, what powers to deceive!
My wit is turned to faith,
And at this moment I believe
In love, and scout at death.
I came from nowhere, and shall be
Strong, steadfast, swift, eternally:
I am a lion, a stone, a tree,
And as the Polar star in me
Is fixed my constant heart on thee.
Ah, may I stay for ever blind
With lions, tigers, leopards, and their kind.

Vita Sackville-West

Intimate Friendship with the Large Cats

I regret that I have never enjoyed an intimate friendship with one of the large cats. I envy those who have been on familiar terms with a lion or a leopard. I met a cheetah once, and I have never been more gratified than when this great lovely cat rolled over and purred when I scratched it under the chin. A friend of mine in Burma once had a leopardess who slept at the foot of his bed for over two years. Then one day when he was being attentive to the little daughter of a high official he noticed a look in Ruth's eyes (Ruth was the name of the leopardess) which made him think she was about to spring. He caught her quickly by the collar, but he felt he could not risk having her loose about the house any more, and so he presented her to the Rangoon Zoo. He used to visit her every day but she pined for him too much when he was away and a fortnight later she died of grief.

I think one would probably have to be a bachelor to win the devotion of a great cat. Siamese cats are intensely jealous, but their jealousy is manageable. A jealous lioness or leopardess would be another matter.

I have read several accounts of lion cubs growing up as domestic pets but I fancy that they always have to be banished soon after they are full grown. My friend's leopardess is the first I have heard of as a friend of man. Lion-taming and tiger-taming disgust me because I believe the relationship is based on fear, not upon affection, and if I had my way I would make performing tigers and lions illegal entertainment.

From 'No Cats About the House' by Compton Mackenzie

Kitty

In 1939 the writer Marcia Davenport received an unusual birthday present from her husband.

My birthday came along shortly after we moved to Great Marsh and Russell was late that day coming out from town. He had driven in his horrible old black Chrysler instead of taking the train. When I heard it come snarling in from the highroad I glanced out of the window of my room where I was changing my dress. Russell had driven down to the barn instead of stopping at the front door. I wondered what he was doing there. It was out of sight of the house. There was a long delay. Then I saw him walking slowly across the lawn. He was holding what looked like a long rope and on the other end of it – 'Damn!' I said aloud. I thought of the arrival of the cows in Vermont. In the dusk I could not see what he was leading but it looked big and tawny in colour. I thought he had bought a Great Dane. I was ready to kill him.

Then my cat Tam who was crouched beneath my hand on the window-sill suddenly began to swell like a blowfish. His spine went up, his claws came out, and he let out a noise that was both a hiss and a yowl. His eyes were sharper than mine. Russell had a lion on the end of a long chain. She was a cub three months old – my birthday present. She was enchanting. I named her Kitty. She was a perfect kitten in maximum. She played with strings and balls and bouncy toys; she rolled over and waved her huge paws when she was happy; she cried when she was lonely; she purred with a noise like a large electric motor. Her affection and enthusiasm were a little dangerous since she had no idea of her own strength – she weighed about sixty pounds – and she would fling herself at me, asking to play, or wrap her paws around my ankles. Stockings went at the rate of dozens a week, and lion scratches, even those from love-pats, can be toxic unlike those of felis domesticus. I settled for strong denim overalls, a long-sleeved jacket, and gloves when I went out to play with my pet. Tam was miserable. When Kitty was not in her loose-box in the barn she was tethered by her chain to a long wire between two trees, and Tam remained in my room, yowling with jealousy on the window-sill.

At first sight Kitty petrified most people, including the ice-man, who asked me, 'Is that there what I think that is?' Her favourite treat and toy on hot days was a lump of ice. She had sprung on to the first piece of ice when it slid off the back of the truck, and thereafter she bounded joyfully on her tether to greet the ice-man whenever he came. I assured him that Kitty was harmless but soon the local game warden came round. He could not make up his mind what he was supposed to do about Kitty. I offered to take out a licence for her.

He hadn't thought of that. In fact, there was no such thing, and no precedent for this situation. Was there a law applicable to Kitty? Well, not exactly. He stood watching Kitty who was amiably playing with a spray of rambler roses. He pushed his hat to the back of his head and said, 'Aw, shucks, it can stay.'

From *Too Strong for Fantasy* by Marcia Davenport

The Giddy Goat

While serving with the military police in Burma in 1893, Hector Hugh Munro (Saki) acquired a pet lion cub which gave him great delight. It was three months old when he wrote this boastful letter to his sister.

I hear you have a Persian kitten; of course I, who have the untamable carnivora of the jungle roaming in savage freedom through my rooms, cannot feel any interest in mere domestic cats, but I am not intolerant and I have no objection to your keeping one or two. My beast does not show any signs of getting morose; it sleeps on a shelf in its cage all day but comes out after dinner and plays the giddy goat all over the place. I should like to get another wild cat to chum with it, there are several species in Burma: the jungle-cat, the bay-cat, the lesser leopard-cat, the tiger-cat, marbled-cat, spotted wild-cat, and rusty-spotted cat; the latter, I have read, make delightful pets.

Saki (H. H. Munro)

Leopard

Gentle hunter
His tail plays on the ground
While he crushes the skull.

Beautiful death
Who puts on a spotted robe
When he goes to his victim.

Playful killer
Whose loving embrace
Splits the antelope's heart.

Yoruba poem

A Playful Panther

A letter from Colette to Maurice Goudeket from Saint-Tropez, August 1932.

Yesterday, about six, Jouve* arrived by car. He brought me a beautiful copy of *Paradis terrestres* on Japan paper . . . but that's nothing. In the car, he had a Congo panther, like the one I had, only more handsome, this one being larger (six or seven months old), with miraculously short ears and a pelt . . . But nothing can compare to this golden coat spotted with pure black. The face is more beautiful than mine too, nobler, more *fauve*. I locked all our animals indoors and rejoined Jouve on the road, where, on a leash and with two chambermaids doing nothing but looking after her, the panther played a game of attacking everything that passed by. She flung herself at my bare legs and we had a grand time. As soon as one pretends to take cover, she leaps with her arms spread wide and roaring with laughter. She began to chew grass, which meant she was thirsty. I opened a bottle of milk, which she gulped down with the noise of a dog, and then resumed playing. She went off to make peepee in the vineyard and tried to get into the garage rooms. She kept spitting at Moune, and Jouve, who knows how to treat animals, said 'Madame Moune is nervous.' With me she got along well from the start, except for a certain antagonism. But she's terribly strong already! She's used to riding in a car and . . . sleeps with her two maids, roars if left alone, and once settled down for the night, becomes tender, soft and well behaved. She's impeccably clean. Once in the car, she played at the lowered window, nibbling at me, offering me her beautiful paws, and spitting gently. But she will attack anything that runs or rolls, unhesitatingly. If you'd been here, you'd have noticed nothing else . . . But to own and love such a beast would amount to taking orders. One would have to retire from the world . . .

From *Letters from Colette*, sel. and trans. Robert Phelps

*Paul Jouve had done the illustrations for a limited edition of Colette's animal portraits called *Paradis terrestres*.

A Grateful Panther

Demetrius, the natural philosopher, relates an equally remarkable instance, in relation to a panther. The animal was lying in the middle of the road, waiting for some one to pass that way, when he was suddenly perceived by the father of one Philinus, an ardent lover of wisdom. Seized with fear, he immediately began to retreat; while the beast rolled itself before him, evidently with the desire of caressing him, at the same time manifesting signs of grief, which could not be misunderstood in a panther even. The animal had young ones, which had happened to fall into a pit at some distance from the place. The first dictates of compassion banished all fear, and the next prompted him to assist the animal. He accordingly followed her, as she gently drew him on by fixing her claws in his garment; and as soon as he discovered what was the cause of her grief and the price of his own safety, he took the whelps out of the pit, and they followed her to the end of the desert; whither he was escorted by her, frisking with joy and gladness, in order that she might more appropriately testify how grateful she was, and how little she had given him in return; a mode of acting which is but rarely found, among men even.

From the *Natural History* by Pliny

Some Especially Ferocious Wild Beasts

In ancient times Meïon became King of Phrygia and Lydia; and marrying Dindymê he begat an infant daughter, but being unwilling to rear her he exposed her on the mountain which was called Cybelus. There, in accordance with some divine providence, both the leopards and some of the other especially ferocious wild beasts offered their nipples to the child and so gave it nourishment and some other women who were tending the flocks in that place witnessed the happening, and being astonished at the strange event took up the babe and called her Cybelê after the name of the place.

Diodorus of Sicily

A Most Disagreeable Odour

There are two species of lions; in the one the body is shorter and more compact, and the mane more crisp and curly; these are more timid than those with a longer body and straight hair, which, in fact, have no fear of wounds. The males raise the leg like the dog, when they pass their urine; which has a most disagreeable odour, the same being the case too with their breath.

From the *Natural History* by Pliny

To Abate Abominable Desires

To foreign countries, also, belongs the lynx, which of all quadrupeds is possessed of the most piercing sight. It is said that in the Isle of Carpathus a most powerful medicament is obtained by reducing to ashes the nails of the lynx, together with the hide; that these ashes, taken in drink, have the effect of checking abominable desires in men; and that, if they are sprinkled upon women, all libidinous thoughts will be restrained. They are good too for the removal of itching sensations in any part of the body. The urine of the lynx is a remedy for strangury; for which reason the animal, it is said, is in the habit of rooting up the ground and covering it the moment it is voided. It is mentioned, too, that this urine is an effectual remedy for pains in the throat. Thus much with reference to foreign animals.

From the *Natural History* by Pliny

Ten Remedies Derived from the Lion

Lion's fat, mixed with oil of roses, protects the skin of the face from all kinds of spots, and preserves the whiteness of the complexion; it is remedial also for such parts of the body as have been frozen by snow, and for swellings in the joints. The frivolous lies of the magicians assert that persons who are anointed with lion's fat, will more readily win favour with kings and peoples; more particularly when the fat has been used that lies between the eyebrows of the animal – a place, in fact, where there is no fat to be found! The like effects they promise also from the possession of a lion's tooth, one from the right side in particular, as also the shaggy hairs that are found upon the lower jaw. The gall, used as an ointment in combination with water, improves the eyesight, and employed with the fat of the same animal, is a cure for epilepsy; but a slight taste only must be taken of it, and the patient must run immediately after swallowing it, in order to digest it. A lion's heart, used as food, is curative of quartan fevers, and the fat, taken with oil of roses, of quotidian fevers. Wild beasts will fly from persons anointed with lion's fat, and it is thought to be a preservative even against treacherous practices.

From the *Natural History* by Pliny

The Food of Lions

Petronius was squeamish about the dining arrangements of lions destined for the amphitheatre.

> Lo! death on death, and wounds of murdered peace:
> Gold buys the forest-lion; Hammon's scoured
> For Afric's end that no beast's fang might be missed
> Of killing value: death brought home, kills man,
> While tigers stalk their gilded cage on board,
> Destined to drink men's blood 'mid cheers of men.

From *Leader of Fashion* by Petronius, transl. Mitchell

Poet-Bellied

Pet lions could not eat Christians, but their nourishment could still be a source of human suffering.

> Numitor can't spare a penny
> For a friend in need, though his mistress never goes short,
> And he scraped up enough (remember?) to purchase that tame lion –
> Not to mention the meat it scoffed. Of course it comes cheaper
> To feed a lion than a poet: poets have bigger bellies.

From *Satire VII* by Juvenal

Waving or Dining

Stevie Smith once proved a tempting morsel for a tiger confined in Edinburgh zoo.

Best of all, is the cat hunting. Then indeed it might be a tiger, and the grass it parts in passing, not our green English, or sooty town grass, but something high in the jungle, and sharp and yellow. But cats have come a long way from tigers, this tiger-strain is also something that can be romanticised. In Edinburgh's beautiful zoo, last summer with some children, I stopped outside the tiger's glass-bound cage. He was pacing narrowly, turning with a fine swing in a narrow turn. Very close to me he was, this glass-confinement needing no guard-rails. I looked in his cold eyes reading cruelty there and great coldness. Cruelty? . . . is not this also a romanticism? To be cruel one must be self-conscious. Animals cannot be cruel, but he was I think hungry. To try it out, to see whether I – this splendid human 'I' – could impinge in any way upon this creature in his anteprandial single-mindedness, I made a quick hissing panting sound, and loud, so that he must hear it – hahr, hahr, hahr, that sort of sound, but loud. At once the great creature paused in his pacing and stood for a moment with his cold eyes close to mine through the protecting glass (and glad I was to have it there). Then suddenly, with my 'hahrs' increasing in violence, this animal grows suddenly mad with anger. Ah then we see what a tiger – a pussycat too? – driven to it, can do with his animal nature and his passion. Up reared my tiger on his hind legs, teeth bared to the high gums, great mouth wide open on the gorge of his terrible throat. There, most beautifully balanced on his hind legs he stood, and danced a little too on these hind paws of his. His forepaws he waved in the air, and from each paw the poor captive claws scratched bare air and would rather have scratched me. This great moment made the afternoon for me, and for the children too and for my old friend, their mama (and for the tiger I daresay) and cosily at tea afterwards in Fullers we could still in mind's eye see our animal, stretched and dancing for anger.

Though pussycat has come so far down the line from his tiger ancestry, from jungle to hearthrug, or to those London graveyards where the grass grows 'as thin as hair in leprosy' as Browning put it, and where I have often seen tib and tom at work, there does still remain a relationship, something as between a Big Cat and a little one, that you will not find between cat big or little and a dog.

From *Me Again* by Stevie Smith

Mountain Lion

Climbing through the January snow, into the Lobo Canyon
Dark grow the spruce-trees, blue is the balsam, water sounds
    still unfrozen, and the trail is still evident.
Men!
Two men!
Men! The only animal in the world to fear!

They hesitate
We hesitate.
They have a gun.
We have no gun.

Then we all advance, to meet.
Two Mexicans, strangers, emerging out of the dark and snow
    and inwardness of the Lobo valley.
What are they doing here on this vanishing trail?

What is he carrying?
Something yellow.
A deer?

Qué tiene, amigo?
León—

He smiles, foolishly, as if he were caught doing wrong.
And we smile, foolishly, as if we didn't know.
He is quite gentle and dark-faced.

It is a mountain lion,
A long, long slim cat, yellow like a lioness.
Dead.

He trapped her this morning, he says, smiling foolishly.
Lift up her face,
Her round, bright face, bright as frost.
Her round, fine-fashioned head, with two dead ears;
And stripes in the brilliant frost of her face, sharp, fine dark
    rays,
Dark, keen, fine rays in the brilliant frost of her face.
Beautiful dead eyes.

Hermoso es!

They go out towards the open;
We go on into the gloom of Lobo.
And above the trees I found her lair,
A hole in the blood-orange brilliant rocks that stick up, a little
    cave.
And bones, and twigs, and a perilous ascent.

So, she will never leap up that way again, with the yellow flash
    of a mountain lion's long shoot!
And her bright striped frost-face will never watch any more,
    out of the shadow of the cave in the blood-orange rock,
Above the trees of the Lobo dark valley-mouth!

Instead, I look out.
And out to the dim of the desert, like a dream, never real;
To the snow of the Sangre de Cristo mountains, the ice of the
    mountains of Picoris,
And near across at the opposite steep of snow, green trees
    motionless standing in snow, like a Christmas toy.

And I think in this empty world there was room for me and a
    mountain lion.
And I think in the world beyond, how easily we might spare a
    million or two of humans
And never miss them.
Yet what a gap in the world, the missing white frost-face of
    that slim yellow mountain lion!

D. H. Lawrence

Heart and Mind

Said the Lion to the Lioness – 'When you are amber dust, -
No more a raging fire like the heat of the Sun
(No liking but all lust) –
Remember still the flowering of the amber blood and bone,
The rippling of bright muscles like a sea,
Remember the rose-prickles of bright paws
Though we shall mate no more
Till the fire of that sun the heart and the moon-cold bone are one.'

From 'Heart and Mind' by Edith Sitwell

Lizzie's Tiger

'Veux-tu voir le grand chat, ma petite?'

Lizzie did not understand what he said, but she knew what he was saying and nodded assent. Mother looked over the head of the good baby in the lace bonnet as her son heaved Lizzie up in his arms for a good look.

'Les poux . . .' she warned, but her son paid her no heed.

'Voilà, ma petite!'

The tiger walked up and down, up and down; it walked up and down like Satan walking about the world and it burned. It burned so brightly, she was scorched. Its tail, thick as her father's forearm, twitched back and forth at the tip. The quick, loping stride of the caged tiger; its eyes like yellow coins of a foreign currency; its round, innocent, toy-like ears; the stiff whiskers sticking out with an artificial look; the red mouth from which the bright noise came. It walked up and down on straw strewn with bloody bones.

The tiger kept its head down, questing hither and thither though in quest of what might not be told. All its motion was slung from the marvellous haunches it held so high you could have rolled a marble down its back, if it would have let you, and the marble would have run down an oblique angle until it rolled over the domed forehead on to the floor. In its hind legs the tense muscles keened and sang. It was a miracle of dynamic suspension. It reached one end of the cage in a few paces and whirled around upon itself in one liquid motion; nothing could be quicker or more beautiful than its walk. It was all raw, vivid, exasperated nerves. Upon its pelt it bore the imprint of the bars behind which it lived.

The young lad who kept hold of her clung tight as she lunged forward towards the beast, but he could not stop her clutching the bars of the cage with her little fingers and he tried but he could not dislodge them. The tiger stopped in its track halfway through its mysterious patrol and looked at her. Her pale-blue Calvinist eyes of New England encountered with a shock the flat, mineral eyes of the tiger.

It seemed to Lizzie that they exchanged this cool regard for an endless time, the tiger and herself.

Then something strange happened. The svelte beast fell to its knees. It was as if it had been subdued by the presence of this child, as if this little child of all the children in the world, might lead it towards a peaceable kingdom where it need not eat meat. But only 'as if'. All we could see was, it knelt. A crackle of shock ran through the tent; the tiger was acting out of character.

Its mind remained, however, a law unto itself. We did not know what it was thinking. How could we?

It stopped roaring. Instead it started to emit a rattling purr. Time somersaulted. Space diminished to the field of attractive force between the child and the tiger. All that existed in the whole world now were Lizzie and the tiger.

Then, oh! then . . . it came towards her, as if she were winding it to her on an invisible string by the exercise of pure will. I cannot tell you how much she loved the tiger, nor how wonderful she thought it was. It was the power of her love that forced it to come to her, on its knees, like a penitent. It dragged its pale belly across the dirty straw towards the bars where the little soft creature hung by its hooked fingers. Behind it followed the serpentine length of its ceaselessly twitching tail.

There was a wrinkle in its nose and it buzzed and rumbled and they never took their eyes off one another, though neither had the least idea what the other meant.

The boy holding Lizzie got scared and pummelled her little fists, but she would not let go a grip as tight and senseless as that of the newborn.

Crack! The spell broke.

The world bounded into the ring.

A lash cracked round the tiger's carnivorous head, and a glorious hero sprang into the cage brandishing in the hand that did not hold the whip a three-legged stool. He wore fawn breeches, black boots, a bright red jacket frogged with gold, a tall hat. A dervish, he; he beckoned, crouched, pointed with the whip, menaced with the stool, leaped and twirled in a brilliant ballet of mimic ferocity, the dance of the Taming of the Tiger, to whom the tamer gave no chance to fight at all.

The great cat unpeeled its eyes off Lizzie's in a trice, rose up on its hind legs and feinted at the whip like our puss Ginger feints at a piece of paper dangled from a string. It batted at the tamer with its enormous paws, but the whip continued to confuse, irritate and torment it and, what with the shouting, the sudden, excited baying of the crowd, the dreadful confusion of the signs surrounding it, habitual custom, a lifetime's training, the tiger whimpered, laid back its ears and scampered away from the whirling man to an obscure corner of the stage, there to cower, while its flanks heaved, the picture of humiliation.

Lizzie let go of the bars and clung, mudstains and all, to her young protector for comfort. She was shaken to the roots by the attack of the trainer upon the tiger and her four-year-old roots were very near the surface.

The tamer gave his whip a final, contemptuous ripple around his adversary's whiskers that made it sink its huge head on the floor. Then he placed one booted foot on the tiger's skull and cleared his throat for speech. He was a hero. He was a tiger himself, but even more so, because he was a man.

'Ladies and gentlemen, boys and girls, this incomparable TIGER known as the Scourge of Bengal, and brought alive-oh to Boston from its native jungle but three short months before this present time, now, at my imperious command, offers you a perfect imitation of docility and obedience. But do not let the brute deceive you. Brute it was, and brute it remains. Not for nothing did it receive the soubriquet of Scourge for, in its native habitat, it thought nothing of consuming a dozen brown-skinned heathen for its breakfast and following up with a couple of dozen more for dinner!'

A pleasing shudder tingled through the crowd.

'This tiger,' and the beast whickered ingratiatingly when he named it, 'is the veritable incarnation of blood lust and fury; in a single instant, it can turn from furry quiescence into three hundred pounds, yes, three hundred POUNDS of death-dealing fury.

'The tiger is the cat's revenge.'

Oh, Miss Ginger, Miss Ginger Cuddles, who sat mewing censoriously on the gatepost as Lizzie passed by; who would have thought you seethed with such resentment!

The man's voice dropped to a confidential whisper and Lizzie, although she was in such a state, such nerves, recognised this was the same man as the one she had met behind the cider stall, although now he exhibited such erect mastery, not a single person in the tent would have thought he had been drinking.

'What is the nature of the bond between us, between the Beast and Man? Let me tell you. It is fear. Fear! Nothing but fear. Do you know how insomnia is the plague of the tamer of cats? How all night long, every night, we pace our quarters, impossible to close our eyes for brooding on what day, what hour, what moment the fatal beast will choose to strike?

'Don't think I cannot bleed, or that they have not wounded me. Under my clothes, my body is a palimpsest of scars, scar upon scar. I heal only to be once more broken open. No skin of mine that is not scar tissue. And I am always afraid, always; all the time in the ring, in the cage, now, this moment – this very moment, boys and girls, ladies and gentlemen, you see before you a man in the grip of mortal fear.

'Here and now I am in terror of my life.

'At this moment I am in this cage within a perfect death trap.'

Theatrical pause.

'But,' and here he knocked the tiger's nose with his whipstock, so that it howled with pain and affront, 'but . . .' and Lizzie saw the secret frog he kept within his trousers shift a little, '. . . BUT I'm not half so scared of the big brute as it is of me!'

He showed his red maw in a laugh.

'For I bring to bear upon its killer instinct a rational man's knowledge of the power of fear. The whip, the stool, are instruments of bluff with which I create his fear in my arena. In my cage, among my cats, I have established a hierarchy of FEAR and among my cats you might well say I am TOP DOG, because I know that all the time they want to kill me, that is their project, that is their intention . . . but as for them, they just don't know what I might do next. No, sir!'

As if enchanted by the notion, he laughed out loud again, but by now the tiger, perhaps incensed by the unexpected blow on the nose, rumbled out a clear and incontrovertible message of disaffection and, with a quick jerk of its sculptured head, flung the man's foot away so that, caught off-balance, he half toppled over. And then the tiger was no longer a thing of stillness, of hard edges and clear outlines, but a whizz of black and red, maw and canines, in the air. On him.

The crowd immediately bayed.

But the tamer, with enormous presence of mind, seeing as how he was drunk, and, in the circumstances, with almost uncanny physical agility, bounced backwards on his boot-heels and thrust the stool he carried in his left hand into the fierce tiger's jaws, leaving the tiger worrying, gnawing, destroying the harmless thing, as a ragged black boy quickly unlatched the cage door and out the tamer leaped, unscathed, amidst hurrahs.

Lizzie's stunned little face was now mottled all over with a curious reddish-purple, with the heat of the tent, with passion, with the sudden access of enlightenment.

To see the rest of the stupendous cat act, the audience would have had to buy another ticket for the Big Top, besides the ticket for the menagerie, for which it had already paid, so, reluctant on the whole to do that, in spite of the promise of clowns and dancing ladies, it soon got bored with watching the tiger splintering the wooden stool, and drifted off.

'*Eh bien, ma petite*,' said her boy-nurse to her in a sweet, singsong, crooning voice. '*Tu as vu la bête! La bête du cauchemar!*'

The baby in the lace bonnet had slept peacefully through all this, but now began to stir and mumble. Its mother nudged her husband with her elbow.

'*On va, Papa?*'

The crooning, smiling boy brought his bright pink lips down on Lizzie's forehead for a farewell kiss. She could not bear that; she struggled furiously and shouted to be put down. With that, her cover broke and she burst out of her disguise of dirt and silence; half the remaining gawpers in the tent had kin been bleakly buried by her father, the rest owed him money. She was the most famous daughter in all Fall River.

'Well, if it ain't Andrew Borden's little girl! What are they Canucks doing with little Lizzie Borden?'

From 'Lizzie's Tiger' by Angela Carter

3

THE MIDDLE AGES AND THE RENAISSANCE

Some, that are mad if they behold a cat;
And others, when the bagpipe sings i' the nose,
Cannot contain their urine.

Shakespeare, *The Merchant of Venice*

The Cat and the Partridge

Your master grieved as though you'd savaged *him*,
When you devoured his partridge, wicked cat.
The hounds which tore Actæon limb from limb,
Fierce man-eaters, did hardly worse than that.
And now so set on partridge is your soul,
The mice can dance and rob your dainty bowl.

Damocharis the Grammarian, transl. W. Bedell Stanford

Hungry Master and Hungry Cat

When my house was bare of skins and pots of meal,
after it had been inhabited, not empty, full of folk and richly prosperous,
I see the mice avoid my house, retiring to the governor's palace.
The flies have called for a move, whether their wings are clipped or whole.
The cat stayed a year in the house and did not see a mouse
shaking its head at hunger, at a life full of pain and spite.
When I saw the pained downcast head, the heat in the belly, I said,
'Patience; you are the best cat my eyes ever saw in a ward.'
He said, 'I have no patience. How can I stay in a desert like the belly of a
    she ass?'
I said, 'Go in peace to a hotel where travellers are many and much trade,
Even if the spider spins in my wine jar, in the jug, and the pot.'

Abu Shamaqmaq, transl. A. S. Tritton

An Embarrassing Incident

During the time of Tse-t'ien [the Empress Wu], a cat and a parrot were
trained to eat food from the same vessel. She ordered Censor P'eng

Hsien-chueh to supervise the exhibition of their friendliness to all the officials at the Court and the Commissioners of the Empire. But before the exhibition was over, the cat was hungry and accordingly bit and killed the parrot and ate it. She felt very much embarrassed.

From *The Ch'ao-yeh Ch'ien-tsai* by Chang Tsu

Morality Claws

According to legend, in eighth-century Ireland St Maeldun encountered an island ruled by a cat. The stories of his travels are said to have inspired the later legend of the voyages of St Brendan. Both saints displayed a healthy circumspection in regard to the beast.

One of the islands visited by Maeldun and his companions in the voyage of Maeldun was the island of the little cat. Here was a great white palace with four stone columns in one of the spacious apartments. A cat leapt from the top of one column to the next. The chamber was filled with treasures of every kind – brooches and torques and swords displayed upon the walls – and here too was an abundance of fine food and drink. The newcomers ate and drank and slept awhile. Next day as they prepared to leave, one of Maeldun's foster brothers took a necklace from the wall. The cat leapt at him like a fiery dart and he fell in a pile of ashes on the floor. Maeldun, who had forbidden the theft, calmed the cat, restored the necklace and scattered the ashes of his dead foster brother on the shore of the island of the little cat.

From *Irish Superstitions and Legends of Birds and Animals*,
ed. Patrick V. O'Sullivan

To a Cat

Poor Puss is gone! 'Tis fate's decree –
Yet I must still her loss deplore,
For dearer than a child was she,
And ne'er shall I behold her more.

With many a sad presaging tear
This morn I saw her steal away,
While she went on without a fear
Except that she should miss her prey.

I saw her to the dove-house climb,
With cautious feet and slow she stept,
Resolved to balance loss of time
By eating faster than she crept.

Her subtle foes were on the watch
And mark'd her course, with fury fraught,
And while she hoped the birds to catch,
An arrow's point the huntress caught.

In fancy she had got them all,
And drunk their blood, and suck'd their breath;
Alas! she only got a fall,
And only drank the draught of death.

Why, why was pigeons' flesh so nice,
That thoughtless cats should love it thus?
Hadst thou but lived on rats and mice,
Thou hadst been living still, poor Puss.

Curst be the taste, howe'er refined,
That prompts us for such joys to wish,
And curst the dainty where we find
Destruction lurking in the dish.

Ibn Alalaf Alnaharwany, transl. J. D. Carlyle

Pangur Ban

To Pangur Ban, my White Cat

Brother artists, he and I
Special crafts elect to ply;
Hunting mice would Pangur choose:
I have different sporting views.

At my books I never tire,
Nor rewards of fame desire:
Proud of inborn talents he
Never thinks of envying me.

Snug indoors who roam abroad?
By ourselves we're never bored:
Countless thrilling tests arise
For our keenest faculties.

He, superbly dexterous,
Many a time entraps the mouse:
Truth elusive I pursue –
Sometimes I can trap her too!

Pangur's pupils, full and bright,
Fix the wainscot in their sight:
Through the walls of science I
Seek with feebler shafts to pry.

Pangur glories in his skill
When his claws achieve a kill:
I am overjoyed to gain
Prizes hunted in the brain.

Thus we live from day to day,
Neither in the other's way,
And our pleasures win apart,
Following each his special art.

Perfect use of eye and limb
Daily practice gives to him:
I my task appointed find
Chasing darkness from the mind.

By a ninth-century Irish monk, transl. Samuel Courtauld

The Sea-cat

According to Taverner, the cat 'wyll not hys feete wette'. He clearly had not encountered the aqueous Irish brute that menaced the second voyage of St Brendan in the ninth century.

After this they rowed for a while over the ocean in a westerly direction, and found a pleasant little island with a number of fishermen in it. As they were going round it they saw in it a little stone church, in which was an aged man, pale and sorrowful, engaged in prayer. And he had neither flesh nor blood, but merely a thin miserable skin over his hard and yellow bones. Then that elder said: 'Flee, Brendan, with all speed,' said he. 'For there is here now a sea-cat as big as a young ox or a three-year-old horse, which has thriven on the fish of the sea and of this island; beware of it now.'

They betake them to their boat, and row over the ocean with all their might. As they were thus, they saw the monstrous sea-cat swimming after them; each of its two eyes was as big as a cauldron, it had tusks like a boar, sharp-pointed bristles, the maw of a leopard, the strength of a lion, and the rage of a mad dog. Then each of them began to pray to God by reason of the great fear which seized them. Then said Brendan: 'O God Almighty,' said he, 'keep off Thy monsters from us, that they may not reach us.'

Then a great sea whale rose up between them and the cat-monster, and each of them set to work to try and drown the other in the depths of the sea, and neither of them ever appeared again. Then Brendan and his company gave thanks to God, and turned back again to the place where the elder was. And the elder wept for the greatness of the joy which possessed him, and said: 'I am of the men of Erin,' said he, 'and twelve of us were there when we came on our pilgrimage, and we brought that bestial sea-cat with us, and we were very fond of it; and it grew afterwards enormously, but it never hurt any of us. And now of our original company eleven have died, and I am left alone, waiting for thee to give me the body and blood of Christ, that therewith I may go to heaven.'

He revealed to them afterwards the little country which they were seeking, that is *the Land of Promise*. And after receiving the body and blood of Christ, the elder went to heaven. He was buried there beside his brethren with great reverence, and with psalms and hymns, in the name of the Father, and of the Son, and of the Holy Ghost.

From *St Brendan*, (the second voyage)

The Law of the Cat

This is the complement of a lawful hamlet: nine buildings and one plough and one kiln and one churn and one cat and one cock and one bull and one herdman.

The animals whose tail, eyes and life are of equal worth: a calf, a filly from common work and a cat, excepting the cat that shall watch the King's barn.

The Vendotian (or North Wales) code
The worth of a cat and her teithi is this:
1. The worth of a kitten from the night it is kittened until it shall open its eyes is a legal penny.
2. And from that time, until it shall kill mice, two legal pence.
3. And after it shall kill mice, four legal pence; and so it always remains.
4. Her teithi are, to see, to hear, to kill mice, to have her claws entire, to rear and not to devour her kittens; and if she be bought, and be deficient in any one of those teithi, let one-third of her worth be returned.

The Gwentian (or South-east) code
1. Whoever shall kill a cat that guards a house and a barn of the King, or shall take it stealthily, it is to be held with its head to the ground and its tail up, the ground being swept, and then clean wheat is to be poured about it, until the tip of its tail be hidden; and that is its worth.
2. A common cat is four legal pence in value.
3. The teithi of a cat are, that it be perfect of ear, perfect of eye, perfect of teeth, perfect of tail, perfect of claw and without marks of fire; and that it will kill mice well; and that it shall not devour its kittens; and that it be not caterwauling on every new moon . . .
5. A pound is the worth of a pet animal of the king.

From *The Codes Enacted by Howel the Good, King of All Wales*

Missing!

In twelfth-century China, the disappearance of a palace cat resulted in a bizarre dragnet.

At six or seven years of age Lady Ch'ung-kuo, granddaughter of Ch'in Kuei, lost a lion-like cat of which she was fond. The prefect of the prefecture of Lin-an was ordered to find it within a certain time. Some hundred persons were arrested; a hundred or so cats were caught, but none of them was the lost one. Then a hundred copies of its likeness were made and they were put up in tea houses and public places. It could not be found after all. Not until a favourite concubine of Ts'ao Yung, the prefect, bribed her with a golden cat and begged her [not to press him to find the lost animal], was the matter dropped.

From *The P'ei-wen Yun-fu Shih-i* compiled by Chang and others

The Story of the Faithful Cat

About sixty years ago, in the summer-time, a man went to pay a visit at a certain house at Osaka, and, in the course of conversation, said –

'I have eaten some very extraordinary cakes to-day,' and on being asked what he meant, he told the following story:–

'I received the cakes from the relatives of a family who were celebrating the hundredth anniversary of the death of a cat that had belonged to their ancestors. When I asked the history of the affair, I was told that, in former days, a young girl of the family, when she was about sixteen years old, used always to be followed about by a tom-cat, who was reared in the house, so much so that the two were never separated for an instant. When her father perceived this, he was very angry, thinking that the tom-cat, forgetting the kindness with which he had been treated for years in the house, had fallen in love with his daughter, and intended to cast a spell upon her; so he determined that he must kill the beast. As he was planning this in secret, the cat overheard him, and that night went to his pillow, and, assuming a human voice, said to him –

'"You suspect me of being in love with your daughter; and although you might well be justified in so thinking, your suspicions are groundless. The fact is this:- There is a very large old rat who has been living for many years in your granary. Now it is this old rat who is in love with my young mistress, and this is why I dare not leave her side for a moment, for fear the old rat should carry her off. Therefore I pray you to dispel your suspicions. But as I, by myself, am no match for the rat, there is a famous cat, named Buchi, at the house of Mr So-and-so, at Ajikawa: if you will borrow that cat, we will soon make an end of the old rat."

'When the father awoke from his dream, he thought it so wonderful, that he told the household of it; and the following day he got up very early and went off to Ajikawa, to inquire for the house which the cat had indicated, and had no difficulty in finding it; so he called upon the master of the house, and told him what his own cat had said, and how he wished to borrow the cat Buchi for a little while.

'"That's a very easy matter to settle," said the other: "pray take him with you at once;" and accordingly the father went home with the cat Buchi in charge. That night he put the two cats into the granary; and after a little while, a frightful clatter was heard, and then all was still again; so the people of the house opened the door, and crowded out to see what had happened; and there they beheld the two cats and the rat all locked together, and panting for breath; so they cut the throat of the rat, which was as big as either of the cats: then they attended to the two cats; but, although they gave them ginseng* and other restoratives, they both got weaker and weaker, until at last they died. So the rat was thrown into the river; but the two cats were buried with all honours in a neighbouring temple.'

*A restorative in high repute. The best sorts are brought from Corea.

From *Tales of Old Japan* by Lord Redesdale

Only a Cat

Ye shall not possess any beast, my dear sisters, except only a cat. An anchoress that hath cattle appears as Martha was, a better housewife than anchoress; nor can she in any wise be Mary, with peacefulness of heart. For then she must think of the cow's fodder, and of the herdsman's hire, flatter the heyward, defend herself when her cattle is shut up in the pinfold, and moreover pay the damage.

From *The Ancren Riwle, a Rule for Nunnes or Recluses*, transl. James Morton

The Vampire Cat of Nabéshima

Cats, foxes and badgers were regarded with reverential fear by the Japanese, who attributed to them the power of assuming the human shape in order to bewitch mankind.

There is a tradition in the Nabéshima* family that, many years ago, the Prince of Hizen was bewitched and cursed by a cat that had been kept by one of his retainers. This prince had in his house a lady of rare beauty, called O Toyo: amongst all his ladies she was the favourite, and there was none who could rival her charms and accomplishments. One day the Prince went out into the garden with O Toyo, and remained enjoying the fragrance of the flowers until sunset, when they returned to the palace, never noticing that they were being followed by a large cat. Having parted with her lord, O Toyo retired to her own room and went to bed. At midnight she awoke with a start, and became aware of a huge cat that crouched watching her; and when she cried out, the beast sprang on her, and, fixing its cruel teeth in her delicate throat, throttled her to death. What a piteous end for so fair a dame, the darling of her prince's heart, to die suddenly, bitten to death by a cat! Then the cat, having scratched out a grave under the verandah, buried the corpse of O Toyo, and assuming her form, began to bewitch the Prince.

But my lord the Prince knew nothing of all this, and little thought that the beautiful creature who caressed and fondled him was an impish and foul beast that had slain his mistress and assumed her shape in order to drain out his life's blood. Day by day, as time went on, the Prince's strength dwindled away; the colour of his face was changed, and became pale and livid; and he was as a man suffering from a deadly sickness. Seeing this, his councillors and his wife became greatly alarmed; so they summoned the physicians, who prescribed various remedies for him; but the more medicine he took, the more serious did his illness appear, and no treatment was of any avail. But most of all did he suffer in the night-time, when his sleep would be troubled and disturbed by hideous dreams. In consequence of this, his councillors nightly appointed a hundred of his retainers to sit up and watch over him; but, strange to say, towards ten o'clock on the very first night that the watch was set, the guard were seized with a sudden and unaccountable drowsiness, which they could not resist, until one by one every man had fallen asleep. Then the false O Toyo came in and harassed the Prince until morning. The following night the same thing occurred, and the Prince was subjected to the imp's tyranny, while his guards slept helplessly around him. Night after night this was repeated, until

*The family of the Prince of Hizen, one of the eighteen chief Daimios of Japan.

at last three of the Prince's councillors determined themselves to sit up on guard, and see whether they could overcome this mysterious drowsiness; but they fared no better than the others, and by ten o'clock were fast asleep. The next day the three councillors held a solemn conclave, and their chief, one Isahaya Buzen, said –

'This is a marvellous thing, that a guard of a hundred men should thus be overcome by sleep. Of a surety, the spell that is upon my lord and upon his guard must be the work of witchcraft. Now, as all our efforts are of no avail, let us seek out Ruiten, the chief priest of the temple called Miyô In, and beseech him to put up prayers for the recovery of my lord.'

And the other councillors approving what Isahaya Buzen had said, they went to the priest Ruiten and engaged him to recite litanies that the Prince might be restored to health.

So it came to pass that Ruiten, the chief priest of Miyô In, offered up prayers nightly for the Prince. One night, at the ninth hour (midnight), when he had finished his religious exercises and was preparing to lie down to sleep, he fancied that he heard a noise outside in the garden, as if some one were washing himself at the well. Deeming this passing strange, he looked down from the window; and there in the moonlight he saw a handsome young soldier, some twenty-four years of age, washing himself, who, when he had finished cleaning himself and had put on his clothes, stood before the figure of Buddha and prayed fervently for the recovery of my lord the Prince. Ruiten looked on with admiration; and the young man, when he had made an end of his prayer, was going away; but the priest stopped him, calling out to him –

'Sir, I pray you to tarry a little: I have something to say to you.'

'At your reverence's service. What may you please to want?'

'Pray be so good as to step up here, and have a little talk.'

'By your reverence's leave;' and with this he went upstairs.

Then Ruiten said –

'Sir, I cannot conceal my admiration that you, being so young a man, should have so loyal a spirit. I am Ruiten, the chief priest of this temple, who am engaged in praying for the recovery of my lord. Pray what is your name?'

'My name, sir, is Itô Sôda, and I am serving in the infantry of Nabéshima. Since my lord has been sick, my one desire has been to assist in nursing him; but, being only a simple soldier, I am not of sufficient rank to come into his presence, so I have no resource but to pray to the gods of the country and to

Buddha that my lord may regain his health.'

When Ruiten heard this, he shed tears in admiration of the fidelity of Itô Sôda, and said –

'Your purpose is, indeed, a good one; but what a strange sickness this is that my lord is afflicted with! Every night he suffers from horrible dreams; and the retainers who sit up with him are all seized with a mysterious sleep, so that not one can keep awake. It is very wonderful.'

'Yes,' replied Sôda, after a moment's reflection, 'this certainly must be witchcraft. If I could but obtain leave to sit up one night with the Prince, I would fain see whether I could not resist this drowsiness and detect the goblin.'

At last the priest said, 'I am in relations of friendship with Isahaya Buzen, the chief councillor of the Prince. I will speak to him of you and of your loyalty, and will intercede with him that you may attain your wish.'

'Indeed, sir, I am most thankful. I am not prompted by any vain thought of self-advancement, should I succeed: all I wish for is the recovery of my lord. I commend myself to your kind favour.'

'Well, then, to-morrow night I will take you with me to the councillor's house.'

'Thank you, sir, and farewell.' And so they parted.

On the following evening Itô Sôda returned to the temple Miyô In, and having found Ruiten, accompanied him to the house of Isahaya Buzen: then the priest, leaving Sôda outside, went in to converse with the councillor, and inquire after the Prince's health.

'And pray, sir, how is my lord? Is he in any better condition since I have been offering up prayers for him?'

'Indeed, no; his illness is very severe. We are certain that he must be the victim of some foul sorcery; but as there are no means of keeping a guard awake after ten o'clock, we cannot catch a sight of the goblin, so we are in the greatest trouble.'

'I feel deeply for you: it must be most distressing. However, I have something to tell you. I think that I have found a man who will detect the goblin; and I have brought him with me.'

'Indeed! who is the man?'

'Well, he is one of my lord's foot-soldiers, named Itô Sôda, a faithful fellow, and I trust that you will grant his request to be permitted to sit up with my lord.'

'Certainly, it is wonderful to find so much loyalty and zeal in a common soldier,' replied Isahaya Buzen, after a moment's reflection; 'still it is impossible to allow a man of such low rank to perform the office of watching over my lord.'

'It is true that he is but a common soldier,' urged the priest; 'but why not raise his rank in consideration of his fidelity, and then let him mount guard?'

'It would be time enough to promote him after my lord's recovery. But come, let me see this Itô Sôda, that I may know what manner of man he is: if he pleases me, I will consult with the other councillors, and perhaps we may grant his request.'

'I will bring him in forthwith,' replied Ruiten, who thereupon went out to fetch the young man.

When he returned, the priest presented Itô Sôda to the councillor, who looked at him attentively, and, being pleased with his comely and gentle appearance, said –

'So I hear that you are anxious to be permitted to mount guard in my lord's room at night. Well, I must consult with the other councillors, and we will see what can be done for you.'

When the young soldier heard this he was greatly elated, and took his leave, after warmly thanking Ruiten, who had helped him to gain his object. The next day the councillors held a meeting, and sent for Itô Sôda, and told him that he might keep watch with the other retainers that very night. So he went his way in high spirits, and at nightfall, having made all his preparations, took his place among the hundred gentlemen who were on duty in the prince's bedroom.

Now the Prince slept in the centre of the room, and the hundred guards around him sat keeping themselves awake with entertaining conversation and pleasant conceits. But, as ten o'clock approached, they began to doze off as they sat; and in spite of all their endeavours to keep one another awake, by degrees they all fell asleep. Itô Sôda all this while felt an irresistible desire to sleep creeping over him, and, though he tried by all sorts of ways to rouse himself, he saw that there was no help for it, but by resorting to an extreme measure, for which he had already made his preparations. Drawing out a piece of oil paper which he had brought with him, and spreading it over the mats, he sat down upon it; then he took the small knife which he carried in the sheath of his dirk, and stuck it into his own thigh. For awhile the pain of the wound kept him awake; but as the slumber by which he was assailed was the work of sorcery, little by little he became drowsy again. Then he twisted the knife round and round in his thigh, so that the pain becoming very violent, he was proof against the feeling of sleepiness, and kept a faithful watch. Now the oil paper which he had spread under his leg was in order to prevent the blood, which might spurt from his wound, from defiling the mats.

So Itô Sôda remained awake, but the rest of the guard slept; and as he watched, suddenly the sliding-doors of the Prince's room were drawn open, and he saw a figure coming in stealthily, and, as it drew nearer, the form was that of a marvellously beautiful woman some twenty-three years of age. Cautiously she looked around her; and when she saw that all the guard were asleep, she smiled an ominous smile, and was going up to the Prince's bedside, when she perceived that in one corner of the room there was a man yet awake. This seemed to startle her, but she went up to Sôda and said –

'I am not used to seeing you here. Who are you?'

'My name is Itô Sôda, and this is the first night that I have been on guard.'

'A troublesome office, truly! Why, here are all the rest of the guard asleep. How is it that you alone are awake? You are a trusty watchman.'

'There is nothing to boast about. I'm asleep myself, fast and sound.'

'What is that wound on your knee? It is all red with blood.'

'Oh! I felt very sleepy; so I stuck my knife into my thigh, and the pain of it has kept me awake.'

'What wondrous loyalty!' said the lady.

'Is it not the duty of a retainer to lay down his life for his master? Is such a scratch as this worth thinking about?'

Then the lady went up to the sleeping prince and said, 'How fares it with my lord to-night?' But the Prince, worn out with sickness, made no reply. But Sôda was watching her eagerly, and guessed that it was O Toyo, and made up his mind that if she attempted to harass the Prince he would kill her on the spot. The goblin, however, which in the form of O Toyo had been tormenting the Prince every night, and had come again that night for no other purpose, was defeated by the watchfulness of Itô Sôda; for whenever she drew near to the sick man, thinking to put her spells upon him, she would turn and look behind her, and there she saw Itô Sôda glaring at her; so she had no help for it but to go away again, and leave the Prince undisturbed.

At last the day broke, and the other officers, when they awoke and opened their eyes, saw that Itô Sôda had kept awake by stabbing himself in the thigh; and they were greatly ashamed, and went home crestfallen.

That morning Itô Sôda went to the house of Isahaya Buzen, and told him all that had occurred the previous night. The councillors were all loud in their praise of Itô Sôda's behaviour, and ordered him to keep watch again that night. At the same hour, the false O Toyo came and looked all round the room, and all the guard were asleep, excepting Itô Sôda, who was wide awake; and so, being again frustrated, she returned to her own apartments.

Now as since Sôda had been on guard the Prince had passed quiet nights, his sickness began to get better, and there was great joy in the palace, and Sôda was promoted and rewarded with an estate. In the meanwhile O Toyo, seeing that her nightly visits bore no fruits, kept away; and from that time forth the night-guard were no longer subject to fits of drowsiness. This coincidence struck Sôda as very strange, so he went to Isahaya Buzen and told him that of a certainty this O Toyo was no other than a goblin. Isahaya Buzen reflected for a while, and said –

'Well, then, how shall we kill the foul thing?'

'I will go to the creature's room, as if nothing were the matter, and try to kill her; but in case she should try to escape, I will beg you to order eight men to stop outside and lie in wait for her.'

Having agreed upon this plan, Sôda went at nightfall to O Toyo's apartment, pretending to have been sent with a message from the Prince. When she saw him arrive, she said –

'What message have you brought me from my lord?'

'Oh! nothing in particular. Be so good as to look at this letter;' and as he spoke, he drew near to her, and suddenly drawing his dirk cut at her; but the goblin, springing back, seized a halberd, and glaring fiercely at Sôda, said –

'How dare you behave like this to one of your lord's ladies? I will have you dismissed;' and she tried to strike Sôda with the halberd. But Sôda fought desperately with his dirk; and the goblin, seeing that she was no match for him, threw away the halberd, and from a beautiful woman became suddenly transformed into a cat, which, springing up the sides of the room, jumped on to the roof. Isahaya Buzen and his eight men who were watching outside shot at the cat, but missed it, and the beast made good its escape.

So the cat fled to the mountains, and did much mischief among the surrounding people, until at last the Prince of Hizen ordered a great hunt, and the beast was killed.

But the Prince recovered from his sickness; and Itô Sôda was richly rewarded.

From Tales of Old Japan by Lord Redesdale

Presbyterian Cat

Hung for Catching a Mouse on the Sabbath.

> Then forth to exe-cu-ti-on,
> Poor Baudrons she was drawn,
> And on a tree they hanged her hie,
> And then they sang a psalm.

Anonymous

The Cat

The cat, if you but singe her tabby skin,
The chimney keeps, and sits content within:
But once grown sleek, will from her corner run,
Sport with her tail and wanton in the sun:
She licks her fair round face, and frisks abroad
To show her fur, and to be catterwaw'd.

From The Prologue to 'The Wife of Bath's Tale' by Geoffrey Chaucer

Mice Before Milk

Go take a Cat and nourish her with milk
And tender fish, and make her couch of silk,
And let her see a mouse go by the wall,
Anon she waiveth milk and flesh and all
And every dainty which is in the house,
Such appetite hath she to eat the mouse.
Behold the domination here of kind,
Appetite drives discretion from her mind.

From 'The Manciple's Tale' by Geoffrey Chaucer,
transl. William Wordsworth

He Falleth on His Feet

The catte hatte *mureligus* and *musio* and hatte also *catus*. And hath that name *mureligus* for he is enemy to mys and to rattes, and communliche ycleped *catus* and hath that name of ravenyng, for he ravyssheth mys and rattes. Other he hath that name *catus* of *catat* that is 'for to see', for he seeth so sharpliche that he overcometh derknesse of the night by schynyng of the light of his yhen. And the name *catus* cometh of grew and is to menynge 'sly and witty', as Ysidorus seith *libro xii*.

And is a beste of uncerteyn here and colour. For som catte is whyte, som reed, and som blak, and som scowed and splenked in the feet and the face and in the eeren, and is most yliche to the lepard. And hath a gret mouth and sawe teeth and scharpe and longe tonge and pliaunt, thynne, and sotile. And lapeth therwith whanne he drynketh as othere bestes doon that haven the nether lip schorter than the over, for bycause of vneuenesse of lippes suche bestes souken nought in drykynge but lapeth and likketh, as Aristotil seith and Plinius also. And he is a ful leccherous beste in southe, swyfte, plaunte, and mery. And lepeth [and] reseth on alle thyng that is tofore him and is yladde by a strawe and pleyeth therwith. And is a wel hevy beste in eelde and ful slepy. And lith sliliche in awayte for mys and is ware where they ben more by smelle than by sight. And hunteth and reseth on hem in privey place. And whanne he taketh a mous he pleyeth therwith and eteth him after the pleye. And is as it were wylde and goth about in tyme of generacioun. Among cattes in tyme of love is hard fightynge for wyves, and oon craccheth and rendeth the other grevousliche with bytyng and with clawes. And he maketh a reweliche noyse and horrible whan oon profreth to fighte with another. And is a cruel beste whanne he is wilde and waonyeth in wodes and hunteth thanne smale wilde bestes, as conynges and hares. And falleth on his owne feet whanne he falleth out of highe place and is unnethe yhurte whanne he is ythrowe doun of an high place. His drytte stynketh ful foule and therfore he hydeth it under erthe and gadereth therupon coverynge with feet and clawes. And whanne he hat a fayre skynne he is as it were prowde thereof and goth faste aboute; and whanne his skynne is ybrende thanne he abydeth at home. And is ofte for his fayre skynne ytake of the skynnere and yslayne and yhulde.

From *De Proprietatibus Rerum* by Bartholomaeus Anglicus,
transl. John of Trevisa

Night Work

The cat, with eyne of burning coal,
Now couches 'fore the mouse's hole;
And crickets sing at the oven's mouth,
As the blither for their drouth.
Hymen hath brought the bride to bed,
Where, by the loss of maidenhead,
A babe is moulded; – Be attent,
And time that is so briefly spent,
With your fine fancies quaintly eche;
What's dumb in show, I'll plain with speech.

From *Pericles, Prince of Tyre* by William Shakespeare

The Rat's Strong Foe

I have (and long shall have) a white great nimble cat,
A king upon a mouse, a strong foe to the rat,
Fine eares, long taile he hath, with Lions curbed clawe,
Which oft he lifteth up, and stayes his lifted pawe,
Deepe musing to himself, which after-mewing showes,
Till with lickt beard, his eye of fire espie his foes.

From the Second Eclogues of the *Arcadia* by Sir Philip Sidney

Ecology

A large part of the bodies which have had life will pass into the bodies of other animals, that is the houses no longer inhabited will pass piecemeal through those which are inhabited, ministering to their needs and bearing away with them what is waste; that is to say, the life of man is made by things which he eats, and these carry with them that part of man which is dead . . . The rat was being besieged in its little dwelling by the weasel which with continual vigilance was awaiting its destruction, and through a tiny chink was considering its great danger. Meanwhile the cat came and suddenly seized hold of the weasel and forthwith devoured it. Whereupon the rat, profoundly grateful to its deity, having offered up some of its hazel-nuts in sacrifice to Jove, came out of its hole in order to repossess itself of the lately lost liberty, and was instantly deprived of this and of life by the cruel claws and teeth of the cat.

From *The Notebooks of Leonardo da Vinci*, ed. Irma A. Richter

Court Cat

Then ran ther a route of ratones, as it were,
And small mys with hem, mo than a thousand,
Comen til a conseil for here commune profit
For a cat of a court cam wher him likede
And overlap him lightliche and laghte him alle at wille,
And playde with some perilously, and putte him ther him likede.

route of ratones: a crowd of rats   til a conseil: to take council
mys: mice   ther: where

From *Piers the Plowman* by William Langland

Anathema of Cats

On all the hole nacyon
Of cattes wylde and tame –
God send them sorowe and shame!
That cat specyally,
That slew so cruelly
My lytell prety sparowe
That I brought up at Carowe!
  O cat of carlyshe kynde,
The fynde was in thy mynde
Whan thou my byrde untwynde!
I wold thou haddest ben blynde!
The leopardes savage,
The lyons in theyr rage,
Myght catche the in theyr pawes,
And gnawe the in theyr jawes!
The serpents of Lybany
Myght stynge the venymously!
The dragones with their tonges
Might poyson thy lyver and longes!
The mantycors of the montaynes
Myght fede them on thy braynes!
  Melancates, that hounde
That plucked Acteon to the grounde,
Gave hym his mortall wounde –
Chaunged to a dere
(The story doth appere)
Was chaunged to an harte:
So thou, foule cat that thou arte,
The selfe-same hounde
Myght the confounde,
That his owne lorde bote
Myght byte asondre thy throte!
  Of Inde the gredy grypes
Myght tere out all thy trypes!
Of Arcady the beares
Might plucke away thyne eares!
The wylde wolfe Lycaon
Byte asondre thy backe bone!

Of Ethna the brennynge hyll
That day and night brenneth styl,
Set in thy tayle a blase
That all the world may gase
And wonder upon the,
From Occyan the great se
Unto the Iles of Orchady,
From Tyllbery fery
To the playne of Salysbery!
So trayterously my byrde to kyll
That never ought the evyll wyll!

From *Phyllyp Sparowe* by John Skelton

Sonnet To My Cats

The sixteenth-century Italian poet Torquato Tasso succumbed to delusion and was interred in an asylum, as was the English poet Christopher Smart three centuries later. Both found the environment conducive to feline verses. The following sonnet was composed in the madhouse of St Anna at Ferrara.

Double the number of Heavenly Bears
Are the cats of the world to-day:
Some are clothed with snowy hairs
Some sable, whilst some are grey:
Some who squall, some minus tail,
One with a camel's dorsal mound –
 I should love to see in a monkey's veil,
Why can't this cat be found?

Mountains enceinte at each other gaze
Awaiting the birth of a miniature mouse.
If this poor creature is born, its days
Are surely numbered by a cat's carouse.

Massara! keep a cool head, I advise
Your eyes on the pot just about on the boil!
Run off, and take in the veal as a prize –
While I must prepare the refrain, lest it spoil.
If this sonnet I spoil I'll set up a wail
Should it no wise resemble a cat with a tail.

Torquato Tasso transl. Evan Morgan

An Enemy to Mice

The beaste is called a Musion for that he is enemie to Myse and Rattes. And he is called a Catte of Greeks because he is slye and wittie; for that he seeth so sharply, that he overcometh darkness of the nighte, by the shyninge lighte of his eyne.

From *The Workes of Armorie* by John Boswell

In Perill on the Sea

The 18. day we abode still at anker, looking for a gale to returne backe, but it was contrary: and the 19. we set saile, but the currant having more force then the winde, we were driven backe, insomuch, that the ship being under saile, we cast the sounding lead, and (nothwithstanding the wind) it remained before the shippe, there we hadde muddie ground at fifteen fadome. The same day about 4. of the clocke, wee set saile again, and sayled West alongst the coast with a fresh sidewinde. It chanced by fortune, that the shippes Cat lept into the Sea, which being downe, kept her selfe very valuantly above water, notwithstanding the great waves, still swimming, but which the master knowing, he caused the Skiffe with half a dosen men to goe towards her and fetch her againe, when she was almost halfe a mile from the shippe, and all this while the shippe lay on staies. I hardly believe they would have made such haste and meanes if one of the company had bene in the like perill. They made the more haste because it was the patrons cat. This I have written onely to note the estimation that cats are in, among the Italiana, for generally they esteem their cattes, as in England we esteeme a good Spaniell. The same night about tenne of the clocke the winde calmed, and because none of the shippe knewe where we were, we let fall an anker about 6 mile from the place we were at before, and there wee had muddie ground at twelve fadome.

From *The Principal Navigations, Voyages, Traffiques and Discoveries of the English Nation* by Richard Hakluyt

Dealing with the Devil

Don Quixote and a hapless cat become the victims of a cruel jest by the Duke and Duchess.

Don Quixote had come to this point in his song, which was heard by the Duke and Duchess, Altisidora and almost all the people in the castle, when suddenly, from a balcony which directly overhung his window, a rope was let down with more than a hundred sheep-bells fastened to it and, immediately afterwards, a great sack, full of cats with smaller bells tied to their tails, was flung after it. The jingling of the bells and the squawking of the cats made such a din that even the Duke and Duchess, who had contrived the joke, were aghast, while Don Quixote was dumbfounded with fear. Now two or three of the cats, as fate would have it, got through the window, and as they rushed about the room it was as if a legion of devils had broken in. They knocked over and put out the candles burning there, and ran about trying to find a way of escape. And all the while the rope with the great sheep-bells on it continued to rise and fall, and the majority of the people of the castle, not being in the secret, remained speechless with astonishment. Finally Don Quixote rose to his feet and, drawing his sword, began to make stabs through the window, crying loudly:

'Avaunt, evil enchanters! Avaunt, crew of sorcerers! For I am Don Quixote de la Mancha, against whom your wicked plots are powerless and of no avail.'

Then, turning round upon the cats, who were running about the room, he dealt them many blows. And all of them rushed to the window and jumped out, except one which, finding itself hard pressed by Don Quixote's sword-thrusts, jumped at his face and dug its claws and teeth into his nose, whereupon Don Quixote began to roar his very loudest in pain. Now when the Duke and Duchess heard him, realizing the probable cause, they ran in great haste to his room and, opening the door with the master-key, found the poor knight struggling with all his might to tear the cat from his face. They went in with lights, and when he saw the unequal struggle the Duke ran up to disengage them, although Don Quixote cried out:

'Let no one pull him off! Leave me to deal with this devil, this wizard, this enchanter, hand to hand. For I will teach him myself what it is to deal with Don Quixote de la Mancha.'

But the cat snarled and held on, heedless of his threats. At last, however, the Duke pulled it off and threw it out of the window, Don Quixote coming off with a scratched face and not too whole a nose. But he was much annoyed at not being left to finish the battle he was fighting so stoutly against that perverse enchanter. Then they sent for oil of Hypericum, and that same Altisidora with her whitest of hands put bandages on all his wounds, saying to him in a soft voice, as she bound them up:

'All these misfortunes befall you, flinty-hearted knight, for your sin of hardness and obstinacy. May it please God that your squire Sancho shall forget to whip himself, so that this beloved Dulcinea of yours may never emerge from her enchantment, and you may never enjoy her nor come to the bridal bed with her, at least while I, who adore you, am alive.'

To all this Don Quixote gave no word of reply, but heaved a deep sigh, and presently lay down on his bed, after thanking the Duke and Duchess for their kindness, not because he had been in any fear of that cattish and hellish rabble of enchanters, but because he realized their good intentions in coming to his rescue. The noble pair left him to rest and went away concerned at the unfortunate result of their joke, for they had not thought the adventure would have proved so tiresome and costly to Don Quixote. But it kept him confined to his room for five days.

From *The Adventures of Don Quixote* by Miguel de Cervantes Saavedra,
transl. J. M. Cohen

A Lick and a Promise

Whan ye se a cat syt in a wyndowe in the sonne, & that she lycke her ars, and that one of her fete be aboue her ere ye nede not doubte but yt shall rayne that daye.

From *A Historie of Four-Footed Beastes* by Edward Topsell

Venomous Cat Brain

It is reported that the flesh of Cats salted and sweetened hath power in it to draw wens from the body, and being warmed to cure the Hemmorhoids and pains in the veins and back, according to the Verse of Ursinus. In Spain and Gallia Norbon, they eat Cats, but first of all take away their head and tail, and hang the prepared flesh a night or two in the open cold air, to exhale the savour of it, finding the flesh thereof almost as sweet as a cony. The flesh of Cats can seldom be free from poison, by reason of their daily food, eating Rats and Mice,

Wrens and other birds which feed on poison, and above all the brain of the Cat is most venomous, for it being above all measure dry, stoppeth the animal spirits, that they cannot pass into the venticle, by reason thereof memory faileth, and the infected person falleth into a Phrenzie. The hair also of a Cat being eaten unawares, stoppeth the artery and causeth suffocation. To conclude this point it appeareth that this is a dangerous beast, and that therefore as for necessity we are constrained to nourish them for the suppressing of small vermin: so with a wary eye we must avoid their harms, making more account of their use than of their persons.

From *A Historie of Four-Footed Beastes* by Edward Topsell

Royalty Statement?

In the midsummer fires formerly kindled on the Place de Grève at Paris it was the custom to burn a basket, barrel, or sack full of live cats, which was hung from a tall mast in the midst of the bonfire; sometimes a fox was burned. The people collected the embers and ashes of the fire and took them home, believing that they brought good luck. The French kings often witnessed these spectacles and even lit the bonfires with their own hands. In 1648 Louis the Fourteenth, crowned with a wreath of roses and carrying a bunch of roses in his hand, kindled the fire, danced at it and partook of the banquet afterwards in the town hall. But this was the last occasion when a monarch presided at the midsummer bonfire in Paris. At Metz midsummer fires were lighted with great pomp on the esplanade, and a dozen cats, enclosed in wicker-cages, were burned alive in them, to the amusement of the people. Similarly at Gap, in the department of the High Alps, cats used to be roasted over the midsummer bonfire.

From *Balder the Beautiful: The Fire Festivals of Europe and the Doctrine of the External Soul* by J. G. Frazer

Royalty Statement? II

When Queen Elizabeth was crowned a feature of the procession was a wicker pope, the interior of which was filled with live cats, who 'squalled in a most hideous manner as soon as they felt the fire.' The culmination of many a religious fête in Germany, France, and England consisted in pitching some wretched puss off a height or into a bonfire. In 1753 certain Frenchmen received a quittance of one hundred *sols parisis* for having furnished during three years all the cats necessary for the fires of the festival of St John.

From *The Tiger in the House* by Carl van Vechten

The Louer

Whose mistresse feared a mouse, declareth that he would become a Cat if he might haue his desire.

> If I might alter kind,
> What, think you, I would bee?
> Nor Fish, nor Foule, nor Fle, nor Frog,
> Nor Squirril on the Tree;
> The Fish the Hooke, the Foule
> The lymed Twig doth catch,
> The Fle the Finger, and the Frog
> The Bustard doth dispatch.
>
> The Squirril thinking nought,
> That feately cracks the Nut,
> The greedie Goshawke wanting pray
> In dread of Death doth put;
> But scorning all these kindes,
> I would become a Cat,
> To combat with the creeping Mouse,
> And scratch the screeking Rat.
>
> I would be present, aye,
> And at my ladie's call;
> To gard her from the fearfull mouse,
> In Parlour and in Hall;
> In Kitchen, for his Lyfe,
> He should not shew his head;
> The Peare in Poke should lie untoucht
> When shee were gone to Bed.
> The Mouse should stand in Feare,
> So should the squeaking Rat;
> And this would I do if I were
> Converted to a Cat.

George Turberville

A Great Company for His Delight

Nicolas-Claude Fabri de Peresc (1580–1637), French writer and antiquarian, became a cat lover by contingency, as is recorded in his biography.

. . . And because we are speaking of his affection to dumb Creatures, it can do no hurt to tell you, that in his Boyes and Youths-Age, he was a great lover of Dogs. And by reason of mice which did gnaw his Books and Papers in his Chamber, be became a Lover of Cats, which he had formerly hated; and whereas at first he kept a few for necessity sake, he had afterwards a great Company for his delight. For, he procured out of the East, Ash-coloured, Dun, and Speckled Cats, beautiful to behold; of the Brood whereof, he sent to Paris, and other places, to his friends. And as nothing could pass his notice, he observed that Cats go with young, exactly nine weeks; that they conceive till they are more than fourteen years old; that they sometimes want a Mid-wife, to assist their bringing forth; that they give suck though they have not conceived; and the like things.

From *The Mirrour of true Nobility and Gentility being the Life of the Renowned Nicholas Claudius Fabricius Lord of Peiresk, Senator of the Parlaiment at Aix*, written by *The Learned Petrus Gassendus, Englished by W. Read Doctor of Physick – 1657*

An Inheritance

Item: I desire my sister, Marie Bluteau, and my niece, Madame Calonge, to look to my cats. If both should survive me, thirty sous a week must be laid out upon them, in order that they may live well.

They are to be served daily, in a clean and proper manner, with two meals of meat soup, the same as we eat ourselves, but it is to be given them separately in two soup-plates. The bread is not to be cut up into the soup, but must be broken into squares about the size of a nut, otherwise they will refuse to eat it. A ration of meat, finely minced, is to be added to it; the whole is then to be mildly seasoned, put into a clean pan, covered close, and carefully simmered before it is dished up. If only one cat should survive, half the sum mentioned will suffice.

From the will of Madame Dupuy

Old Tomcat into Damsel Gay

In strictest secrecy I've heard
And promised not to say a word
About a certain Lady's age,
Her name and face and parentage;
This Lady had a Cat whom she
Adored quite immoderately;
For his amusement once, her whim
Invented a disguise for him.
With tresses cleverly attached,
And precious earrings nicely matched,
The Cat's head she adorned, then she
Regarded him admiringly:
About his neck she hung fine pearls
Larger than the eyes of Merles;
A fine, white, laundered, linen shirt,
A little jacket and a skirt,
A collar and a neckerchief
Made, with the help of her belief,
Old Tomcat into Damsel gay.
Not quite a beauty,
But adequate, at least, to stir
The Dame who'd decorated her.
Then up before a looking-glass
The Lady held this darling lass:
This Cat who showed no evidence
Of being surprised, or of pretense
At joy for being by fool caressed,
Or seeing himself an Idol dressed.
Whatever happened then took place
Because she failed to embrace
Her Cat as closely as she might.
Without considering wrong or right,
The good Cat gained the stair,
And then the attic, and from there
Out upon the tiles he strayed;
Loudly crying, the Lady prayed
Her servants instantly to be
Out after him assiduously:

But in the country of the tiles
Wary Tomcats show their wiles.
They searched for him until they tired,
And the next day they enquired
Of the neighbours; some averred
They couldn't credit what they heard,
Others their belief asserted;
All were very much diverted;
And all the while the Cat uncaged
Never returned; the Lady raged
Less for the necklace's expense
Than for her Tomcat vanished thence.

Paul Scarron

4

CLASSIC CAT STORIES

True happiness, paradise . . . is where one is locked up and beaten, wherever there is meat.

Émile Zola, 'The Cat's Paradise'

Who Was to Blame?

As my uncle Pyotr Demyanitch, a lean, bilious collegiate councillor, exceedingly like a stale smoked fish with a stick through it, was getting ready to go to the high school, where he taught Latin, he noticed that the corner of his grammar was nibbled by mice.

'I say, Praskovya,' he said, going into the kitchen and addressing the cook, 'how is it we have got mice here? Upon my word! yesterday my top hat was nibbled, to-day they have disfigured my Latin grammar. . . . At this rate they will soon begin eating my clothes!'

'What can I do? I did not bring them in!' answered Praskovya.

'We must do something! You had better get a cat, hadn't you?'. . . .

'I've got a cat, but what good is it?'

And Praskovya pointed to the corner where a white kitten, thin as a match, lay curled up asleep beside a broom.

'Why is it no good?' asked Pyotr Demyanitch.

'It's young yet, and foolish. It's not two months old yet.'

'H'm. . . . Then it must be trained. It had much better be learning instead of lying there.'

Saying this, Pyotr Demyanitch sighed with a careworn air and went out of the kitchen. The kitten raised his head, looked lazily after him, and shut his eyes again.

The kitten lay awake thinking. Of what? Unacquainted with real life, having no store of accumulated impressions, his mental processes could only be instinctive, and he could but picture life in accordance with the conceptions that he had inherited, together with his flesh and blood, from his ancestors, the tigers (*vide* Darwin). His thoughts were of the nature of day-dreams. His feline imagination pictured something like the Arabian desert, over which flitted shadows closely resembling Praskovya, the stove, the broom. In the midst of the shadows there suddenly appeared a saucer of milk; the saucer began to grow paws, it began moving and displayed a tendency to run; the kitten made a bound, and with a thrill of bloodthirsty sensuality thrust his claws into it. . . . When the saucer had vanished into obscurity a piece of meat appeared, dropped by Praskovya; the meat ran away with a cowardly squeak, but the kitten made a bound and got his claws into it. . . . Everything that rose before the imagination of the young dreamer had for its starting-point leaps, claws, and teeth. . . . The soul of another is darkness, and a cat's soul more than most, but how near the visions just described are to the truth may be seen from the following fact: under the influence of his day-dreams the kitten suddenly leaped up, looked with flashing eyes at Praskovya, ruffled up his coat, and making one bound, thrust his claws into the cook's skirt. Obviously he was born a mouse catcher, a worthy son of his bloodthirsty ancestors. Fate had destined him to be the terror of cellars, store-rooms and cornbins, and had it not been for education . . . we will not anticipate, however.

On his way home from the high school, Pyotr Demyanitch went into a general shop and bought a mouse-trap for fifteen kopecks. At dinner he fixed a little bit of his rissole on the hook, and set the trap under the sofa, where there were heaps of the pupils' old exercise-books, which Praskovya used for various domestic purposes. At six o'clock in the evening, when the worthy Latin master was sitting at the table correcting his pupils' exercises, there was a sudden 'klop!' so loud that my uncle started and dropped his pen. He went at once to the sofa and took out the trap. A neat little mouse, the size of a thimble, was sniffing the wires and trembling with fear.

'Aha,' muttered Pyotr Demyanitch, and he looked at the mouse malignantly, as though he were about to give him a bad mark. 'You are cau—aught, wretch! Wait a bit! I'll teach you to eat my grammar!'

Having gloated over his victim, Pyotr Demyanitch put the mouse-trap on the floor and called:

'Praskovya, there's a mouse caught! Bring the kitten here!'

'I'm coming,' responded Praskovya, and a minute later she came in with the descendant of tigers in her arms.

'Capital!' said Pyotr Demyanitch, rubbing his hands. 'We will give him a lesson. . . . Put him down opposite the mouse-trap . . . that's it. . . . Let him sniff it and look at it. . . . That's it. . . .'

The kitten looked wonderingly at my uncle, at his arm-chair, sniffed the mouse-trap in bewilderment, then, frightened probably by the glaring lamplight and the attention directed to him, made a dash and ran in terror to the door.

'Stop!' shouted my uncle, seizing him by the tail, 'stop, you rascal! He's afraid of a mouse, the idiot! Look! It's a mouse! Look! Well? Look, I tell you!'

Pyotr Demyanitch took the kitten by the scruff of the neck and pushed him with his nose against the mouse-trap.

'Look, you carrion! Take him and hold him, Praskovya. . . . Hold him opposite the door of the trap. . . . When I let the mouse out, you let him go instantly. . . . Do you hear?. . . Instantly let go! Now!'

My uncle assumed a mysterious expression and lifted the door of the trap. . . . The mouse came out irresolutely, sniffed the air, and flew like an arrow under the sofa. . . . The kitten on being released darted under the table with his tail in the air.

'It has got away! got away!' cried Pyotr Demyanitch, looking ferocious. 'Where is he, the scoundrel? Under the table? You wait. . . .'

My uncle dragged the kitten from under the table and shook him in the air.

'Wretched little beast,' he muttered, smacking him on the ear. 'Take that, take that! Will you shirk it next time? Wr-r-r-etch. . . .'

Next day Praskovya heard again the summons.

'Praskovya, there is a mouse caught! Bring the kitten here!'

After the outrage of the previous day the kitten had taken refuge under the stove and had not come out all night. When Praskovya pulled him out and, carrying him by the scruff of the neck into the study, set him down before the mouse-trap, he trembled all over and mewed piteously.

'Come, let him feel at home first,' Pyotr Demyanitch commanded. 'Let him look and sniff. Look and learn! Stop, plague take you!' he shouted, noticing that the kitten was backing away from the mouse-trap. 'I'll thrash you! Hold him by the ear! That's it. . . . Well now, set him down before the trap. . . .'

My uncle slowly lifted the door of the trap . . . the mouse whisked under the very nose of the kitten, flung itself against Praskovya's hand and fled under the cupboard; the kitten, feeling himself free, took a desperate bound and retreated under the sofa.

'He's let another mouse go!' bawled Pyotr Demyanitch. 'Do you call that a cat? Nasty little beast! Thrash him! thrash him by the mouse-trap!'

When the third mouse had been caught, the kitten shivered all over at the sight of the mouse-trap and its inmate, and scratched Praskovya's hand. . . . After the fourth mouse my uncle flew into a rage, kicked the kitten, and said:

'Take the nasty thing away! Get rid of it! Chuck it away! It's no earthly use!'

A year passed, the thin, frail kitten had turned into a solid and sagacious tom-cat. One day he was on his way by the back yards to an amatory interview. He had just reached his destination when he suddenly heard a rustle, and thereupon caught sight of a mouse which ran from a water-trough towards a stable; my hero's hair stood on end, he arched his back, hissed, and trembling all over, took to ignominious flight.

Alas! sometimes I feel myself in the ludicrous position of the flying cat. Like the kitten, I had in my day the honour of being taught Latin by my uncle. Now, whenever I chance to see some work of classical antiquity, instead of being moved to eager enthusiasm, I begin recalling, *ut consecutivum*, the irregular verbs, the sallow grey face of my uncle, the ablative absolute. . . . I turn pale, my hair stands up on my head, and, like the cat, I take to ignominious flight.

Anton Chekhov, transl. Constance Garnett

The Cat's Paradise

I was then two years old, and was at the same time the fattest and most naive cat in existence. At that tender age I still had all the presumptuousness of an animal who is disdainful of the sweetness of home.

How fortunate I was, indeed, that providence had placed me with your aunt! That good woman adored me. I had at the bottom of a wardrobe a veritable sleeping salon, with feather cushions and triple covers. My food was equally excellent; never just bread, or soup, but always meat, carefully chosen meat.

Well, in the midst of all this opulence, I had only one desire, one dream, and that was to slip out of the upper window and escape on to the roofs. Caresses annoyed me, the softness of my bed nauseated me, and I was so fat that it was disgusting even to myself. In short, I was bored the whole day long just with being happy.

I must tell you that by stretching my neck a bit, I had seen the roof directly in front of my window. That day four cats were playing with each other up there; their fur bristling, their tails high, they were romping around with every indication of joy on the blue roof slates baked by the sun. I had never before watched such an extraordinary spectacle. And from then on I had a definitely fixed belief: out there on that roof was true happiness, out there beyond the window which was always closed so carefully. In proof of that contention I remembered that the doors of the chest in which the meat was kept were also closed, just as carefully!

I resolved to flee. After all there had to be other things in life besides a comfortable bed. Out there was the unknown, the ideal. And then one day they forgot to close the kitchen window. I jumped out on to the small roof above it.

How beautiful the roofs were! The wide eaves bordering them exuded delicious smells. Carefully I followed those eaves, where my feet sank into fine mud that smelled tepid and infinitely sweet. It felt as if I were walking on velvet. And the sun shone with a good warmth that caressed my plumpness.

I will not hide from you the fact that I was trembling all over. There was something overwhelming in my joy. I remember particularly the tremendous emotional upheaval which actually made me lose my footing on the slates, when three cats rolled down from the ridge of the roof and approached with excited miaows. But when I showed signs of fear, they told me I was a silly fat goose and insisted that their miaowing was only laughter.

I decided to join them in their caterwauling. It was fun, even though the three stalwarts weren't as fat as I was and made fun of me when I rolled like a ball over the roof heated by the sun.

An old tomcat belonging to the gang honoured me particularly with his friendship. He offered to take care of my education, an offer which I accepted with gratitude.

Oh, how far away seemed all the soft things of your aunt! I drank from the gutters, and never did sugared milk taste half as fine! Everything was good and beautiful.

A female cat passed by, a ravishing she, and the very sight of her filled me with strange emotions. Only in my dreams had I up to then seen such an exquisite creature with such a magnificently arched back. We dashed forward to meet the newcomer, my three companions and myself. I was actually ahead of the others in paying the enchanting female my compliments; but then one of my comrades gave me a nasty bite in the neck, and I let out a shriek of pain.

'Pshaw!' said the old tomcat, dragging me away. 'You will meet plenty of others.'

After a walk that lasted an hour I had a ravenous appetite.

'What does one eat on these roofs?' I asked my friend the tom.

'Whatever one finds,' he replied laconically.

This answer embarrassed me somewhat for, hunt as I might, I couldn't find a thing. Finally I looked through a dormer window and saw a young workman preparing his breakfast. On the table, just above the windowsill, lay a chop of a particularly succulent red.

'There is my chance,' I thought, rather naively.

So I jumped on to the table and snatched the chop. But the workingman saw me and gave me a terrific wallop across my back with a broom. I dropped the meat, cursed rather vulgarly and escaped.

'What part of the world do you come from?' asked the tomcat. 'Don't you know that meat on tables is meant only to be admired from afar? What we've got to do is look in the gutters.'

I have never been able to understand why kitchen meat shouldn't belong to cats. My stomach began to complain quite bitterly. The tom tried to console me by saying it would only be necessary to wait for the night. Then, he said, we would climb down from the roofs into the streets and forage in the garbage heaps.

Wait for the night! Confirmed philosopher that he was, he said it calmly while the very thought of such a protracted fast made me positively faint.

Night came ever so slowly, a misty night that made me shiver. To make things worse, rain began to fall, a thin, penetrating rain whipped up by brisk howling gusts of wind.

How desolate the streets looked to me! There was nothing left of the good warmth, of the big sun, of those roofs where one could play so pleasantly. My paws slipped on the slimy pavement, and I began to think with some longing of my triple covers and my feather pillow.

We had hardly reached the street when my friend, the tom, began to tremble. He made himself small, quite small, and glided surreptitiously along the walls of the houses, warning me under his breath to be quick about it. When we reached the shelter of a house door, he hid behind it and purred with satisfaction. And when I asked him the reason for his strange conduct, he said:

'Did you see that man with the hook and the basket?'

'Yes.'

'Well, if he had seen us, we would have been caught, fried on the spit and eaten!'

'Fried on the spit and eaten!' I exclaimed. 'Why, then the street is really not for the likes of us. One does not eat, but is eaten instead!'

In the meantime, however, they had begun to put the garbage out on the sidewalks. I inspected it with growing despair. All I found there were two or three dry bones that had obviously been thrown in among the ashes. And then and there I realized how succulent a dish of fresh meat really is!

My friend, the tom, went over the heaps of garbage with consummate artistry. He made me rummage around until morning, inspecting every cobblestone, without the least trace of hurry. But after ten hours of almost incessant rain my whole body was trembling. Damn the street, I thought, damn liberty! And how I longed for my prison!

When day came, the tomcat noticed that I was weakening.

'You've had enough, eh?' he asked in a strange voice.

'Oh, yes,' I replied.

'Do you want to go home?'

'I certainly do. But how can I find my house?'

'Come along. Yesterday morning when I saw you come out I knew immediately that a cat as fat as you isn't made for the joys of liberty. I know where you live. I'll take you back to your door.'

He said this all simply enough, the good, dignified tom. And when we finally got there, he added, without the slightest show of emotion:

'Goodbye, then.'

'No, no!' I protested. 'I shall not leave you like this. You come with me! We shall share bed and board. My mistress is a good woman . . .'

He didn't even let me finish.

'Shut up!' he said brusquely. 'You are a fool. I'd die in that stuffy softness. Your abundant life is for weaklings. Free cats will never buy your comforts and your featherbeds at the price of being imprisoned. Goodbye!'

With these words he climbed back on to the roof. I saw his proud thin shadow shudder deliciously as it began to feel the warmth of the morning sun.

When I came home your aunt acted the martinet and administered a corrective which I received with profound joy. I revelled in being punished and voluptuously warm. And while she cuffed me, I thought with delight of the meat she would give me directly afterwards.

You see – an afterthought, while stretched out before the embers – true happiness, paradise, my master, is where one is locked up and beaten, wherever there is meat.

I speak for cats.

Émile Zola

The Squaw

Nurnberg at the time was not so much exploited as it has been since then. Irving had not been playing *Faust* and the very name of the old town was hardly known to the great bulk of the travelling public. My wife and I being in the second week of our honeymoon, naturally wanted someone else to join our party, so that when the cheery stranger, Elias P. Hutcheson, hailing from Isthmian City, Bleeding Gulch, Maple Tree County, Neb. turned up at the station at Frankfurt, and casually remarked that he was going on to see the most all-fired old Methuselah of a town in Yurrup, and that he guessed that so much travelling alone was enough to send an intelligent, active citizen into the melancholy ward of a daft house, we took the pretty broad hint and suggested that we should join forces. We found, on comparing notes afterwards, that we had each intended to speak with some diffidence or hesitation so as not to appear too eager, such not being a good compliment to the success of our married life; but the effect was entirely marred by our both beginning to speak at the same instant – stopping simultaneously and then going on together again. Anyhow, no matter how, it was done; and Elias P. Hutcheson became one of our party. Straightway Amelia and I found the pleasant benefit; instead of quarrelling, as we had been doing, we found that the restraining influence of a third party was such that we now took every opportunity of spooning in odd corners. Amelia declares that ever since she has, as the result of that experience, advised all her friends to take a friend on the honeymoon. Well, we 'did' Nurnberg together, and much enjoyed the racy remarks of our Transatlantic friend, who, from his quaint speech and his wonderful stock of adventures, might have stepped out of a novel. We kept for the last object of interest in the city to be visited the Burg, and on the day appointed for the visit strolled round the outer wall of the city by the eastern side.

The Burg is seated on a rock dominating the town and an immensely deep fosse guards it on the northern side. Nurnberg has been happy in that it was never sacked; had it been it would certainly not be so spick and span perfect as it is at present. The ditch has not been used for centuries, and now its base is spread with tea-gardens and orchards, of which some of the trees are of quite respectable growth. As we wandered round the wall, dawdling in the hot July sunshine, we often paused to admire the views spread before us, and in especial the great plain covered with towns and villages and bounded with a blue line of hills, like a landscape of Claude Lorraine. From this we always turned with new delight to the city itself, with its myriad of quaint old gables and acrewide red roofs dotted with dormer windows, tier upon tier. A little to our right rose the towers of the Burg, and nearer still, standing grim, the Torture Tower, which was, and is, perhaps, the most interesting place in the city. For centuries the tradition of the Iron Virgin of Nurnberg has been handed down as an instance of the horrors of cruelty of which man is capable; we had long looked forward to seeing it; and here at last was its home.

In one of our pauses we leaned over the wall of the moat and looked down. The garden seemed quite fifty or sixty feet below us, and the sun pouring into it with an intense, moveless heat like that of an oven. Beyond rose the grey, grim wall seemingly of endless height, and losing itself right and left in the angles of bastion and counterscarp. Trees and bushes crowned the wall, and above again towered the lofty houses on whose massive beauty Time has only set the hand of approval. The sun was hot and we were lazy; time was our own, and we lingered, leaning on the wall. Just below us was a pretty sight – a great black cat lying stretched in the sun, whilst round her gambolled prettily a tiny black kitten. The mother would wave her tail for the kitten to play with, or would raise her feet and push away the little one as an encouragement to further play. They were just at the foot of the wall, and Elias P. Hutcheson, in order to help the play, stooped and took from the walk a moderate sized pebble.

'See!' he said, 'I will drop it near the kitten, and they will both wonder where it came from.'

'Oh, be careful,' said my wife; 'you might hit the dear little thing!'

'Not me, ma'am,' said Elias P. 'Why, I'm as tender as a Maine cherry-tree. Lor, bless ye, I wouldn't hurt the poor pooty little critter more'n I'd scalp a

baby. An' you may bet your variegated socks on that! See, I'll drop it fur away
on the outside so's not to go near her!' Thus saying, he leaned over and held
his arm out at full length and dropped the stone. It may be that there is some
attractive force which draws lesser matters to greater; or more probably that
the wall was not plumb but sloped to its base – we not noticing the inclination
from above; but the stone fell with a sickening thud that came up to us through
the hot air, right on the kitten's head, and shattered out its little brains then
and there. The black cat cast a swift upward glance, and we saw her eyes like
green fire fixed an instant on Elias P. Hutcheson; and then her attention was
given to the kitten, which lay still with just a quiver of her tiny limbs, whilst a
thin red stream trickled from a gaping wound. With a muffled cry, such as a
human being might give, she bent over the kitten licking its wounds and moaning. Suddenly she seemed to realise that it was dead, and again threw her eyes
up at us. I shall never forget the sight, for she looked the perfect incarnation
of hate. Her green eyes blazed with lurid fire, and the white, sharp teeth
seemed to almost shine through the blood which dabbled her mouth and
whiskers. She gnashed her teeth, and her claws stood out stark and at full
length on every paw. Then she made a wild rush up the wall as if to reach us,
but when the momentum ended fell back, and further added to her horrible
appearance for she fell on the kitten, and rose with her black fur smeared with
its brains and blood. Amelia turned quite faint, and I had to lift her back from
the wall. There was a seat close by in shade of a spreading plane-tree, and here
I placed her whilst she composed herself. Then I went back to Hutcheson, who
stood without moving, looking down on the angry cat below.

As I joined him, he said:

'Wall, I guess that air the savagest beast I ever see – 'cept once when an
Apache squaw had an edge on a half-breed what they nicknamed "Splinters"
'cos of the way he fixed up her papoose which he stole on a raid just to show
that he appreciated the way they had given his mother the fire torture. She got
that kinder look so set on her face that it jest seemed to grow there. She followed Splinters mor'n three year till at last the braves got him and handed him
over to her. They did say that no man, white or Injun, had ever been so long
a-dying under the tortures of the Apaches. The only time I ever see her smile
was when I wiped her out. I kem on the camp just in time to see Splinters pass
in his checks, and he wasn't sorry to go either. He was a hard citizen, and
though I never could shake with him after that papoose business – for it was
bitter bad, and he should have been a white man, for he looked like one – I see
he had got paid out in full. Durn me, but I took a piece of his hide from one
of his skinnin' posts an' had it made into a pocket-book. It's here now!' and he
slapped the breast pocket of his coat.

Whilst he was speaking the cat was continuing her frantic efforts to get up the wall. She would take a run back and then charge up, sometimes reaching an incredible height. She did not seem to mind the heavy fall which she got each time but started with renewed vigour; and at every tumble her appearance became more horrible. Hutcheson was a kind-hearted man – my wife and I had both noticed little acts of kindness to animals as well as to persons – and he seemed concerned at the state of fury to which the cat had wrought herself.

'Wall, now!' he said, 'I du declare that that poor critter seems quite desperate. There! there! poor thing, it was all an accident – thought that won't bring back your little one to you. Say! I wouldn't have had such a thing happen for a thousand! Just shows what a clumsy fool of a man can do when he tries to play! Seems I'm too darned slipperhanded to even play with a cat. Say Colonel!' – it was a pleasant way he had to bestow titles freely – 'I hope your wife don't hold no grudge against me on account of this unpleasantness? Why, I wouldn't have had it occur on no account.'

He came over to Amelia and apologised profusely, and she with her usual kindness of heart hastened to assure him that she quite understood that it was an accident. Then we all went again to the wall and looked over.

The cat missing Hutcheson's face had drawn back across the moat, and was sitting on her haunches as though ready to spring. Indeed, the very instant she saw him she did spring, and with a blind unreasoning fury, which would have been grotesque, only that it was so frightfully real. She did not try to run up the wall, but simply launched herself at him as though hate and fury could lend her wings to pass straight through the great distance between them. Amelia, womanlike, got quite concerned, and said to Elias P. in a warning voice:

'Oh! you must be very careful. That animal would try to kill you if she were here; her eyes look like positive murder.'

He laughed out jovially. 'Excuse me, ma'am,' he said, 'but I can't help laughin'. Fancy a man that has fought grizzlies an' Injuns bein' careful of bein' murdered by a cat!'

When the cat heard him laugh, her whole demeanour seemed to change. She no longer tried to jump or run up the wall, but went quietly over, and sitting again beside the dead kitten began to lick and fondle it as though it were alive.

'See!' said I, 'the effect of a really strong man. Even that animal in the midst of her fury recognises the voice of a master, and bows to him!'

'Like a squaw!' was the only comment of Elias P. Hutcheson, as we moved on our way round the city fosse. Every now and then we looked over the wall and each time saw the cat following us. At first she had kept going back to the dead kitten, and then as the distance grew greater took it in her mouth and so followed. After a while, however, she abandoned this, for we saw her following all alone; she had evidently hidden the body somewhere. Amelia's alarm grew at the cat's persistence, and more than once she repeated her warning; but the American always laughed with amusement, till finally, seeing that she was beginning to be worried, he said:

'I say, ma'am, you needn't be skeered over that cat. I go heeled, I du!' Here he slapped his pistol pocket at the back of his lumbar region. 'Why sooner'n have you worried, I'll shoot the critter, right here, an' risk the police interferin' with a citizen of the United States for carryin' arms contrairy to reg'lations!' As he spoke he looked over the wall, but the cat on seeing him, retreated, with a growl, into a bed of tall flowers, and was hidden. He went on: 'Blest if that ar critter ain't got more sense of what's good for her than most Christians. I guess we've seen the last of her! You bet, she'll go back now to that busted kitten and have a private funeral of it, all to herself!'

Amelia did not like to say more, lest he might, in mistaken kindness to her, fulfil his threat of shooting the cat: and so we went on and crossed the little wooden bridge leading to the gateway whence ran the steep paved roadway between the Burg and the pentagonal Torture Tower. As we crossed the bridge we saw the cat again down below us. When she saw us her fury seemed to return, and she made frantic efforts to get up the steep wall. Hutcheson laughed as he looked down at her, and said:

'Goodbye, old girl. Sorry I injured your feelin's, but you'll get over it in time! So long!' And then we passed through the long, dim archway and came to the gate of the Burg.

When we came out again after our survey of this most beautiful old place which not even the well-intentioned efforts of the Gothic restorers of forty years ago have been able to spoil – though their restoration was then glaring white – we seemed to have quite forgotten the unpleasant episode of the morning. The old lime tree with its great trunk gnarled with the passing of nearly nine centuries, the deep well cut through the heart of the rock by those captives of old, and the lovely view from the city wall whence we heard, spread over almost a full quarter of an hour, the multitudinous chimes of the city, had all helped to wipe out from our minds the incident of the slain kitten.

We were the only visitors who had entered the Torture Tower that morning – so at least said the old custodian – and as we had the place all to ourselves were able to make a minute and more satisfactory survey than would have otherwise been possible. The custodian, looking to us as the sole source of his gains for the day, was willing to meet our wishes in any way. The Torture Tower is truly a grim place, even now when many thousands of visitors have sent a stream of life, and the joy that follows life, into the place; but at the time I mention it wore its grimmest and most gruesome aspect. The dust of ages seemed to have settled on it, and the darkness and the horror of its memories seem to have become sentient in a way that would have satisfied the Pantheistic souls of Philo or Spinoza. The lower chamber where we entered was seemingly, in its normal state, filled with incarnate darkness; even the hot sunlight streaming in through the door seemed to be lost in the vast thickness of the walls, and only showed the masonry rough as when the builder's scaffolding had come down, but coated with dust and marked here and there with patches of dark stain which, if walls could speak, could have given their own dread memories of fear and pain. We were glad to pass up the dusty wooden staircase, the custodian leaving the outer door open to light us somewhat on our way; for to our eyes the one long-wick'd, evil-smelling candle stuck in a sconce on the wall gave an inadequate light. When we came up through the open trap in the corner of the chamber overhead, Amelia held on to me so tightly that I could actually feel her heart beat. I must say for my own part that I was not surprised at her fear, for this room was even more gruesome than that below. Here there was certainly more light, but only just sufficient to realise the horrible surroundings of the place. The builders of the tower had evidently intended that only they who should gain the top should have any of the joys of light and prospect. There, as we had noticed from below, were ranges of windows, albeit of mediaeval smallness, but elsewhere in the tower were only a very few narrow slits such as were habitual in places of mediaeval defence. A few of these only lit the chamber, and these so high up in the wall that from no part could the sky be seen through the thickness of the walls. In racks, and leaning in disorder against the walls, were a number of headsmen's swords, great double-handed weapons with broad blade and keen edge. Hard by were several blocks whereon the necks of the victims had lain, with here and there deep notches where the steel had bitten through the guard of flesh and shored into the wood. Round the chamber, placed in all sorts of irregular ways, were many implements of torture which made one's heart ache to see – chairs full of spikes which gave instant and excruciating pain; chairs and couches with dull knobs whose torture was seemingly less, but which, though slower, were equally efficacious; racks, belts, boots, gloves, collars, all made for compressing at will; steel baskets in which the head could be slowly crushed into a pulp if necessary; watchmen's hooks with long handle and knife that cut at resistance – this a speciality of the old Nurnberg police system; and many, many other devices for man's injury to man. Amelia grew quite pale with the horror of the things, but fortunately did not faint, for being a little overcome she sat down on a torture chair, but jumped up again with a shriek, all tendency to faint gone. We both pretended that it was the injury done to her dress by the dust of the chair, and the rusty spikes which had upset her, and Mr Hutcheson acquiesced in accepting the explanation with a kind-hearted laugh.

But the central object in the whole of this chamber of horrors was the engine known as the Iron Virgin, which stood near the centre of the room. It was a rudely-shaped figure of a woman, something of the bell order, or, to make a closer comparison, of the figure of Mrs Noah in the children's Ark, but without that slimness of waist and perfect *rondeur* of hip which marks the aesthetic type of the Noah family. One would hardly have recognised it as intended for a human figure at all had not the founder shaped on the forehead a rude semblance of a woman's face. This machine was coated with rust without, and covered with dust; a rope was fastened to a ring in the front of the figure, about where the waist should have been, and was drawn through a pulley, fastened on the wooden pillar which sustained the flooring above. The custodian pulling this rope showed that a section of the front was hinged like a door at one side; we then saw that the engine was of considerable thickness, leaving just room enough inside for a man to be placed. The door was of equal thickness and of great weight, for it took the custodian all his strength, aided though he was by the contrivance of the pulley, to open it. This weight was partly due to the fact that the door was of manifest purpose hung so as to throw its weight downwards, so that it might shut of its own accord when the strain was released. The inside was honeycombed with rust – nay more, the rust alone that comes through time would hardly have eaten so deep into the iron walls; the rust of the cruel stains was deep indeed! It was only, however, when we came to look at the inside of the door that the diabolical intention was manifest to the full. Here were several long spikes, square and massive, broad at the base and sharp at the points, placed in such a position that when the door should close the upper ones would pierce the eyes of the victim, and the lower ones his heart and vitals. The sight was too much for poor Amelia, and this time she fainted dead off, and I had to carry her down the stairs, and place her on a bench outside till she recovered. That she felt it to the quick was afterwards shown by the fact that my eldest son bears to this day a rude birthmark on his breast, which has, by family consent, been accepted as representing the Nurnberg Virgin.

When we got back to the chamber we found Hutcheson still opposite the Iron Virgin; he had been evidently philosophising, and now gave us the benefit of his thought in the shape of a sort of exordium.

'Wall, I guess I've been learnin' somethin' here while madam has been gettin' over her faint. 'Pears to me that we're a long way behind the times on our side of the big drink. We uster think out on the plains that the Injun could give

us points in tryin' to make a man uncomfortable; but I guess your old mediaeval law-and-order party could raise him every time. Splinters was pretty good
in his bluff on the squaw, but this here young miss held a straight flush all high
on him. The points of them spikes air sharp enough still, though even the
edges air eaten out by what uster be on them. It'd be a good thing for our
Indian section to get some specimens of this here play-toy to send round to the
Reservations jest to knock the stuffin' out of the bucks, and the squaws too, by
showing them as how old civilisation lays over them at their best. Guess but
I'll get in that box a minute jest to see how it feels!'

'Oh no! no!' said Amelia. 'It is too terrible!'

'Guess, ma'am, nothin's too terrible to the explorin' mind. I've been in some
queer places in my time. Spent a night inside a dead horse while a prairie fire
swept over me in Montana Territory – an' another time slept inside a dead
buffler when the Comanches was on the war path an' I didn't keer to leave my
kyard on them. I've been two days in a caved-in tunnel in the Billy Broncho
gold mine in New Mexico, an' was one of the four shut up for three parts of a
day in the caisson what slid over on her side when we was settin' the founda-
tions of the Buffalo Bridge. I've not funked an odd experience yet, an' I don't
propose to begin now!'

We saw that he was set on the experiment, so I said: 'Well, hurry up, old
man, and get through it quick!'

'All right, General,' said he, 'but I calculate we ain't quite ready yet. The
gentlemen, my predecessors, what stood in that thar canister, didn't volunteer
for the office – not much! And I guess there was some ornamental tyin' up
before the big stroke was made. I want to go into this thing fair and square, so
I must get fixed up proper first. I dare say this old galoot can rise some string
and tie me up accordin' to sample?'

This was said interrogatively to the old custodian, but the latter, who understood the drift of his speech, though perhaps not appreciating to the full the
niceties of dialect and imagery, shook his head. His protest was, however, only
formal and made to be overcome. The American thrust a gold piece into his
hand, saying: 'Take it, pard! it's your pot; and don't be skeer'd. This ain't no
necktie party that you're asked to assist in!' He produced some thin frayed
rope and proceeded to bind our companion with sufficient strictness for the
purpose. When the upper part of his body was bound, Hutcheson said:

'Hold on a moment, Judge. Guess I'm too heavy for you to tote into the canister. You jest let me walk in, and then you can wash up regardin' my legs!'

Whilst speaking he had backed himself into the opening which was just
enough to hold him. It was a close fit and no mistake. Amelia looked on with
fear in her eyes, but she evidently did not like to say anything. Then the cus-

todian completed his task by tying the American's feet together so that he was now absolutely helpless and fixed in his voluntary prison. He seemed to really enjoy it, and the incipient smile which was habitual to his face blossomed into actuality as he said:

'Guess this here Eve was made out of the rib of a dwarf! There ain't much room for a full-grown citizen of the United States to hustle. We uster make our coffins more roomier in Idaho territory. Now, Judge, you just begin to let this door down, slow, on to me. I want to feel the same pleasure as the other jays had when those spikes began to move toward their eyes!'

'Oh no! no! no!' broke in Amelia hysterically. 'It is too terrible! I can't bear to see it! – I can't! I can't!' But the American was obdurate. 'Say, Colonel,' said he, 'why not take Madame for a little promenade? I wouldn't hurt her feelin's for the world; but now that I am here, havin' kem eight thousand miles, would-n't it be too hard to give up the very experience I've been pinin' an' pantin' fur? A man can't get to feel like canned goods every time! Me and the Judge here'll fix up this thing in no time, an' then you'll come back, an' we'll all laugh together!'

Once more the resolution that is born of curiosity triumphed, and Amelia stayed holding tight to my arm and shivering whilst the custodian began to slacken slowly inch by inch the rope that held back the iron door. Hutcheson's face was positively radiant as his eyes followed the first movement of the spikes.

'Wall!' he said, 'I guess I've not had enjoyment like this since I left Noo York. Bar a scrap with a French sailor at Wapping – an' that warn't much of a picnic neither – I've not had a show fur real pleasure in this dod-rotted Continent, where there ain't no b'ars nor no Injuns, an' wheer nary man goes heeled. Slow there, Judge! Don't you rush this business! I want a show for my money this game – I du!'

The custodian must have had in him some of the blood of his predecessors in that ghastly tower, for he worked the engine with a deliberate and excruci-ating slowness which after five minutes, in which the outer edge of the door had not moved half as many inches, began to overcome Amelia. I saw her lips whiten, and felt her hold upon my arm relax. I looked around an instant for a place whereon to lay her, and when I looked at her again found that her eye had become fixed on the side of the Virgin. Following its direction I saw the black cat crouching out of sight. Her green eyes shone like danger lamps in the gloom of the place, and their colour was heightened by the blood which still smeared her coat and reddened her mouth. I cried out:

'The cat! look out for the cat!' for even then she sprang out before the engine. At this moment she looked like a triumphant demon. Her eyes blazed with ferocity, her hair bristled out till she seemed twice her normal size, and her tail lashed about as does a tiger's when the quarry is before it. Elias P. Hutcheson when he saw her was amused, and his eyes positively sparkled with fun as he said:

'Darned if the squaw hain't got on all her war paint! Jest give her a shove off if she comes any of her tricks on me, for I'm so fixed everlastingly by the boss, that durn my skin if I can keep my eyes from her if she wants them! Easy there, Judge! don't you slack that ar rope or I'm euchered!'

At this moment Amelia completed her faint, and I had to clutch hold of her round the waist or she would have fallen to the floor. Whilst attending to her I saw the black cat crouching for a spring, and jumped up to turn the creature out.

But at that instant, with a sort of hellish scream, she hurled herself, not as we expected at Hutcheson, but straight at the face of the custodian. Her claws seemed to be tearing wildly as one sees in the Chinese drawings of the dragon rampant, and as I looked I saw one of them light on the poor man's eye, and actually tear through it and down his cheek, leaving a wide band of red where the blood seemed to spurt from every vein.

With a yell of sheer terror which came quicker than even his sense of pain, the man leaped back, dropping as he did so the rope which held back the iron door. I jumped for it, but was too late, for the cord ran like lightning through the pulley-block, and the heavy mass fell forward from its own weight.

As the door closed I caught a glimpse of our poor companion's face. He seemed frozen with terror. His eyes stared with a horrible anguish as if dazed, and no sound came from his lips.

And then the spikes did their work. Happily the end was quick, for when I wrenched open the door they had pierced so deep that they had locked in the bones of the skull through which they had crushed, and actually tore him – it – out of his iron prison till, bound as he was, he fell at full length with a sickly thud upon the floor, the face turning upward as he fell.

I rushed to my wife, lifted her up and carried her out, for I feared for her very reason if she should wake from her faint to such a scene. I laid her on the bench outside and ran back. Leaning against the wooden column was the custodian moaning in pain whilst he held his reddening handkerchief to his eyes. And sitting on the head of the poor American was the cat, purring loudly as she licked the blood which trickled through the gashed socket of his eyes.

I think no one will call me cruel because I seized one of the old executioner's swords and shore her in two as she sat.

From *Dracula's Guest* by Bram Stoker

An Incident

Morning. Brilliant sunshine is piercing through the frozen lacework on the window-panes into the nursery. Vanya, a boy of six, with a cropped head and a nose like a button, and his sister Nina, a short, chubby, curly-headed girl of four, wake up and look crossly at each other through the bars of their cots.

'Oo-oo-oo! naughty children!' grumbles their nurse. 'Good people have had their breakfast already, while you can't get your eyes open.'

The sunbeams frolic over the rugs, the walls, and nurse's skirts, and seem inviting the children to join in their play, but they take no notice. They have woken up in a bad humour. Nina pouts, makes a grimace, and begins to whine:

'Brea-eakfast, nurse, breakfast!'

Vanya knits his brows and ponders what to pitch upon to howl over. He has already begun screwing up his eyes and opening his mouth, but at that instant the voice of mamma reaches them from the drawing-room, saying: 'Don't forget to give the cat her milk, she has a family now!'

The children's puckered countenances grow smooth again as they look at each other in astonishment. Then both at once begin shouting, jump out of their cots, and filling the air with piercing shrieks, run barefoot, in their nightgowns, to the kitchen.

'The cat has puppies!' they cry. 'The cat has got puppies!'

Under the bench in the kitchen there stands a small box, the one in which Stepan brings coal when he lights the fire. The cat is peeping out of the box. There is an expression of extreme exhaustion on her grey face; her green eyes, with their narrow black pupils, have a languid, sentimental look. . . . From her face it is clear that the only thing lacking to complete her happiness is the presence in the box of 'him,' the father of her children, to whom she had abandoned herself so recklessly! She wants to mew, and opens her mouth wide, but nothing but a hiss comes from her throat; the squealing of the kittens is audible.

The children squat on their heels before the box, and, motionless, holding their breath, gaze at the cat. . . . They are surprised, impressed, and do not hear nurse grumbling as she pursues them. The most genuine delight shines in the eyes of both.

Domestic animals play a scarcely noticed but undoubtedly beneficial part in the education and life of children. Which of us does not remember powerful but magnanimous dogs, lazy lapdogs, birds dying in captivity, dull-witted but haughty turkeys, mild old tabby cats, who forgave us when we trod on their tails for fun and caused them agonizing pain? I even fancy, sometimes, that the patience, the fidelity, the readiness to forgive, and the sincerity which are characteristic of our domestic animals have a far stronger and more definite effect on the mind of a child than the long exhortations of some dry, pale Karl Karlovitch, or the misty expositions of a governess, trying to prove to children that water is made up of hydrogen and oxygen.

'What little things!' says Nina, opening her eyes wide and going off into a joyous laugh. 'They are like mice!'

'One, two, three,' Vanya counts. 'Three kittens. So there is one for you, one for me, and one for somebody else, too.'

'Murrm . . . murrm . . .' purrs the mother, flattered by their attention. 'Murrm.'

After gazing at the kittens, the children take them from under the cat, and begin squeezing them in their hands, then, not satisfied with this, they put them in the skirts of their nightgowns, and run into the other rooms.

'Mamma, the cat has got pups!' they shout.

Mamma is sitting in the drawing-room with some unknown gentleman. Seeing the children unwashed, undressed, with their nightgowns held up high, she is embarrassed, and looks at them severely.

'Let your nightgowns down, disgraceful children,' she says. 'Go out of the room, or I will punish you.'

But the children do not notice either mamma's threats or othe presence of a stranger. They put the kittens down on the carpet, and go off into deafening squeals. The mother walks round them, mewing imploringly. When, a little afterwards, the children are dragged off to the nursery, dressed, made to say their prayers, and given their breakfast, they are full of a passionate desire to get away from these prosaic duties as quickly as possible, and to run to the kitchen again.

Their habitual pursuits and games are thrown completely into the background.

The kittens throw everything into the shade by making their appearance in the world, and supply the great sensation of the day. If Nina or Vanya had been offered forty pounds of sweets or ten thousand kopecks for each kitten, they would have rejected such a barter without the slightest hesitation. In spite of the heated protests of the nurse and the cook, the children persist in sitting by the cat's box in the kitchen, busy with the kittens till dinner-time. Their faces are earnest and concentrated and express anxiety. They are worried not so much by the present as by the future of the kittens. They decide that one kitten shall remain at home with the old cat to be a comfort to her mother, while the second shall go to their summer villa, and the third shall live in the cellar, where there are ever so many rats.

'But why don't they look at us?' Nina wondered. 'Their eyes are blind like the beggars'.'

Vanya, too, is perturbed by this question. He tries to open one kitten's eyes, and spends a long time puffing and breathing hard over it, but his operation is unsuccessful. They are a good deal troubled, too, by the circumstance that the kittens obstinately refuse the milk and the meat that is offered to them. Everything that is put before their little noses is eaten by their grey mamma.

'Let's build the kittens little houses,' Vanya suggests. 'They shall live in different houses, and the cat shall come and pay them visits. . . .'

Cardboard hat-boxes are put in the different corners of the kitchen and the kittens are installed in them. But this division turns out to be premature: the cat, still wearing an imploring and sentimental expression on her face, goes the round of all the hat-boxes, and carries off her children to their original position.

'The cat's their mother,' observed Vanya, 'but who is their father?'

'Yes, who is their father?' repeats Nina.

'They must have a father.'

Vanya and Nina are a long time deciding who is to be the kittens' father, and in the end, their choice falls on a big dark-red horse without a tail, which is lying in the store-cupboard under the stairs, together with other relics of toys that have outlived their day. They drag him up out of the store-cupboard and stand him by the box.

'Mind now!' they admonish him, 'stand here and see they behave themselves properly.'

All this is said and done in the gravest way, with an expression of anxiety on their faces. Vanya and Nina refuse to recognize the existence of any world but the box of kittens. Their joy knows no bounds. But they have to pass through bitter, agonizing moments, too.

Just before dinner, Vanya is sitting in his father's study, gazing dreamily at the table. A kitten is moving about by the lamp, on stamped notepaper. Vanya is watching its movements, and thrusting first a pencil, then a match into its little mouth. . . . All at once, as though he has sprung out of the floor, his father is beside the table.

'What's this?' Vanya hears, in an angry voice.

'It's . . . it's the kitty, papa. . . .'

'I'll give it you; look what you have done, you naughty boy! You've dirtied all my paper!'

To Vanya's great surprise his papa does not share his partiality for the kittens, and, instead of being moved to enthusiasm and delight, he pulls Vanya's ear and shouts:

'Stepan, take away this horrid thing.'

At dinner, too, there is a scene. . . . During the second course there is suddenly the sound of a shrill mew. They begin to investigate its origin, and discover a kitten under Nina's pinafore.

'Nina, leave the table!' cries her father angrily. 'Throw the kittens in the cesspool! I won't have the nasty things in the house. . .!'

Vanya and Nina are horrified. Death in the cesspool, apart from its cruelty, threatens to rob the cat and the wooden horse of their children, to lay waste the cat's box, to destroy their plans for the future, that fair future in which one cat will be a comfort to its old mother, another will live in the country, while the third will catch rats in the cellar. The children begin to cry and entreat that the kittens may be spared. Their father consents, but on the condition that the children do not go into the kitchen and touch the kittens.

After dinner, Vanya and Nina slouch about the rooms, feeling depressed. The prohibition of visits to the kitchen has reduced them to dejection. They refuse sweets, are naughty, and are rude to their mother. When their uncle Petrusha comes in the evening, they draw him aside, and complain to him of their father, who wanted to throw the kittens into the cesspool.

'Uncle Petrusha, tell mamma to have the kittens taken to the nursery,' the children beg their uncle, 'do-o tell her.'

'There, there . . . very well,' says their uncle, waving them off. 'All right.'

Uncle Petrusha does not usually come alone. He is accompanied by Nero, a big black dog of Danish breed, with drooping ears, and a tail as hard as a stick. The dog is silent, morose, and full of a sense of his own dignity. He takes not the slightest notice of the children, and when he passes them hits them with his tail as though they were chairs. The children hate him from the bottom of their hearts, but on this occasion, practical considerations override sentiment.

'I say, Nina,' says Vanya, opening his eyes wide. 'Let Nero be their father, instead of the horse! The horse is dead and he is alive, you see.'

They are waiting the whole evening for the moment when papa will sit down to his cards and it will be possible to take Nero to the kitchen without being observed. . . . At last, papa sits down to cards, mamma is busy with the samovar and not noticing the children. . . .

The happy moment arrives.

'Come along!' Vanya whispers to his sister.

But, at that moment, Stepan comes in and, with a snigger announces:

'Nero has eaten the kittens, madam.'

Nina and Vanya turn pale and look at Stepan with horror.

'He really has . . .' laughs the footman,' 'he went to the box and gobbled them up.'

The children expect that all the people in the house will be aghast and fall upon the miscreant Nero. But they all sit calmly in their seats, and only express surprise at the appetite of the huge dog. Papa and mamma laugh. Nero walks about by the table, wags his tail and licks his lips complacently . . . the cat is the only one who is uneasy. With her tail in the air she walks about the rooms, looking suspiciously at people and mewing plaintively.

'Children, it's past nine,' cries mamma, 'it's bedtime.'

Vanya and Nina go to bed, shed tears, and spend a long time thinking about the injured cat, and the cruel, insolent, and unpunished Nero.

From *Selected Tales of Tchehov* transl. Constance Garnett

John Mortonson's Funeral

John Mortonson was dead: his lines in 'the tragedy of "Man"' had all been spoken and he had left the stage.

The body rested in a fine mahogany coffin fitted with a plate of glass. All arrangements for the funeral had been so well attended to that had the deceased known he would doubtless have approved. The face, as it showed under the glass, was not disagreeable to look upon: it bore a faint smile, and as the death had been painless, had not been distorted beyond the repairing power of the undertaker. At two o'clock of the afternoon the friends were to assemble to pay their last tribute of respect to one who had no further need of friends and respect. The surviving members of the family came severally every few minutes to the casket and wept above the placid features beneath the glass. This did them no good; it did no good to John Mortonson; but in the presence of death reason and philosophy are silent.

As the hour of two approached the friends began to arrive and after offering such consolation to the stricken relatives as the proprieties of the occasion required, solemnly seated themselves about the room with an augmented consciousness of their importance in the scheme funereal. Then the minister came, and in that overshadowing presence the lesser lights went into eclipse. His entrance was followed by that of the widow, whose lamentations filled the room. She approached the casket and after leaning her face against the cold glass for a moment was gently led to a seat near her daughter. Mournfully and low the man of God began his eulogy of the dead, and his doleful voice, mingled with the sobbing which it was its purpose to stimulate and sustain, rose and fell, seemed to come and go, like the sound of a sullen sea. The gloomy day grew darker as he spoke; a curtain of cloud underspread the sky and a few drops of rain fell audibly. It seemed as if all nature were weeping for John Mortonson.

When the minister had finished his eulogy with prayer a hymn was sung and the pallbearers took their places beside the bier. As the last notes of the hymn died away the widow ran to the coffin, cast herself upon it and sobbed hysterically. Gradually, however, she yielded to dissuasion, becoming more composed; and as the minister was in the act of leading her away her eyes sought the face of the dead beneath the glass. She threw up her arms and with a shriek fell backward insensible.

The mourners sprang forward to the coffin, the friends followed, and as the clock on the mantel solemnly struck three all were staring down upon the face of John Mortonson, deceased.

They turned away, sick and faint. One man, trying in his terror to escape the awful sight, stumbled against the coffin so heavily as to knock away one of its frail supports. The coffin fell to the floor, the glass shattered to bits by the concussion.

From the opening crawled John Mortonson's cat, which lazily leapt to the floor, sat up, tranquilly wiped its crimson muzzle with a forepaw, then walked with dignity from the room.

Ambrose Bierce

Dick Baker's Cat

One of my comrades there – another of those victims of eighteen years of unrequited toil and blighted hopes – was one of the gentlest spirits that ever bore its patient cross in a weary exile; grave and simple Dick Baker, pocket-miner of Dead-Horse Gulch. He was forty-six, grey as a rat, earnest, thoughtful, slenderly educated, slouchily dressed and clay-soiled, but his heart was finer metal than any gold his shovel ever brought to light – than any, indeed, that ever was mined or minted.

Whenever he was out of luck and a little down-hearted, he would fall to mourning over the loss of a wonderful cat he used to own (for where women and children are not, men of kindly impulses take up with pets, for they must love something). And he always spoke of the strange sagacity of that cat with the air of a man who believed in his secret heart that there was something human about it – maybe even supernatural.

I heard him talking about this animal once. He said:

'Gentlemen, I used to have a cat here, by the name of Tom Quartz, which you'd 'a' took an interest in, I reckon – most anybody would. I had him here eight year – and he was the remarkablest cat *I* ever see. He was a large grey one of the Tom specie, an' he had more hard, natchral sense than any man in this camp – 'n' a *power* of dignity – he wouldn't let the Gov'ner of Californy be familiar with him. He never ketched a rat in his life – 'peared to be above it. He never cared for nothing but mining. He knowed more about mining, that cat did, than any man *I* ever, ever see. You couldn't tell *him* noth'n' 'bout placer-diggin's – 'n' as for pocket-mining, why he was just born for it. He would dig out after me an' Jim when we went over the hills prospect'n', and he would trot along behind us for as much as five mile, if we went so fur. An' he had the best judgment about mining-ground – why, you never see anything like it. When we went to work, he'd scatter a glance round, 'n' if he didn't think much of the indications, he would give a look as much as to say, "Well, I'll have to get you to excuse *me*" – 'n' without another word he'd hyste his nose in the air 'n' shove for home. But if the ground suited him, he would lay low 'n' keep dark till the first pan was washed, 'n' then he would sidle up 'n' take a look, an' if there was about six or seven grains of gold *he* was satisfied – he didn't want no better prospect 'n' that – 'n' then he would lay down on our coats and snore like a steamboat till we'd struck the pocket, an' then get up 'n' superintend. He was nearly lightnin' on superintending.

'Well, by an' by, up comes this yer quartz excitement. Everybody was into it – everybody was pick'n' 'n' blast'n' instead of shovellin' dirt on the hillside – everybody was putt'n' down a shaft instead of scrapin' the surface. Noth'n' would do Jim, but *we* must tackle the ledges, too, 'n' so we did. We commenced putt'n' down a shaft, 'n' Tom Quartz he begin to wonder what in the dickens it was all about. *He* hadn't ever seen any mining like that before, 'n' he was all upset, as you may say – he couldn't come to a right understanding of it no way – it was too many for *him*. He was down on it too, you bet you – he was down on it powerful – 'n' always appeared to consider it the cussedest foolishness out. But that cat, you know, was *always* agin' new-fangled arrangements – somehow he never could abide 'em. *You* know how it is with old habits. But by an' by Tom Quartz begin to git sort of reconciled a little though he never *could* altogether understand that eternal sinkin' of a shaft an' never pannin' out anything. At last he got to comin' down in the shaft, hisself, to try to cipher it out. An' when he'd git the blues, 'n' feel kind o' scruffy, 'n' aggravated 'n' disgusted – knowin' as he did, that the bills was runnin' up all the time an' we warn't makin' a cent – he would curl up on a gunny-sack in the corner an' go to sleep. Well, one day when the shaft was down about eight foot, the rock got so hard that we had to put in a blast – the first blast'n' we'd ever done since Tom Quartz was born. An' then we lit the fuse 'n' clumb out 'n' got off 'bout fifty yards – 'n' forgot 'n' left Tom Quartz sound asleep on the gunny-sack. In 'bout a minute we seen a puff of smoke bust up out of the hole, 'n' then everything let go with an awful crash, 'n' about four million tons of rocks 'n' dirt 'n' smoke 'n' splinters shot up 'bout a mile an' a half into the air, an' by George, right in the dead centre of it was old Tom Quartz a-goin' end over end, an' a-snortin' an' a-sneezn'n, an' a-clawin' an' a-reach'n' for things like all possessed. But it warn't no use, you know, it warn't no use. An' that was the last we see of *him* for about two minutes 'n' a half, an' then all of a sudden it begin to rain rocks and rubbage an' directly he come down ker-whoop about ten foot off f'm where we stood. Well, I reckon he was p'raps the orneriest-lookin' beast you ever see. One ear was sot back on his neck, 'n' his tail was stove up, 'n' his eye-winkers was singed off, 'n' he was all blacked up with powder an' smoke, an' all sloppy with mud 'n' slush f'm one end to the other. Well, sir, it warn't no use to try to apologize – we couldn't say a word. He took a sort of a disgusted look at hisself, 'n' then he looked at us – an' it was just exactly the same as if he had said – "Gents, maybe *you* think it's smart to take advantage of a cat that ain't had no experience of quartz-minin', but I think *different*" – an' then he turned on his heel 'n' marched off home without ever saying another word.

That was jest his style. An' maybe you won't believe it, but after that you never see a cat so prejudiced agin' quartz-mining as what he was. An' by an' by when he *did* get to goin' down in the shaft agin', you'd 'a' been astonished at his sagacity. The minute we'd tetch off a blast 'n' the fuse'd begin to sizzle, he'd give a look as much as to say, "Well, I'll have to git you to excuse *me*," an' it was surpris'n' the way he'd shin out of that hole 'n' go f'r a tree. Sagacity? It ain't no name for it. 'Twas inspiration!'

I said, 'Well, Mr Baker, his prejudice against quartz-mining *was* remarkable, considering how he came by it. Couldn't you ever cure him of it?'

'*Cure him*! No! When Tom Quartz was sot once, he was *always* sot – and you might 'a' blowed him up as much as three million times 'n' you'd never 'a' broken him of his cussed prejudice agin' quartz-mining.'

Mark Twain

The Reticence of Lady Anne

Egbert came into the large, dimly lit drawing-room with the air of a man who is not certain whether he is entering a dovecote or a bomb factory, and is prepared for either eventuality. The little domestic quarrel over the luncheon-table had not been fought to a definite finish, and the question was how far Lady Anne was in a mood to renew or forgo hostilities. Her pose in the arm-chair by the tea-table was rather elaborately rigid; in the gloom of a December afternoon Egbert's pince-nez did not materially help him to discern the expression of her face.

By way of breaking whatever ice might be floating on the surface he made a remark about a dim religious light. He or Lady Anne were accustomed to make that remark between 4.30 and 6 on winter and late autumn evenings; it was a part of their married life. There was no recognized rejoinder to it, and Lady Anne made none.

Don Tarquinio lay astretch on the Persian rug, basking in the firelight with superb indifference to the possible ill-humour of Lady Anne. His pedigree was as flawlessly Persian as the rug, and his ruff was coming into the glory of its second winter. The page-boy, who had Renaissance tendencies, had christened him Don Tarquinio. Left to themselves, Egbert and Lady Anne would unfailingly have called him Fluff, but they were not obstinate.

Egbert poured himself out some tea. As the silence gave no sign of breaking on Lady Anne's initiative, he braced himself for another Yermak effort.

'My remark at lunch had a purely academic application,' he announced; 'you seem to put an unnecessarily personal significance into it.'

Lady Anne maintained her defensive barrier of silence. The bullfinch lazily filled in the interval with an air from *Iphigénie en Tauride*. Egbert recognized it immediately, because it was the only air the bullfinch whistled, and he had come to them with the reputation for whistling it. Both Egbert and Lady Anne would have preferred something from *The Yeoman of the Guard*, which was their favourite opera. In matters artistic they had a similarity of taste. They leaned towards the honest and explicit in art, a picture, for instance, that told its own story, with generous assistance from its title. A riderless warhorse with harness in obvious disarray, staggering into a courtyard full of pale swooning women, and marginally noted 'Bad News,' suggested to their minds a distinct interpretation of some military catastrophe. They could see what it was meant to convey, and explain it to friends of duller intelligence.

The silence continued. As a rule Lady Anne's displeasure became articulate and markedly voluble after four minutes of introductory muteness. Egbert seized the milk-jug and poured some of its contents into Don Tarquinio's saucer; as the saucer was already full to the brim an unsightly overflow was the result. Don Tarquinio looked on with a surprised interest that evanesced into elaborate unconsciousness when he was appealed to by Egbert to come and drink up some of the spilt matter. Don Tarquinio was prepared to play many rôles in life, but a vacuum carpet-cleaner was not one of them.

'Don't you think we're being rather foolish?' said Egbert cheerfully.

If Lady Anne thought so she didn't say so.

'I daresay the fault has been partly on my side,' continued Egbert, with evaporating cheerfulness. 'After all, I'm only human, you know. You seem to forget that I'm only human.'

He insisted on the point, as if there had been unfounded suggestions that he was built on Satyr lines, with goat continuations where the human left off.

The bullfinch recommenced its air from *Iphigénie en Tauride*. Egbert began to feel depressed. Lady Anne was not drinking her tea. Perhaps she was feeling unwell. But when Lady Anne felt unwell she was not wont to be reticent on the subject. 'No one knows what I suffer from indigestion' was one of her favourite statements; but the lack of knowledge can only have been caused by defective listening; the amount of information available on the subject would have supplied material for a monograph.

Evidently Lady Anne was not feeling unwell.

Egbert began to think he was being unreasonably dealt with; naturally he began to make concessions.

'I daresay,' he observed, taking as central a position on the hearth-rug as Don Tarquinio could be persuaded to concede him, 'I may have been to blame. I am willing, if I can thereby restore things to a happier standpoint, to undertake to lead a better life.'

He wondered vaguely how it would be possible. Temptations came to him, in middle age, tentatively and without insistence, like a neglected butcher-boy who asks for a Christmas box in February for no more hopeful reason than that he didn't get one in December. He had no more idea of succumbing to them than he had of purchasing the fish-knives and fur boas that ladies are impelled to sacrifice through the medium of advertisement columns during twelve months of the year. Still, there was something impressive in this unasked-for renunciation of possibly latent enormities.

Lady Anne showed no sign of being impressed.

Egbert looked at her nervously through his glasses. To get the worst of an argument with her was no new experience. To get the worst of a monologue was a humiliating novelty.

'I shall go and dress for dinner,' he announced in a voice into which he intended some shade of sternness to creep.

At the door a final access of weakness impelled him to make a further appeal.

'Aren't we being very silly?'

'A fool,' was Don Tarquinio's mental comment as the door closed on Egbert's retreat. Then he lifted his velvet forepaws in the air and leapt lightly on to a bookshelf immediately under the bullfinch's cage. It was the first time he had seemed to notice the bird's existence, but he was carrying out a long-formed theory of action with the precision of mature deliberation. The bullfinch, who had fancied himself something of a despot, depressed himself of a sudden into a third of his normal displacement; then he fell to a helpless wing-beating and shrill cheeping. He had cost twenty-seven shillings without the cage, but Lady Anne made no sign of interfering. She had been dead for two hours.

Hector Hugh Munro (Saki)

5

THE RESTORATION AND THE EIGHTEENTH CENTURY

The cat is an unfaithful domestic, and kept only from the necessity we find of opposing him to the domestics still more incommodius.

Georges de Buffon, *Histoire Naturelle*

Frost-eyebrows

In the middle of the Chia-ching period [A.D. 1522–1566] there was a cat in the palace. She was of faintly blue colour but her two eyebrows were clearly jade-white and she was called Shuang-mei [Frost-eyebrows]. She surmised the Emperor's intentions very well. Whomever His Majesty summoned and wherever her Imperial master went, she always led. She waited upon the Emperor until he slept and then she lay still like a stump. His Majesty was very fond of her, and, when she died, ordered that she should be buried in the north side of the Wan-sui mountains [in Peking, now Peping]. By her grave was erected a stone tablet inscribed with three characters: 'Ch'iu-lung Chung' ['Grave of a Dragon with two horns'].

From *The Erh-t'an* by Wang T'ung-kuei, transl. Mr Z. L. Yih

The Diminutive Lyon

All cats were at first wild, but were at length tamed by the industry of Mankind: it is a Beast of prey, even the tame one, more especially the wild, it being in the opinion of many nothing but a diminutive Lyon.

From *The Compleat English Physician* by William S. Salmon

Grimalkin

Grimalkin to Domestick Vermin sworn
An everlasting Foe, with watchful Eye
Lies nightly brooding o'er a chinky Gap
Protending her fell Claws, to thoughtless Mice
Sure Ruin.

From *The Splendid Shilling* by John Philips

An Unfaithful Domestic

The cat is an unfaithful domestic, and kept only from the necessity we find of opposing him to the domestics still more incommodius, and which cannot be hunted: for we value not those people who, being fond of all brutes, foolishly keep cats for their amusement.

From the *Histoire Naturelle* by Georges de Buffon

An Unaccountable Animosity

The conceit that a cat has nine lives has cost at least nine lives in ten of the whole race of 'em: scarce a boy in the streets but has in this point outdone Hercules himself, who was famous for killing a monster that had but three lives. Whether the unaccountable animosity against this useful domestic may be any cause of the general persecution of owls (who are a sort of feathered cats) or whether it be only an unreasonable pique the moderns have taken to a serious countenance, I shall not determine. Though I am inclined to believe the former; since I observe the sole reason alleged for the destruction of frogs is because they are like toads. Yet amidst all the misfortunes of these unfriended creatures, 'tis some happiness that we have not yet taken a fancy to eat them: for should our countrymen refine upon the French never so little, 'tis not to be conceived to what unheard-of torments, owls, cats, and frogs may be yet reserved.

From 'The Fate of Cats' by Alexander Pope

A Mutual Entertainment

. . . as the learned and ingenious Montaigne says like himself freely, When my cat and I entertain each other with mutual apish tricks, as playing with a garter, who knows but that I make my cat more sport than she makes me? Shall I conclude her to be simple, that has her time to begin or refuse to play as freely as I myself have? Nay, who knows but that it is a defect of my not understanding her language (for doubtless cats talk and reason with one another) that we agree no better? And who knows but that she pities me for being no wiser than to play with her, and laughs and censures my folly for making sport for her, when we two play together?

From *The Compleat Angler* by Izaak Walton

A Very Curious Kitten

April 20 [1644] when comming to Orleans, and lying at the White-Cross (where I found Mr John Nicholas, eldest sonne to Mr Secretary) there kitten'd a Cat on my bed, which left on it a Young one having 6 Eares, eight leggs, two bodys from the navil downewards, & two tayles: which strange Monster, I found dead; but warme by me in the Morning when I awaked.

From *The Diary of John Evelyn*, ed. E. S. de Beer

The Cat and the Rain

Careful observers may foretell the hour
(By sure prognostics) when to dread a shower;
While rain depends, the pensive cat gives o'er
Her frolics, and pursues her tail no more.

Jonathan Swift

A Fable of the Widow and Her Cat

A widow kept a favourite cat.
  At first a gentle creature;
But when he was grown sleek and fat,
With many a mouse, and many a rat,
  He soon disclosed his nature.

The fox and he were friends of old,
  Nor could they now be parted;
They nightly slunk to rob the fold,
Devoured the lambs, the fleeces sold,
  And puss grew lion-hearted.

He scratched her maid, he stole the cream,
  He tore her best laced pinner;
Nor Chanticleer upon the beam,
Nor chick, nor duckling 'scapes, when Grim
  Invites the fox to dinner.

The dame full wisely did decree,
  For fear he should dispatch more,
That the false wretch should worried be:
But in a saucy manner he
  Thus speeched it like a Lechmere.

'Must I, against all right and law,
  Like pole-cat vile be treated?
I! who so long with tooth and claw
Have kept domestic mice in awe,
  And foreign foes defeated!

'Your golden pippins, and your pies,
  How oft have I defended?
'Tis true, the pinner which you prize
I tore in frolic; to your eyes
  I never harm intended.

'I am a cat of honour—' 'Stay,'
  Quoth she, 'no longer parley;
Whate'er you did in battle slay,
By law of arms become your prey,
  I hope you won it fairly.

'Of this, we'll grant you stand acquit,
  But not of your outrages:
Tell me, perfidious! was it fit
To make my cream a *perquisite*,
  And steal to mend your wages!

'So flagrant is thy insolence,
  So vile thy breach of trust is;
That longer with thee to dispense,
Were want of power, or want of sense:
  Here, Towser!— Do him justice.'

                                        Jonathan Swift

On the Tiles

Men ride many miles,
Cats tread many tiles,
Both hazard their necks in the fray;
Only Cats, when they fall
From a house or a wall,
Keep their feet, mount their tails, and away!

From 'An Appeal to Cats in the Business of Love' by Thomas Flatman

An Increase of Family

Robinson Crusoe's anxiety over a lost cat was soon replaced by a different misgiving.

In this season, I was much surprised with the increase of my family. I had been concerned for the loss of one of my cats, who run away from me, or, as I thought, had been dead, and I heard no more tale or tidings of her, till, to my astonishment, she came home about the end of August with three kittens. This was the more strange to me, because, though I had killed a wild cat, as I called it, with my gun, yet I thought it was a quite different kind from our European cats; yet the young cats were the same kind of house-breed like the old one; and both my cats being females, I thought it very strange. But from these three cats I afterwards came to be so pestered with cats, that I was forced to kill them like vermin, or wild beasts, and to drive them from my house as much as possible. . . . As for my cats, they multiplied, as I have observed, to that degree, that I was obliged to shoot several of them at first to keep them from devouring me and all I had; but at length, when the two old ones I brought with me were gone, and after some time continually driving them from me, and letting them have no provision with me, they all ran wild into the woods, except two or three favourites, which I kept tame, and whose young, when they had any, I always drowned; and these were part of my family.

From *Robinson Crusoe* by Daniel Defoe

Hodge

I never shall forget the indulgence with which he treated Hodge, his cat; for whom he himself used to go out and buy oysters, lest the servants having that trouble should take a dislike to the poor creature. I am, unluckily, one of those who have an antipathy to a cat, so that I am uneasy when in the room with one; and I own, I frequently suffered a good deal from the presence of the same Hodge. I recollect him one day scrambling up Dr Johnson's breast, apparently with much satisfaction, while my friend, smiling and half-whistling, rubbed down his back, and pulled him by the tail; and when I observed he was a fine cat, saying, 'Why, yes, Sir, but I have had cats whom I liked better than this'; and then, as if perceiving Hodge to be out of countenance, adding, 'but he is a very fine cat, a very fine cat indeed.'

From the *Life of Johnson* by James Boswell

Full of Cunning

The *domesticus*, or tame cat, is so well known, that it requires no description. It is a useful, but deceitful domestic. Although when young they are playful and gay, they possess at the same time an innate malice and perverse disposition, which increases as they grow up, and which education learns them to conceal, but never to subdue. Constantly bent upon theft and rapine, though in a domestic state, they are full of cunning and dissimulation; they conceal all their designs; seize every opportunity of doing mischief, and then fly from punishment. They easily take on the habits of society, but never its manners; for they have only the appearance of friendship and attachment. This disingenuity of character is betrayed by the obliquity of their movements and the ambiguity of their looks. In a word, the cat is totally destitute of friendship; he thinks and acts for himself alone.

From the *Encyclopaedia Britannica* (1787)

A Small Operation

I had a poor little cat, that had one of her ribs broke and that laid across her belly, and we could not tell what it was, and she was in great pain. I therefore with a small pen knife this morning, opened one side of her and took it out, and performed the operation very well, and afterwards sewed it up and put Friars Balsam to it, and she was much better after, the incision was half an inch. It grieved me much to see the poor creature in such pain before, and therefore made me undertake the above, which I hope will preserve the life of the poor creature.

From *The Diary of a Country Parson* by James Woodforde, ed. John Beresford

A Cat's Tail

The Stiony on my right Eye-lid still swelled and inflamed very much. As it is commonly said that the Eye-lid being rubbed by the tail of a black Cat would do it much good if not entirely cure it, and having a black Cat, a little before dinner I made a trial of it, and very soon after dinner I found my Eye-lid much abated of the swelling and almost free from Pain. I cannot therefore but conclude it to be of the greatest service to a Stiony on the Eye-lid. Any other Cats Tail may have the above effect in all probability – but I did my Eye-lid with my own black Tom Cat's Tail.

From *The Diary of a Country Parson* by James Woodforde, ed. John Beresford

My Cat Jeoffrey

For I will consider my Cat Jeoffrey.
For he is the servant of the Living God, duly and daily serving him.
For at the first glance of the glory of God in the East he worships in his way.
For this is done by wreathing his body seven times round with elegant
    quickness.
For then he leaps up to catch the musk, which is the blessing of God upon
    his prayer.
For he rolls upon prank to work it in.
For having done duty and received blessing he begins to consider himself.
For this he performs in ten degrees.
For first he looks upon his fore-paws to see if they are clean.
For secondly he kicks up behind to clear away there.
For thirdly he works it upon stretch with the fore-paws extended.
For fourthly he sharpens his paws by wood.
For fifthly he washes himself.
For sixthly he rolls upon wash.

For Seventhly he fleas himself, that he may not be interrupted upon the beat.

For Eighthly he rubs himself against a post.

For Ninthly he looks up for his instructions.

For Tenthly he goes in quest of food.

For having consider'd God and himself he will consider his neighbour.

For if he meets another cat he will kiss her in kindness.

For when he takes his prey he plays with it to give it a chance.

For one mouse in seven escapes by his dallying.

For when his day's work is done his business more properly begins.

For he keeps the Lord's watch in the night against the adversary.

For he counteracts the powers of darkness by his electrical skin & glaring eyes.

For he counteracts the Devil, who is death, by brisking about the life.

For in his morning orisons he loves the sun and the sun loves him.

For he is of the tribe of Tiger.

For the Cherub Cat is a term of the Angel Tiger.

For he has the subtlety and hissing of a serpent, which in goodness he suppresses.

For he will not do destruction, if he is well fed, neither will he spit without provocation.

For he purrs in thankfulness, when God tells him he's a good Cat.

For he is an instrument for the children to learn benevolence upon.

For every house is incomplete without him and a blessing is lacking in the spirit.

For the Lord commanded Moses concerning the cats at the departure of the Children of Israel from Egypt.

For every family had one cat at least in the bag.

For the English Cats are the best in Europe.

For he is the cleanest in the use of his fore-paws of any quadrupede.

For the dexterity of his defence is an instance of the love of God to him exceedingly.

For he is the quickest to his mark of any creature.

For he is tenacious of his point.

For he is a mixture of gravity and waggery.

For he knows that God is his Saviour.

For there is nothing sweeter than his peace when at rest.

For there is nothing brisker than his life when in motion.

For he is of the Lord's poor and so indeed is he called by benevolence perpetually – Poor Jeoffry! poor Jeoffry! the rat has bit thy throat.

For I bless the name of the Lord Jesus that Jeoffry is better.

For the divine spirit comes about his body to sustain it in complete cat.

For his tongue is exceedingly pure so that it has in purity what it wants in music.

For he is docile and can learn certain things.

For he can set up with gravity which is patience upon approbation.

For he can fetch and carry, which is patience in employment.

For he can jump over a stick which is patience upon proof positive.

For he can spraggle upon waggle at the word of command.

For he can jump from an eminence into his master's bosom.

For he can catch the cork and toss it again.

For he is hated by the hypocrite and miser.

For the former is afraid of detection.

For the latter refuses the charge.

For he camels his back to bear the first notion of business.

For he is good to think on, if a man would express himself neatly.

For he made a great figure in Egypt for his signal services.

For he killed the Ichneumon-rat very pernicious by land.

For his ears are so acute that they sting again.

For from this proceeds the passing quickness of his attention.

For by stroking of him I have found out electricity.

For I perceived God's light upon him both wax and fire.

For the Electrical fire is the spiritual substance, which God sends from heaven to sustain the bodies both of man and beast.

For God has blessed him in the variety of his movements.

For, tho he cannot fly, he is an excellent clamberer.

For his motions upon the face of the earth are more than any other quadrupede.

For he can tread to all the measures upon the music.

For he can swim for life.

For he can creep.

From *Jubilate Agno* by Christopher Smart

The Cat Organ

Christopher Smart wrote his *Jubilate Agno* while in Bedlam, suffering from a mild bout of lunacy. The following letter, addressed some years earlier to the Royal Society and written under Smart's pseudonym, 'Mary Midnight', suggests that he was already richly eccentric.

A letter from Mrs Mary Midnight to the Royal Society, containing some new and curious Improvements upon the CAT-ORGAN.

Gentlemen,

I need not inform persons of your infinite experience and erudition, that the Cat-Organ, as it has hitherto been made use of, was no more than what followeth, *viz.* A plain harpsichord, which instead of having strings and jacks, consists of cats of different sizes, included in boxes, whose voices express every note in the gamut, which is extorted from the imprison'd animals, by placing their tails in grooves, which are properly squeezed by the impression of the organist's fingers on the keys. – This instrument, unimproved as it was, I have often heard with incredible delight; but especially in the Grand and the plaintive – This delight grew upon me every time I was present at its performance. At length I shut myself up for seven years to study some additions and improvements, which I have at length accomplished, agreeable to my warmest wishes, and which I with all due submission now lay before you.

In the first place then it is universally known and acknowledged that these animals, at the time of their amours, are the most musical creatures in nature; I would therefore recommend it to all and singular Cat-Organists, to have a most especial regard to the time of caterwawling, particularly if they have any thing very august or affecting to exhibit.

Secondly, it is also very well known that the best voices are improved by castration. I therefore never have less than eight geldings in my treble cleft. – And here I cannot help informing you of an experiment I lately made on an Italian boar-cat, and an English one of the same gender; and I solemnly protest that, after the operation, my country animal had every whit as delicate, piercing, and comprehensive a tone as the foreigner. – And I make no sort of doubt but some of our harmonious Englishmen would shine with an equal lustre, if they had the same ADVANTAGES as the Italians. – This may be worth the consideration of the people in power: – For, if this experiment had been tryed with success, how many thousand pounds would it have save this nation?

Thirdly, of the forte and Piano. – I must not omit to tell you, gentlemen, that my Cat-Organ resembles a double harpsichord; for as that has two rows of keys, so mine has two layers of cats. – The upper row on which I play piano, or softly, consists of cats, both of a lesser size, and whose tails are squeezed by a much less degree of pressure; that is, by nothing but the bare extremity of the key. – But the lower row, on which I play forte, or loudly, contains an harmonious society of banging grimalkins; and whose tails are severely pricked by brass-pins, inserted at the end of the key for that purpose.

Fourthly, Of the shake [a trill-like ornament in keyboard playing]. – There was one enormous defect in this instrument, before I took it in hand, and that was in the shake; the imperfectness of which gave me great offence. – But as it is now managed, it has the most ravishing effect in the world. – There are between all the keys little wires fixed almost imperceptibly. – These go underneath 'till they reach each puss's throat. – At the extremity of these wires are placed horizontally wrens' quills, about the length of a quarter of an inch. – when the artist therefore has a mind to form his shake, he touches the wires, which soon sends the quills in a tickle, tickle, tickle, up to the cat's throat, and causes the most gurgling, warbling, shaking, quaking, trembling, murmuring sound in the World . . .

> I am,
> Gentlemen,
> Your most obedient humble Servant
> M. MIDNIGHT

> From *The Midwife, or Old Woman's Magazine*

Cat and Hare

DEAR SIR,

> . . . admôrunt ubera tigres.

We have remarked in a former letter how much incongruous animals, in a lonely state, may be attached to each other from a spirit of sociality; in this it may not be amiss to recount a different motive which has been known to create as strange a fondness.

My friend had a little helpless leveret brought to him, which the servants fed with milk in a spoon, and about the same time his cat kittened and the young were dispatched and buried. The hare was soon lost, and supposed to be gone the way of most foundlings, to be killed by some dog or cat. However, in about a fortnight, as the master was sitting in his garden in the dusk of the evening, he observed his cat, with tail erect, trotting towards him, and calling with little short inward notes of complacency, such as they use towards their kittens, and something gamboling after, which proved to be the leveret that the cat had supported with her milk, and continued to support with great affection.

Thus was a graminivorous animal nurtured by a carnivorous and predaceous one!

Why so cruel and sanguinary a beast as a cat, of the ferocious genus of *Feles*, the *murium leo*,* as Linnæus calls it, should be affected with any tenderness towards an animal which is its natural prey, is not so easy to determine.

This strange affection probably was occasioned by that *desiderium*, those tender maternal feelings, which the loss of her kittens had awakened in her breast; and by the complacency and ease she derived to herself from the procuring her teats to be drawn, which were too much distended with milk, till, from habit, she became as much delighted with this foundling as if it had been her real offspring.

This incident is no bad solution of that strange circumstance which grave historians as well as the poets assert, of exposed children being sometimes nurtured by female wild beasts that probably had lost their young. For it is not one whit more marvellous that Romulus and Remus, in their infant state, should be nursed by a she-wolf, than that a poor little sucking leveret should be fostered and cherised by a bloody grimalkin.

> From a letter to the Hon. Daines Barrington, 9 May 1776,
> in *The Natural History of Selborne* by Gilbert White

*That is, the lion of mice.

Dogged By the Hare

The poet William Cowper, a lifelong cat lover, was also very keen on his three buck hares, oddly named Puss, Tiny and Bess, and allowed the two species to sort out their own differences.

. . . I always admitted them into the parlour after supper, when, the carpet affording their feet a firm hold, they would frisk, and bound, and play a thousand gambols, in which Bess, being remarkably strong and fearless, was always superior to the rest, and proved himself the Vestris of the party. One evening the cat, being in the room, had the hardiness to pat Bess upon the cheek, an indignity which he resented by drumming upon her back with such violence, that the cat was happy to escape from under his paws, and hide herself . . .

From an essay by William Cowper in *The Gentleman's Magazine*, June 1784

Cat and Fish

There is a propensity belonging to common house-cats that is very remarkable; I mean their violent fondness for fish, which appears to be their most favourite food: and yet nature in this instance seems to have planted in them an appetite that, unassisted, they know not how to gratify: for of all quadrupeds cats are the least disposed towards water; and will not, when they can avoid it, deign to wet a foot, much less to plunge into that element.

From *The Natural History of Selborne* by Gilbert White

Ode on the Death of a Favourite Cat, Drowned in a Tub of Gold Fishes

'Twas on a lofty vase's side
Where China's gayest art had dyed
The azure flowers, that blow;
Demurest of the tabby kind,
The pensive Selima, reclined,
Gazed on the lake below.

Her conscious tail her joy declared;
The fair round face, the snowy beard,
The velvet of her paws,
Her coat, that with the tortoise vies,
Her ears of jet, and emerald eyes,
She saw; and purr'd applause.

Still had she gazed; but 'midst the tide
Two angel forms were seen to glide,
The genii of the stream:
Their scaly armour's Tyrian hue
Through richest purple to the view
Betray'd a golden gleam.

The hapless nymph with wonder saw:
A whisker first, and then a claw,
  With many an ardent wish,
She stretch'd, in vain, to reach the prize.
What female heart can gold despise?
  What cat's averse to fish?

Presumptuous maid! with looks intent
Again she stretch'd, again she bent,
  Nor knew the gulf between.
(Malignant Fate sat by, and smiled)
The slipp'ry verge her feet beguiled,
  She tumbled headlong in.

Eight times emerging from the flood
She mew'd to ev'ry wat'ry God,
  Some speedy aid to send.
No Dolphin came, no Nereid stirr'd:
Nor cruel Tom, nor Susan heard.
  A fav'rite has no friend!

From hence, ye beauties, undeceived,
Know, one false step is ne'er retrieved,
  And be with caution bold.
Not all that tempts your wand'ring eyes
And heedless hearts is lawful prize.
  Nor all that glitters, gold.

                                        Thomas Gray

The Retired Cat

A drawer, it chanced, at bottom lined
With linen of the softest kind,
With such as merchants introduce
From India, for the ladies' use,
A drawer impending o'er the rest,
Half open in the topmost chest,
Of depth enough, and none to spare,
Invited her to slumber there;
Puss with delight beyond expression
Surveyed the scene, and took possession.
Recumbent at her ease, ere long,
And lulled by her own humdrum song,
She left the cares of life behind,
   And slept as she would sleep her last,
When in came, housewifely inclined,
The chambermaid, and shut it fast;
By no malignity impelled,
But all unconscious whom it held.
   Awakened by the shock (cried Puss)
'Was ever cat attended thus?
'The open drawer was left, I see,
'Merely to prove a nest for me,
'For soon as I was well composed,
'Then came the maid, and it was closed.
'How smooth these 'kerchiefs, and how sweet!
'Oh what a delicate retreat!
'I will resign myself to rest
'Till Sol, declining in the west,
'Shall call to supper, when, no doubt
'Susan will come and let me out.'
   The evening came, the sun descended,
And Puss remained still unattended.
The night rolled tardily away,
(With her indeed, 'twas never day,)
The sprightly morn her course renewed,
The evening gray again ensued,
And Puss came into mind no more

Than if entombed the day before.
With hunger pinched, and pinched for room,
She now presaged approaching doom
Nor slept a single wink or purred,
Conscious of jeopardy incurred.
  That night, by chance, the poet watching,
Heard an inexplicable scratching;
His noble heart went pit-a-pat,
And to himself he said – 'What's that?'
He drew the curtain at his side,
And forth he peeped, but nothing spied.
Yet, by his ear directed, guessed
Something imprisoned in the chest,
And, doubtful what, with prudent care
Resolved it should continue there.
At length a voice which well he knew,
A long and melancholy mew,
Saluting his poetic ears,
Consoled him and dispelled his fears:
He left his bed, he trod the floor,
He 'gan in haste the drawers to explore,
The lowest first, and without stop
The rest in order to the top.
For 'tis a truth well known to most
That whatsoever thing is lost,
We seek it, ere it come to light,
In every cranny but the right.
Forth skipped the cat, not now replete
As erst with airy self-conceit,
Nor in her own fond apprehension
A theme for all the world's attention
But modest, sober, cured of all
Her notions hyperbolical,
And wishing for a place of rest
Anything rather than a chest.

From *The Retired Cat* by William Cowper

An Humble Petition Presented to
Madame Helvétius by Her Cats

Benjamin Franklin wanted to marry Madame Helvétius, the Parisian *salonnière* whose eighteen cats dined only on breast of chicken. This petition was turned down but there is no record of her response to the following one.

W e shall not endeavour to defend ourselves equally from devouring as many sparrows, blackbirds, and thrushes, as we can possibly catch. But here we have to plead in extenuation, that our most cruel enemies, your Abbés themselves, are incessantly complaining of the ravages made by these birds among the cherries and other fruit. The Sieur Abbé Morellet, in particular, is always thundering the most violent anathemas against the blackbirds and thrushes, for plundering your vines, which they do with as little mercy as he himself. To us, however, most illustrious Lady, it appears that the grapes may just as well be eaten by *blackbirds* as *Abbés*, and that our warfare against the winged plunderers will be fruitless, if you encourage other biped and featherless pilferers, who make ten times more havoc.

We know that we are also accused of eating nightingales, who never plunder, and sing, as they say, most enchantingly. It is indeed possible that we may now and then have gratified our palates with a delicious morsel in this way, but we can assure you that it was in utter ignorance of your affection for the species; and that, resembling sparrows in their plumage, we, who make no pretensions to being connoisseurs in music, could not distinguish the song of the one from that of the other, and therefore supposed ourselves regaling only on sparrows. A cat belonging to M. Piccini has assured us, that they who only know how to *mew*, cannot be any judges of the art of singing; and on this we rest for our justification. However, we will henceforward exert our utmost endeavours to distinguish the *Gluckists*, who are, as we are informed, the sparrows, from the *Piccinists*, who are the nightingales. We only intreat of you to pardon the inadvertence into which we may possibly fall, if, in roving after nests, we may sometimes fall upon a brood of *Piccinists*, who, being then destitute of plumage, and not having learnt to sing, we will have no mark by which to distinguish them.

Benjamin Franklin

Lord Nelson

In the autumn of the year 1803, when I entered upon this place of abode, I found the hearth in possession of two Cats, whom my nephew Hartley Coleridge (then in the 7th year of his age) had named Lord Nelson, and Bona Marietta. The former one was an ugly specimen of the streaked-carrotty, or Judas-coloured kind; which is one of the ugliest varieties. But *nimium ne crede colori*. In spite of his complexion, there was nothing treacherous about him. He was altogether a good Cat, affectionate, vigilant and brave; and for services performed against the Rats was deservedly raised in succession to the rank of Baron, Viscount and Earl.

There are still some of Lord Nelson's descendants in the town of Keswick. Two of the family were handsomer than I should have supposed any Cats of this complexion could have been; but their fur was fine, the colour a rich carrot, and the striping like that of the finest tyger or tabby kind. I named one of them William Rufus; the other Danayr le Roux, after a personage in the Romance of Gyron le Courtoys.

Robert Southey

Waiting for the Roast

The first day we had the honour of dining at the palace of the Archbishop of Taranto, at Naples, he said to me, 'You must pardon my passion for cats (la mia passione gattesca), but I never exclude them from my dining-room, and you will find they make excellent company.'

Between the first and second course, the door opened, and several enormously large and beautiful cats were introduced, by the names of Pantalone, Desdemona, Otello, and other dramatic *cognomine*. They took their places on chairs near the table, and were as silent, as quiet, as motionless, and as well behaved, as the most bon ton table in London could require. On the Bishop requesting one of the chaplains to help the signora Desdemona to something, the butler stept up to his Lordship and observed, 'Desdemona will prefer waiting for the roast.' After dinner they were sent to walk on the terrace, and I had the honour of assisting at their coucher, for which a number of comfortable cushions were prepared in the Bishop's dressing-room.

Anon.

The Farmer, the Spaniel and the Cat

As at his board a farmer sat,
Replenish'd by his homely treat,
His favourite Spaniel near him stood,
And with his master shar'd the food;
The crackling bones his jaws devour'd,
His lapping tongue the trenchers scour'd,
Till sated, now supine he lay,
And snor'd the rising fumes away.
  The hungry Cat in turn drew near,
And humbly crav'd a servant's share;
Her modest worth the Master knew,
And straight the fattening morsel threw;
Enrag'd the snarling Cur awoke,
And this with spiteful envy spoke:
  'They only claim a right to eat
Who earn by services their meat:
Me zeal and industry inflame
To scour the fields and spring the game,
Or plunging in the wintry wave
For man the wounded bird to save.
With watchful diligence I keep
From prowling wolves his fleecy sheep,
At home his midnight hours secure,
And drive the robber from the door:
For this his breast with kindness glows,
For this his hand the food bestows;
And shall thy indolence impart
A warmer friendship to his heart,
That thus he robs me of my due,
To pamper such vile things as you?'
  'I own (with meekness Puss replied)
Superior merit on your side;
Nor does my breast with envy swell
To find it recompens'd so well;
Yet I, in what my nature can,
Contribute to the good of man.
Whose claws destroy the pilfering mouse?
Who drives the vermin from the house?

Or, watchful for the labouring swain,
From lurking rats secures the grain?
From hence if he rewards bestow,
Why should your heart with gall o'erflow?
Why pine my happiness to see,
Since there's enough for you and me?'
  'Thy words are just,' the Farmer cried,
And spurn'd the snarler from his side.

From 'The Farmer, the Spaniel and the Cat' by Edward Moore

6

CAT SAYINGS

A French writer says, the three animals that waste most time over their toilet are cats, flies and women.

Charles H. Ross, *The Book of Cats*

When rats infest the palace a lame cat is better than the swiftest horse.

Chinese proverb

Even the smallest feline is a work of art.

Leonardo da Vinci

Cats are intended to teach us that not everything in nature has a function.

Garrison Keillor

Cats do not need to be shown how to have a good time, for they are unfailingly ingenious in that respect.

James Mason

There are two means of refuge from the miseries of life: music and cats.

Albert Schweitzer

It's almost as if we're put here on earth to show how silly they [cats] aren't.

Russell Hoban

Cats can be very funny and have the oddest way of showing they're glad to see you.

W. H. Auden

Once you have been presented with a mouse by your cat, you will never be the same again. She can use you for a doormat. And she will, too.

Paul Gallico

The soul of another is a mystery, and a cat's soul is even more so.

Anton Chekhov

If a fish is the movement of water embodied, given shape, then a cat is a diagram and pattern of subtle air.

Doris Lessing

The cat pretends to sleep that it may see the more clearly.

Chateaubriand

If you say 'Hallelujah' to a cat, it will excite no fixed set of fibres in connection with any other set and the cat will exhibit none of the phenomena of consciousness. But if you say 'Me-e-at', the cat will be there in a moment.

Samuel Butler

When I was young, no public man would have dared acknowledge himself a cat enthusiast; now even MPs can do so without danger of being laughed at.

Louis Wain (cat cartoonist)

All dogs look up to you. All cats look down to you. Only a pig looks at you as an equal.

Winston Churchill (attrib.)

Beautiful present sufficingness of a cat's imagination! Confined to the snug circle of her sides, and the next two inches of rug or carpet.

Leigh Hunt

Cats are a mysterious kind of folk. There is more passing in their minds than we are aware of.

Sir Walter Scott

If you want to write, keep a cat.

Aldous Huxley

Wherever a cat sits, there shall happiness be found.

Stanley Spencer

The catte wyll fyshe eate, but she wyll not her feete wette.

John Taverner

How can we be interested in an animal that did not know how to achieve a place in the night sky, where all the animals scintillate, from the bear and dog to the lion, the bull, the ram and the fish?

Voltaire

A French writer says, the three animals that waste most time over their toilet are cats, flies and women.

Charles H. Ross

If the cat had a dowry she would often be kissed.

Irish proverb

You always ought to have tom-cats arranged, you know – it makes 'em more companionable.

Noël Coward

Cat *n.* a soft indestructible automaton provided by nature to be kicked when things go wrong in the domestic circle.

Ambrose Bierce

When I play with my cat, who knows whether she is not amusing herself with me more than I with her?

Michel de Montaigne

More ways of killing a cat than choking her with cream.

Charles Kingsley

The cat is mighty dignified until the dog comes by.

Southern folk saying

If man could be crossed with the cat, it would improve man but deteriorate the cat.

Mark Twain

The cat is a dilettante in fur.

Théophile Gautier

Honest as the cat when the meat is out of reach.

English proverb

To please himself only the cat purrs.

Irish proverb

In a cat's eyes, all things belong to cats.

English proverb

God save all here, except the cat.

Irish household greeting

They say that the test of literary power is whether a man can write an inscription. I say, 'Can he name a kitten?'

Samuel Butler

Most cemeteries, he says, provide a dog's toilet and a cat's motel.

Evelyn Waugh

7

THE NINETEENTH CENTURY

They are the friends of learning, and of sexual bliss

Charles Baudelaire, *Flowers of Evil*

The Cat

Come, my fine cat, against my loving heart;
    Sheathe your sharp claws, and settle.
And let my eyes into your pupils dart
    Where agate sparks with metal.

Now while my fingertips caress at leisure
    Your head and wiry curves,
And that my hand's elated with the pleasure
    Of your electric nerves,

I think about my woman – how her glances
    Like yours, dear beast, deep-down
And cold, can cut and wound one as with lances;

    Then, too, she has that vagrant
And subtle air of danger that makes fragrant
    Her body, lithe and brown.

                    Charles Baudelaire, transl. Roy Campbell

Marigold

She moved through the garden in glory, because
She had very long claws at the end of her paws.
Her back was arched, her tail was high,
A green fire glared in her vivid eye;
And all the Toms, though never so bold,
Quailed at the martial Marigold.

                            Richard Garnett

She Sights a Bird

She sights a Bird – she chuckles –
She flattens – then she crawls –
She runs without the look of feet –
Her eyes increase to Balls –

Her Jaws stir – twitching – hungry –
Her Teeth can hardly stand –

She leaps, but Robin leaped the first –
Ah, Pussy, of the Sand,

The Hopes so juicy ripening –
You almost bathed your Tongue –
When Bliss disclosed a hundred Toes –
And fled with every one –

Emily Dickinson

Cats

No-one but indefatigable lovers and old
Chilly philosophers can understand the true
Charm of these animals serene and potent, who
Likewise are sedentary and suffer from the cold.

They are the friends of learning and of sexual bliss;
Silence they love, and darkness where temptation breeds.
Erebus would have made them his funereal steeds,
Save that their proud free nature would not stoop to this.

Like those great sphinxes lounging through eternity
In noble attitudes upon the desert sand,
They gaze incuriously at nothing, calm and wise.

Their fecund loins give forth electric flashes, and
Thousands of golden particles drift ceaselessly,
Like galaxies of stars, in their mysterious eyes.

From *Flowers of Evil* by Charles Baudelaire, transl. George Dillon

The Sleep of the Cat

The sleep of the Cat, though generally very light, is, however, sometimes so profound, that the animal requires to be shaken pretty briskly before it can be awakened. This particularity takes place chiefly in the depth of winter, and especially on the approach of snowy weather. At such periods also, as well as some others, the animal diffuses a fragrant smell somewhat like that of cloves.

Rev. W. Bingley

Cat and Lady

They were at play, she and her cat,
And it was marvellous to mark
The white paw and the white hand pat
Each other in the deepening dark.

The stealthy little lady hid
Under her mittens' silken sheath
Her deadly agate nails that thrid
The silk-like dagger points of death.

The cat purred primly and drew in
Her claws that were of steel filed thin:
The devil was in it all the same.

And in the boudoir, while a shout
Of laughter in the air rang out,
Four sparks of phosphor shone like flame.

Paul Verlaine, transl. Arthur Symonds

A Cure for Warts

'You take your cat and go and get in the graveyard long before midnight when someone that was wicked has been buried; and when it's midnight a devil will come . . . you heave your cat after 'em and say, "Devil follow corpse, cats follow devil, warts follow cat, I'm done with ye."'

From *The Adventures of Tom Sawyer* by Mark Twain

A Remedy for Singing

A Malteese soprano kat, about 12 months old, singing old hundred on a picket fence, late last thursda nite, whichever persons owns sed kat will find him (or her, according to circumstancis) in a vakant lot, just bak ov our hous, still butiful in death.

From *The Farmer's Allminax* by Henry Wheeler Shaw

Cat and Colossus

Mark Twain was delighted by a curious loyalty which he observed on a visit to Marseille.

In the great Zoological Gardens we found specimens of all the animals the world produces, I think. . . . The boon companion of the colossal elephant was a common cat! This cat had a fashion of climbing up the elephant's hind legs, and roosting on his back. She would sit up there, with her paws curved under her breast, and sleep in the sun half the afternoon. It used to annoy the elephant at first, and he would reach up and take her down, but she would go aft and climb up again. She persisted until she finally conquered the elephant's prejudices, and now they are inseparable friends. The cat plays about her comrade's forefeet or his trunk often, until dogs approach, and then she goes aloft out of danger. The elephant has annihilated several dogs lately, that pressed his companion too closely.

Mark Twain

Having a Canary

Sir, –

Here is the story of a cat and a bird. Two young ladies dwelt together, – one the owner of a canary, which she petted and played with; the other was the mistress of a beautiful cat, which was nursed and patted and petted also. They were a happy and united family. The owner of the cat went abroad for a time, and pussy grew sad and melancholy, and at last became jealous of the bird, which was daily petted as usual, while she was sadly neglected. Pussy could not, and would not, stand this treatment; her jealousy grew day by day till at last, in a fit of rage, she made a dash at the little bird and tore him limb from limb. Then seized by remorse she fled, but the owner of the bird was frantic, and she beat the cat and mourned for her bird; and the owner of the cat when she heard of the catastrophe shed sad tears, not, indeed, because the bird was dead, but because her pussy had been beaten; and so the peace of that happy family was destroyed for a time. Pussy, overwhelmed with remorse at the crime she had committed, was found the next day curled up and asleep in the little bird's cage. Now, the problem for psychologists required to be solved is, why did that cat go into that cage? The only solution that suggests itself to the persons concerned is, that by going there she thought she might regain the favour of the mistress whose happiness she had so ruthlessly destroyed, by taking the place of the bird, and so, perhaps, in due time, be changed into a little petted bird herself. –

I am, Sir, &c.,

Catalonia

From the *Spectator*, 19 October 1895

Not Having a Canary

I am sorry for your cat's Influenza (It is a clear case of Influenza!) but it would have been worse if she had given way to passion, as her mother has just done, and done no end of mischief in attempting a great crime! For several days there had been *that* in her eyes when raised to my canary, which filled my heart with alarm. I sent express for a carpenter, and had the cage attached to the drawing room ceiling, with an elaborate apparatus of chain and pulley and weight. 'Most expensive!' (as my Scotch servant exclaimed with clasped hands over a Picture of the *Virgin and Child* in the National Gallery!) and there had it swung for two days, to Mr C's intense disgust, who regards thy pet as '*the most inanely chimerical of all*' – the cat meanwhile spending all its spare time in gazing up at the bird with eyes aflame! But it was safe *now* – I thought! and went out for a walk. On my return Charlotte met me with 'Oh! whatever *do* you think the cat has gone and done?' 'Eaten my canary?' – 'No, *far worse*! – pulled down the cage and the weight, and broke the chain and upset the little table and broken everything on it!' – 'And not eaten the canary?' – 'Oh, I suppose the dreadful crash she made frightened *herself*; for I met *her* running downstairs as I ran up – tho' the cage was on the floor, and the door open and the canary in *such* a way!' You never saw such a scene of devastation. The carpet was covered with fragments of a pretty terra cotta basket given me by Lady Airlie – and fragments of the glass which

covered it, and with the earth and ferns that had been growing in it, and with birdseed, and bits of brass chain, and I can't tell what all! That is what one gets by breeding up a cat! – She had rushed right out by the back door and didn't show her face for twenty-four hours after! And now I don't know where the poor bird will be safe.
Come soon.

Affectionately yours,
Jane Carlyle.

Part of a letter from Thomas Carlyle's wife, Jane Welsh Carlyle, to Mr Thomas Woolner; from *New Letters and Memorials of Jane Welsh Carlyle*

A Green Chicken

'Madame Théophile', a reddish cat with a white breast, a pink nose and blue eyes, so called because she lived with us in an intimacy which was quite conjugal, sleeping at the foot of our bed, dreaming on the arm of our chair while we wrote, going down to the garden in order to follow us in our walks, assisting at our meals, and sometimes even intercepting a tit-bit from our plate to our mouth.

One day a friend of ours who was going away for a few days brought us his parrot to look after during his absence. The bird, feeling himself to be among strangers, had climbed to the top of his perch by the help of his beak, and was rolling his eyes, which were like brass-headed nails, and blinking the white skin which served him for eyelids in a decidedly frightened way.

'Madame Théophile' had never seen a parrot, and this new creature evidently caused her much surprise.

Motionless as an embalmed Egyptian cat in its wrappings she watched the bird with an air of profound meditation, putting together all the notions of natural history which she had been able to gather on the roof, in the yard, or the garden. The shadow of her thoughts passed across her opalescent eyes, and we could read in them this summary of her investigations:

'This is decidedly a green chicken. . . .'

The parrot followed the cat's movements with feverish anxiety. . . . His instinct told him that this was an enemy meditating some evil deed.

As to the cat's eyes, which were fixed on the bird with fascinating intensity, they said in language which the parrot understood perfectly, for there was nothing ambiguous about it, 'Although it is green, this chicken must be good to eat.'

We followed this scene with interest, ready to intervene if necessity arose.

Madame Théophile had insensibly drawn nearer. Her pink nose quivered, she half closed her eyes, and her contractile claws went in and out. Little shivers ran down her spine. . . . Suddenly her back was bent like a bow, and in one vigorous, elastic bound she alighted on the perch. The parrot, perceiving the danger, promptly exclaimed in a bass voice, as solemn and deep as that of Monsieur Joseph Prudhomme, 'As tu déjeuné, Jacquot?' (Have you breakfasted, Jacquot?) This speech caused the cat to spring back in unspeakable terror. . . . All her ornithological ideas were upset.

The parrot continued:

'Et de quoi? De roti du roi.' (And on what? Off the joint of the king.)

The cat's face clearly expressed: 'It is not a bird; it is a gentleman; he is speaking!' . . .

She cast a look full of interrogation at us, and not being satisfied with our reply she went and hid herself under the bed, from where it was impossible to get her out for the rest of the day.

From 'Madame Théophile' by Théophile Gautier

No Chicken

Agentleman who lived in the neighbourhood of Portsmouth, had a cat, which kittened four or five days after a hen had brought out a brood of chickens. As he did not wish to keep more than one cat at a time, the kittens were all drowned, and the same day the cat and one chicken went amissing. Diligent search was immediately made in every place that could be thought of, both in and out of the house, but to no purpose; it was then concluded that some mischance had befallen both. Four days afterwards, however, the servant having occasion to go into an unfrequented part of the cellar, discovered, to his great astonishment, the cat lying in one corner, with the chicken hugged close to her body, and one paw laid over it as if to preserve it from injury. The cat and adopted chicken were brought into a closet in the kitchen, where they continued some days, the cat treating the chicken in every respect as a kitten. Whenever the chicken left the cat to eat, she appeared very uneasy, but, on its return, she received it with the affection of a mother, pressed it to her body, purred, and seemed perfectly happy. If the chicken was carried to the hen, it immediately returned to the cat. The chicken was by some accident killed, and the cat would not eat for several days afterwards, being inconsolable for its loss.

From *Interesting Anecdotes of the Animal Kingdom* by Thomas Brown

Punch Drunk

My cat has taken to mulled port and rum punch. Poor old dear! he is all the better for it. Dr W. B. Richardson says that the lower animals always refuse alcoholic drinks, and gives that as a reason why humans should do so too.

A very pretty reason, is it not?

Part of a letter from a Miss Savage to Samuel Butler; from *Samuel Butler, Author of Erewhon (1835–1902): A Memoir* by Henry Festing Jones

A Depraved Appetite

Cats sometimes behave like dogs. The writer possessed an animal that used to come to his whistle just as a terrier would, and in the night time, when dogs and pedestrians were not about, used to accompany him in his walks in May Fair.

This cat was not formed like others of its species. It was a tabby, with rather longish hair and with a thick tail, which was not more than six inches long. How the remainder was lost was a question; but from its extreme irritability when its tip was touched, a butcher-boy's chopper was suspected. The cat was odd in other ways; when her master was at his desk writing, she would always select a small piece of writing paper on which she sat down, no doubt putting herself on a literary footing with him. Her diet was also extraordinary; she would eat pickles and drink brandy-and-water. One day she rose suddenly and sprang up the chimney, a fire burning in the grate all the time. A couple of hundred years ago the writer would without doubt have been burned as a wizard for keeping a familiar. The cat when she found the top of the register too hot for her feet came down, a little blacker than when she went up. One day, however, poor puss suddenly rushed round the room in a circle for a few seconds, and then fell down dead. This finale explained many of her peculiarities when alive. She suffered from epileptic fits, and these always affect the brain in a singular manner, and no doubt accounted for the depraved nature of her appetite.

From *Fruit Between the Leaves* by Andrew Wynter

The Successor

No, I will not have any Persian cat; it is undertaking too much responsibility. I must have a cat whom I find homeless, wandering about the court, and to whom, therefore, I am under no obligation. There is a Clifford's Inn euphemism about cats which the laundresses use quite gravely: they say people come to this place 'to lose their cats.' They mean that, when they have a cat they don't want to kill and don't know how to get rid of, they bring it here, drop it inside the railings of our grass-plot, and go away under the impression that they have been 'losing' their cat. Well, this happens very frequently and I have already selected a dirty little drunken wretch of a kitten to be successor to my poor old cat. I don't suppose it drinks anything stronger than milk and water but then, you know, so much milk and water must be bad for a kitten that age – at any rate it looks as if it drank; but it gives me the impression of being affectionate, intelligent, and fond of mice, and I believe, if it had a home, it would become more respectable; at any rate I will see how it works.

Letter from Samuel Butler to his sister; from *Samuel Butler, Author of Erewhon (1835–1902): A Memoir* by Henry Festing Jones

Drunk as a Duke

Now, as to what she drinks, a well-bred cat is always particular, and at times even fastidious; but two things they must have – water and milk. They will often prefer the former to the latter . . .

But do keep their dishes clean. Disease is often brought on from neglect of this precaution. Cats will drink tea or beer, and I have seen a Tom get as drunk as a duke on oatmeal and whisky. An old lady, an acquaintance of mine, has a fine red-and-white Tom, and whenever he is ailing she gives him 'just a leetle drop o' brandy, sir.' Tom, I think, must have had two little drops o' brandy yesterday, when he rode my fox-terrier, Princie, all round the paddock. Those naughty drops o' brandy!

From *The Domestic Cat* by Gordon Stables

A Moral Haggardness

As the dogs of shy neighbourhoods usually betray a slinking consciousness of being in poor circumstances – for the most part manifested in an aspect of anxiety, an awkwardness in their play, and a misgiving that somebody is going to harness them to something, to pick up a living – so the cats of shy neighbourhoods exhibit a strong tendency to relapse into barbarism. Not only are they made selfishly ferocious by ruminating on the surplus population around them, and on the densely crowded state of all the avenues to cat's meat; not only is there a moral and politico-economical haggardness in them, traceable to these reflections; but they evince a physical deterioration. Their linen is not clean, and is wretchedly got up; their black turns rusty, like old mourning; they wear very indifferent fur; and take to the shabbiest cotton velvet, instead of silk velvet. I am on terms of recognition with several small streets of cats, about the Obelisk in Saint George's Fields, and also in the vicinity of Clerkenwell-green, and also in the back settlements of Drury-lane. In appearance, they are very like the women among whom they live. They seem to turn out of their unwholesome beds into the street, without any preparation. They leave their young families to stagger about the gutters, unassisted, while they frouzily quarrel and swear and scratch and spit, at street corners. In particular, I remark that when they are about to increase their families (an event of frequent recurrence) the resemblance is strongly expressed in a certain dusty dowdiness, down-at-heel self-neglect, and general giving up of things. I cannot honestly report that I have ever seen a feline matron of this class washing her face when in an interesting condition.

From *The Uncommercial Traveller* by Charles Dickens

A Shocking Mother

She could have learnt from the few animals in the house, if she had never opened a book. Minouche in particular interested her. Four times a year, the rakish creature would go on a wild spree. She who was normally so fastidious, constantly preening herself, so scared of getting dirty that she never set a paw outside without a shudder, would vanish for two or three days at a time. She could be heard cursing and fighting, and the eyes of all the toms in Bonneville could be seen gleaming in the dark like candles. Then she would come home in a shocking state, all bedraggled, her fur so torn and dirty that she had to spend a whole week licking herself clean. After that she would resume her supercilious airs, rubbing herself against people's faces without seeming to notice that her belly was growing rounder. And one fine morning, she would be found with a litter of kittens. Véronique used to carry them all off in a corner of her apron to drown them. And Minouche, a shocking mother, did not even miss them; she was used to being rid of them in this fashion, and thought that she had fulfilled all her maternal duties. She would go on licking herself, purring, giving herself airs, until one evening she went off again shamelessly to collect a fresh bellyful, to the accompaniment of mewing and scratching. Mathieu [the dog] was a far better father to these children that were not his own, for he would walk whining after Véronique's apron; he loved licking helpless little creatures clean.

'Oh, auntie, do let's leave her one this time,' Pauline would say on each occasion, shocked and delighted by the cat's amorous airs and graces. But Véronique snapped: 'No, indeed! she'd only drag it about all over the place. And besides she doesn't care about them; she has all the fun and none of the burden.'

From *Zest for Life* by Émile Zola, transl. Jean Stewart

The Sorrows of Cats in a Poor Neighbourhood

It seems almost too horrible for belief that a creature exquisitely sensitive, daintily fastidious, superlatively clean by choice, capable of reasoning and gifted with emotional faculties of a high type should lead the fugitive, vagabond, and persecuted life which she is allowed to do in our cultivated cities. The only excuse for the apathy of the public is that the details of cat life are unknown to influential persons, of such cat life I mean as lived in crowded centres. Otherwise the cruel meanness of neglecting to protect a faithful servant merely because he is cheap and tenacious of life would strike them.

It is not by day but by night, it is less in rich and fashionable than in slummy neighbourhoods that the utterly deplorable nature of feline existence can be realized. It is not a tempting invitation I know, but I challenge anybody who has the courage to see for himself or herself what the cat population of a poor district is, and how it lives when it turns out *en masse* after dark. Almost any back street or alley will furnish ample corroboration of what I say, – that the treatment of cats in England is a discredit to a land professedly civilized. As soon as the streets are comparatively empty, and there is a shadowy chance that some vile fragments may be picked up in the gutter without interruption, out steals one phantom-like creature after another from the lurking places where they have hidden all day.

They seem to flit along instead of running, so swift are they to disappear on the least alarm. They are gaunt, famine-stricken, covered, many of them, with sores and wounds. Even this meal of offscourings they pick up in a clandestine and guilty haste. Here and there are the broken limbed or lame, and these seem half crazy from want, owing to being handicapped in the general scrimmage of food. After howling and fighting like fiends, a single conqueror swallows the disgusting offal, from which his soul revolts, while he must eat or perish. He tears in frantic haste the entrails which he has found, lest some other cat, fiercer and stronger than he, should wrest the booty from him; his torn and bleeding ears are pricked to listen for the least sound, though there is now less danger from dogs and stone-throwers than in broad daylight. His shoulder bones are sticking through his skin, his tail is a mere wisp, his eyes glare and seem to occupy half his face. Here you will find a creature who snarls when you go near him, snatching up his prey and vanishing with it like a wild beast into the gloomy shades of some cellar, or through a broken window into a disused and empty house. There you may see 'the poor remains of beauty once admired,' – a Puss who still believes in humanity in spite of all, clings to the legends of her youth, timidly touches your feet, and lifts appealing eyes to yours. She will follow you for half a mile or more if you do but throw a kind word to her.

Even on snowy nights these scenes go on just the same. Perhaps there is some excuse for not believing what one has not seen, especially when it is so much more comfortable and conducive to one's night's rest to be incredulous. I can but say that I have seen and must believe.

I do not think that any words or pictures could overpaint the sorrows of cats in a poor neighbourhood. In one small street alone, in a single poor district of Bristol, no less than three cats were found frozen to death in one night. Of course nobody troubles himself to gather statistics of dead cats; besides, no numbers could fitly express the amount of distress spread through a hundred streets of a thousand towns. If obtainable, these statistics could not indicate, even faintly, the sufferings of shelterless cats before the frost mercifully benumbs those fortunate enough to die.

From *The Cat: Her Place in Society and Treatment* by Edith Carrington

A Painless Sleep

Charles Dodgson was one of those nineteenth-century authors who could not countenance the suffering of animals. He invented his own humane mousetrap, and when the Common Room cat at Christ Church had to be destroyed, he felt compelled to write to Sir James Paget.

It seems a shame to occupy your time and attention with so trivial a matter as a pet-cat: but all the modes you suggest, except the poisoned meat, would be unsuitable. To shut it up in a cage would produce an agony of terror: and the same may be said of the hypodermic injection (which would have to be done by a stranger, I suppose), and, most of all, of the journey to London. Is there no kind of poison which would *not* involve the risk of being vomited, and which would produce a painless sleep? My own idea would have been to give *laudanum*, (I don't know what quantity, say a drachm) mixed with some meat or fish – Would not this do?

From *Carroll: An Illustrated Biography* by Derek Hudson

A Rescued Kitten

Rescued a little kitten that was perched in the sill of the round window at the sink over the gasjet and dared not jump down. I heard her mew a piteous long time till I could bear it no longer; but I make a note of it because of her gratitude after I had taken her down, which made her follow me about and at each turn of the stairs as I went down leading her to the kitchen ran back a few steps up and try to get up to lick me through the bannisters from the flight above.

From the diary of Gerard Manly Hopkins

An Obituary

Charlotte Bronte added this poignant post-script to a letter to her friend Ellen Nussey, on 1 July 1841.

PS. – Also, little black Tom is dead. Every cup, however, sweet, has its drop of bitterness in it. Probably you will be at a loss to ascertain the identity of black Tom, but, do not fret about it. I'll tell you when you come.

Horrible and Terrible

At Godwin's with Northcote, Coleridge, &c. Coleridge made himself very merry at the expense of Fuseli, whom he always called Fuzzle or Fuzly. He told a story of Fuseli's being on a visit at Liverpool at a time when unfortunately he had to divide the attention of the public with a Prussian soldier, who had excited a great deal of notice by his enormous powers of eating. And the annoyance was aggravated by persons persisting in considering the soldier as Fuseli's countryman. He spent his last evening at Dr Crompton's, when Roscoe (whose visitor Fuseli was) took an opportunity of giving a hint to the party that no one should mention the glutton. The admonition unfortunately was not heard by a lady, who, turning to the great Academician and lecturer, said, 'Well, sir, your countryman has been surpassing himself!' – 'Madam,' growled the irritated painter, 'the fellow is no countryman of mine.' – 'He is a foreigner! Have you heard what he has been doing? He has eaten a live cat!' – 'A live cat!' everyone exclaimed, except Fuseli, whose rage was excited by the suggestion of a lady famous for her blunders: 'Dear me, Mr Fuseli, that would be a fine subject for your pencil.' 'My pencil, madam?' – 'To be sure, sir, as the horrible is your forte.' – 'You mean the *terrible*, madam,' he replied with an assumed composure, muttering at the same time between his teeth, 'if a silly woman can mean anything.'

From the diary of Henry Crabb Robinson

Wery Like Weal

'Weal pie,' said Mr Weller, soliloquising, as he arranged the eatables on the grass. 'Wery good thing is a weal pie, when you know the lady as made it, and is quite sure it an't kittens; and arter all, though, where's the odds, when they're so like weal that the wery piemen themselves don't know the difference?'

'Don't they, Sam?' said Mr Pickwick.

'Not they, sir,' replied Mr Weller, touching his hat. 'I lodged in the same house with a pieman once, sir, and a wery nice man he was – reg'lar clever chap, too – make pies out o' anything, he could. "What a number o' cats you keep, Mr Brooks," says I, when I'd got intimate with him. "Ah," says he, "I do – a good many," says he. "You must be wery fond o' cats," says I. "Other people is," says he, a winkin' at me; "they an't in season till the winter, though," says he. "Not in season!" says I. "No," says he, "fruits is in, cats is out." "Why, what do you mean?" says I. "Mean?" says he. "That I'll never be a party to the combination o' the butchers, to keep up the prices o' meat," says he. "Mr Weller," says he, a squeezing my hand wery hard, and vispering in my ear – "don't mention this here agin – but it's the seasonin' as does it. They're all made o' them noble animals," says he, a pointing to a wery nice little tabby kitten, "and I seasons 'em for beef-steak, weal, or kidney, 'cordin to the demand. And more than that," says he, "I can make a weal a beef-steak, or a beef-steak a kidney, or any one on 'em a mutton, at a minute's notice, just as the market changes, and appetites wary!"'

'He must have been a very ingenious young man, that, Sam,' said Mr Pickwick with a slight shudder.

'Just was, sir,' replied Mr Weller, continuing his occupation of emptying the basket, 'and the pies was beautiful.'

From *The Posthumous Papers of the Pickwick Club* by Charles Dickens

The Rabbit of the Jungles

Phileas Fogg eats a detestable dinner in Bombay.

After leaving the passport office, Phileas Fogg quietly returned to the station, and there had dinner served. Among other dishes, the landlord thought he ought to recommend to him a certain giblet of 'native rabbit', of which he spoke in the highest terms. Phileas Fogg accepted the giblet and tasted it conscientiously; but in spite of the spiced sauce, he found it detestable. He rang for the landlord.

'Sir,' he said, looking at him steadily, 'is that rabbit?'

'Yes, my lord,' replied the rogue boldly, 'the rabbit of the jungles.'

'And that rabbit did not mew when it was killed?'

'Mew! oh, my lord! a rabbit! I swear to you—'

'Landlord,' replied Mr Fogg coolly, 'don't swear, and recollect this: in former times, in India, cats were considered sacred animals. That was a good time.'

'For the cats, my lord?'

'And perhaps also for the travellers!'

After this observation Mr Fogg went on quietly with his dinner.

From *Around the World in Eighty Days* by Jules Verne

A Stolen Cat

A widow resents the theft of her pet, but not its appalling fate, in Mrs Gaskell's novel *North and South*.

'How is old Betty Barnes?'

'I don't know,' said the woman, rather shortly. 'We'se not friends.'

'Why not?' asked Margaret, who had formerly been the peacemaker of the village.

'She stole my cat.'

'Did she know it was yours?'

'I don't know. I reckon not.'

'Well! could not you get it back again when you told her it was yours?'

'No! for she burnt it.'

'Burnt it?' exclaimed both Margaret and Mr Bell.

'Roasted it!' explained the woman.

It was no explanation. By dint of questioning, Margaret extracted from her the horrible fact that Betty Barnes, having been induced by a gipsy fortune-teller to lend the latter her husband's Sunday clothes, on promise of having them faithfully returned on the Saturday night before Goodman Barnes should have missed them, became alarmed by their non-appearance, and her consequent dread of her husband's anger; and as, according to one of the savage country superstitions, the cries of a cat, in the agonies of being boiled or roasted alive, compelled (as it were) the powers of darkness to fulfil the wishes of the executioner, resort had been had to the charm.

The poor woman evidently believed in its efficacy; her only feeling was indignation that her cat had been chosen out from all others for a sacrifice. Margaret listened in horror; and endeavoured in vain to enlighten the woman's mind; but she was obliged to give it up in despair. Step by step, she got the woman to admit certain facts, of which the logical connection and sequence was perfectly clear to Margaret; but, at the end, the bewildered woman simply repeated her first assertion, namely, that 'it were very cruel for sure, and she should not like to do it; but that there were nothing like it for giving a person what they wished for; she had heard it all her life; but it were very cruel for all that.'

From *North and South* by Elizabeth Gaskell

Revolting Animals

There are signs that the domestic animals are revolting. From Holborn comes news that one Mr Ashton, returning home, discovered his black tom had two visitors in the passage, whom Mr Ashton proceeded to eject, but all three set on him, and after a violent struggle Mr Ashton was driven precipitously out at the front door, and fell into the arms of two policemen who took him to the hospital.

On their return, they found old Mrs Ashton the mother had retreated into the back drawing-room badly scratched, and she also was conveyed to the hospital. The two policemen returned a second time and had a tremendous battle, in which one cat jumped on the leading policeman's helmet. However, the two strangers were killed at last. Unfortunately the blackie leader took warning and escaped through a back window, since which a large body of cats are said to have been seen moving towards Oxford Street.

I don't consider cats thoroughly domesticated animals. I have twice been attacked by two which had not kittens, when trying to turn them out of the garden. Once I retreated at full speed, the other time I had a most unpleasant fight with a heavy walking stick.

From *The Journal of Beatrix Potter from 1881 to 1897*

Lady Jane

A large grey cat leaped from some neighbouring shelf on his shoulder, and startled us all.

'Hi! show 'em how you scratch. Hi! Tear, my lady!' said her master.

The cat leaped down, and ripped at a bundle of rags with her tigerish claws, with a sound that it set my teeth on edge to hear.

'She'd do as much for any one I was to set her on,' said the old man. 'I deal in cat-skins among other general matters, and hers was offered to me. It's a very fine skin, as you may see, but I didn't have it stripped off! *That* warn't like Chancery practice though, says you!'

From *Bleak House* by Charles Dickens

The Pain-killer

Aunt Polly procures a remedy for Tom Sawyer and Tom finds a taker for his aunt's revolting medicine.

Now she heard of Pain-killer for the first time. She ordered a lot at once. She tasted it and was filled with gratitude. It was simply fire in a liquid form. She dropped the water treatment and everything else, and pinned her faith to Pain-killer. She gave Tom a teaspoonful and watched with the deepest anxiety for the result. Her troubles were instantly at rest, her soul at peace again; for the 'indifference' was broken up. The boy could not have shown a wilder, heartier interest if she had built a fire under him.

Tom felt that it was time to wake up; this sort of life might be romantic enough, in his blighted condition but it was getting to have too little sentiment and too much distracting variety about it. So he thought over various plans for relief, and finally hit upon that of professing to be fond of Pain-killer. He asked for it so often that he became a nuisance, and his aunt ended by telling him to help himself and quit bothering her. If it had been Sid, she would have had no misgivings to alloy her delight; but since it was Tom, she watched the bottle clandestinely. She found that the medicine did really diminish, but it did not occur to her that the boy was mending the health of a crack in the sitting-room floor with it.

One day Tom was in the act of dosing the crack when his aunt's yellow cat came along, purring, eying the teaspoon avariciously, and begging for a taste. Tom said:

'Don't ask for it unless you want it, Peter.'

But Peter signified that he did want it.

'You better make sure.'

Peter was sure.

'Now you've asked for it, and I'll give it to you, because there ain't anything mean about *me*; but if you find you don't like it, you mustn't blame anybody but your own self.'

Peter was agreeable. So Tom pried his mouth open and poured down the Pain-killer. Peter sprang a couple of yards in the air, and then delivered a war-whoop and set off round and round the room, banging against furniture, upsetting flower-pots, and making general havoc. Next he rose on his hind feet and pranced around, in a frenzy of enjoyment, with his head over his shoulder and his voice proclaiming his unappeasable happiness. Then he went tearing around the house again spreading chaos and destruction in his path. Aunt Polly entered in time to see him throw a few double somersets, deliver a final mighty hurrah, and sail through the open window, carrying him 'thout any more feeling than if he was a human!

Aunt Polly felt a sudden pang of remorse. This was putting the thing in a new light; what was cruelty to a cat *might* be cruelty to a boy, too. She began to soften; she felt sorry. Her eyes watered a little, and she put her hand on Tom's head and said gently:

'I was meaning for the best, Tom. And, Tom, it *did* do you good.'

Tom looked up in her face with just a perceptible twinkle peeping through his gravity:

'I know you was meaning for the best, auntie, and so was I with Peter. It done *him* good, too. I never see him get around so since—'

From *The Adventures of Tom Sawyer* by Mark Twain

The Purge

One of the best-loved episodes from Elizabeth Gaskell's *Cranford* concerns the narrow escape of Mrs Forrester's lace fichu, as recounted to Lady Glenmire.

'Yes,' said that lady, 'such lace cannot be got now for either love or money; made by the nuns abroad they tell me. They say that they can't make it now, even there. But perhaps they can now they've passed the Catholic Emancipation Bill. I should not wonder. But, in the meantime, I treasure up my lace very much. I daren't even trust the washing of it to my maid' (the little charity school-girl I have named before, but who sounded well as 'my maid'). 'I always wash it myself. And once it had a narrow escape. Of course, your ladyship knows that such lace must never be starched or ironed. Some people wash it in sugar and water; and some in coffee, to make it the right yellow colour; but I myself have a very good receipt for washing it in milk, which stiffens it enough, and gives it a very good creamy colour. Well, ma'am, I had tacked it together (and the beauty of this fine lace is, that when it is wet, it goes into a very little space), and put it to soak in milk, when, unfortunately, I left the room; on my return I found pussy on the table, looking very like a thief, but gulping very uncomfortably as if she was half-choked with something she wanted to swallow, and could not. And, would you believe it? At first I pitied her, and said, "Poor pussy! poor pussy!" till, all at once, I looked and saw the cup of milk empty – cleaned out! "You naughty cat!" said I; and I believe I was provoked enough to give her a slap, which did no good, but only helped the lace down – just as one slaps a choking child on the back. I could have cried, I was so vexed; but I determined I would not give the lace up without a struggle for it. I hoped the lace might disagree with her at any rate; but it would have been too much for Job, if he had seen, as I did, that cat come in, quite placid and purring, not a quarter of an hour after, and almost expecting to be stroked. "No, pussy!" said I; "if you have any conscience, you ought not to expect that!" And then a thought struck me; and I rang the bell for my maid, and sent her to Mr Hoggins with my compliments, and would he be kind enough to lend me one of his top-boots for an hour? I did not think there was anything odd in the message; but Jenny said, the young men in the surgery laughed as if they would be ill, at my wanting a top-boot. When it came, Jenny and I put pussy in, with her fore-feet straight down, so that they were fastened, and could not scratch, and we gave her a teaspoonful of currant-jelly, in which (your ladyship must excuse me) I had mixed some tartar emetic. I shall never forget how anxious I was for the next half-hour. I took pussy to my own room, and spread a clean towel on the floor. I could have kissed her when she returned the lace to sight, very much as it had gone down. Jenny had boiling water ready, and we soaked it and soaked it, and spread it on a lavender bush in the sun, before I could touch it again, even to put it in milk. But now, your ladyship would never guess that it had been in pussy's inside.'

From *Cranford* by Elizabeth Gaskell

A Cat and Bull Story

'Wickham,' retorted Mrs Pipchin, colouring, 'is a wicked, impudent bold-faced hussy.'

'What's that?' inquired Paul.

'Never you mind, Sir,' retorted Mrs Pipchin. 'Remember the story of the little boy that was gored to death by a mad bull, for asking questions.'

'If the bull was mad,' said Paul, 'how did *he* know the boy had asked questions? Nobody can go and whisper secrets to a mad bull. I don't believe that story.'

'You don't believe it, Sir?' repeated Mrs Pipchin amazed.

'No,' said Paul.

'Not if it should happen to have been a tame bull, you little Infidel?' said Mrs Pipchin.

As Paul had not considered the subject in that light, and had founded his conclusions on the alleged lunacy of the bull, he allowed himself to be put down for the present. But he sat turning it over in his mind, with such an obvious intention of fixing Mrs Pipchin presently, that even that hardy old lady deemed it prudent to retreat until he should have forgotten the subject.

From that time, Mrs Pipchin appeared to have something of the same odd kind of attraction towards Paul, as Paul had towards her. She would make him move his chair to her side of the fire, instead of sitting opposite; and there he would remain in a nook between Mrs Pipchin and the fender, with all the light of his little face absorbed into the black bombazeen drapery, studying every line and wrinkle of her countenance, and peering at the hard grey eye, until Mrs Pipchin was sometimes fain to shut it on pretence of dozing. Mrs Pipchin had an old black cat, who generally lay coiled upon the centre foot of the fender, purring egotistically, and winking at the fire until the contracted pupils of his eyes were like two notes of admiration. The good old lady might have been – not to record it disrespectfully – a witch, and Paul and the cat her two familiars, as they all sat by the fire together. It would have been quite in keeping with the appearance of the party if they had all sprung up the chimney in a high wind one night, and never been heard of any more.

This, however, never came to pass. The cat, and Paul, and Mrs Pipchin, were constantly to be found in their usual places after dark; and Paul, eschewing the companionship of Master Bitherstone, went on studying Mrs Pipchin, and the cat, and the fire, night after night, as if they were a book of necromancy, in three volumes.

From *Dombey and Son* by Charles Dickens

Eye Contact

After this cat's departure Agnes took to heart a kitten, who was very fond of her. This kitten, the first night she slept in her room, on wakening in the morning looked up from the hearth at Agnes, who was lying awake, but with her eyes half-shut, and marked all pussy's motions; after looking some instants, puss jumped up on the bed, crept softly forward and put her paw, with its glove on, upon one of Miss Baillie's eyelids and pushed it gently up. Miss Baillie looked at her fixedly, and Puss, as if satisfied that her eyes were *there* and safe, went back to her station on the hearth and never troubled herself more about the matter.

Part of a letter from Maria Edgeworth to Lucy Edgeworth; from *Behold This Dreamer*, ed. Walter de la Mare

A Musical Critique

Another favourite cat of Gautier's, called Madame Théophile, loved perfumes, some kinds of which sent her into ecstasies of delight. This cat was also fond of music, but shrill notes displeased her and, as cats will, she would try to silence the singer by placing a velvet paw on his mouth.

From 'Madame Théophile' by Théophile Gautier

A Kiss on the Nose

Florence Nightingale had about sixty cats and refused to travel without them. All Persians, they were named after prominent men of the day, such as Disraeli, Gladstone and Bismark. As the following episode, told by herself, reveals, she clearly found them an improving example.

I learn the lesson of life from a little kitten of mine, one of two. The old cat comes in and says, very cross, 'I didn't ask you in here, I like to have my Missus to myself!' And he runs at them. The bigger and handsomer kitten runs away, but the littler one *stands her ground*, and when the old enemy comes near enough kisses his nose, and makes the peace. That is the lesson of life, to kiss one's enemy's nose, always standing one's ground.

From *Florence Nightingale* by Elspeth Huxley

A Profitable Accomplishment

Four cats, belonging to one of my friends, had taught themselves the art of begging like a dog. They had frequently seen the dog practise that accomplishment at the table, and had observed that he generally received a reward for so doing. By a process of inductive reasoning, they decided that if they possessed the same accomplishment, they would in all probability receive the same reward. Acting on this opinion, they waited until they saw the dog sit up in a begging posture, and immediately assumed the attitude with imperturbable gravity. Of course their ingenuity was not suffered to pass unrewarded and they always found that their newly-discovered accomplishment was an unfailing source of supplies for them.

From *Sketches and Anecdotes of Animal Life* by the Revd James Wood

Cat Map

I have a cat who, if I hold her up in front of the map of London, will place her paw upon any principal building I like to name. The cat has been used to be carried round the room to catch flies on the wall. The principal buildings in the map are marked with square black spots, which she naturally mistakes for flies, so you have only to hold her in front of the map nearest to the spot you want her to touch, and slightly elevate your voice when you name the place, and the thing is done.

From *The Domestic Cat* by Gordon Stables

The Milky Way

My friend Captain Noble, of Maresfield, informs me that he has himself known a cat which was in the habit of catching starlings by getting on a cow's back and waiting till the cow happened to approach the birds, which little suspected what the approaching inoffensive beast bore crouching upon it. He assures me he has himself witnessed this elaborate trick, by means of which the cat managed to catch starlings which otherwise it could never have got near. Many cats will readily learn the signification of certain words, and will answer to their names and come when called. Very strange is the power which cats may show of finding their way home by routes which they have never before traversed. We cannot explain this (as it has been sought to explain the like power in dogs), by the power of smell being the predominate sense, so that a passed succession of smells can be retraversed in reverse order, as a number of places seen in succession on a journey may be retraversed in reverse order by ourselves. On the whole, it seems probable that the power in question may be due to a highly developed 'sense of direction', like that which enables some men so much to excel others in finding their way about cities, or that which enables the inhabitants of Siberia to find their way through woods or over hummocky ice, and who, though constantly changing the direction they immediately pursue, yet keep their main direction unchanged.

From *The Cat: An Introduction to the Study of Backboned Animals* by St George Mivart

A Great Usefulness

Edgar Allan Poe's child-wife, Virginia Clemm (known as Sissy to him) died in miserable circumstances in 1844, comforted by her immediate family and a heroic pet, according to a Mrs Grove-Nichols who wrote an account of the event. There is no record of Mrs Poe's view of the proceedings, which seem entirely to the advantage of the cat.

The autumn came, and Mrs Poe sank rapidly in consumption. I saw her in her bedchamber. Everything here was so neat, so purely clean, so scant and poverty-stricken, that I saw the poor sufferer with such a heartache. . . . There was no clothing on the bed, which was only straw, but a snow-white counterpane and sheets. The weather was cold, and the sick lady had the dreadful chills, that accompany the hectic fever of consumption. She lay on the straw-bed, wrapped in her husband's great coat, with a large tortoiseshell cat in her bosom. The wonderful cat seemed conscious of her great usefulness. The coat and the cat were the sufferer's only means of warmth; except as her husband held her hands, and her mother her feet.

An account written by Mrs Grove-Nichols

Cats, Large and Noisy

While living in his mistress's villa in Ravenna, Lord Byron accumulated a remarkable menagerie including peacocks, birds of prey, guinea fowl, monkeys, eight dogs and five cats. Shelley stayed there in 1821 and wrote about his encounter with five peacocks, two guinea hens and an Egyptian crane on the grand staircase. Their impudence may have accounted for the condition of the cats, which Byron later recorded in his journal.

The crow is lame of a leg – wonder how it happened – some fool trod upon his toe, I suppose. The falcon pretty brisk – the cats large and noisy – the monkeys I have not looked to since the cold weather, as they suffer by being brought out.

From *Byron's Ravenna Journal*

Mother

In 1819 John Keats, a cat lover, was catless. While staying with his friend Charles Brown in Hampstead, 'Mother', a cat belonging to his neighbours, Mr and Mrs Charles Dilke, took it upon herself to remedy this situation.

Mrs Dilke has two Cats – a Mother and a Daughter – now the Mother is a tabby and the daughter a black and white like the spotted child – Now it appears ominous to me for the doors of both houses are opened frequently – so that there is a complete thoroughfare for both Cats (there being no board up to the contrary) they may one and several of them come into my room ad libitum. But no – the Tabby only comes – whether from sympathy from ann the maid or me I can not tell – or whether Brown has left behind him any atmosphere spirit of Maidenhood I can not tell. The Cat is not an old Maid herself – her daughter is a proof of it – I have questioned her – I have look'd at the lines of her paw – I have felt her pulse – to no purpose – why should the *old* Cat come to me? I ask myself – and myself has not a word to answer.

Part of a letter from Keats to his brother George, 3 January 1819

Singular Attachments

The cat, like many other animals, will often form singular attachments. One would sit in my horse's manger and purr and rub his nose, which undoubtedly the horse enjoyed, for he would frequently turn his head purposely to be so treated . . . while another would cosset up close to a sitting hen, and allow her fresh-hatched chickens to seek warmth by creeping under her. Again, they will rear other animals such as rats, squirrels, rabbits, puppies, hedgehogs; and, when motherly inclined, will take to almost anything, even to a young pigeon.

From *Our Cats* by Harrison Weir

A Light Diversion

Charles Dickens was a dog lover, but it was a nameless kitten who was permitted to disturb him at his work.

On account of our birds, cats were not allowed in the house; but from a friend in London I received a present of a white kitten – Williamina – and she and her numerous offspring had a happy home at 'Gad's Hill'. She became a favorite with all the household, and showed particular devotion to my father.

I remember on one occasion when she had presented us with a family of kittens, she selected a corner of father's study for their home. She brought them one by one from the kitchen and deposited them in her chosen corner. My father called to me to remove them, saying that he could not allow the kittens to remain in his room. I did so, but Williamina brought them back again, one by one. Again they were removed. The third time, instead of putting them in the corner, she placed them all, and herself beside them, at my father's feet, and gave him such an imploring glance that he could resist no longer, and they were allowed to remain. As the kittens grew older they became more and more frolicsome, swarming up the curtains, playing about on the writing table and scampering behind the book shelves. But they were never complained of and lived happily in the study until the time came for finding them other homes. One of these kittens was kept, who, as he was quite deaf, was left unnamed, and became known by the servants as 'the master's cat', because of his devotion to my father. He was always with him, and used to follow him about the garden like a dog, and sit with him while he wrote. One evening we were all, except father, going to a ball, and when we started, left 'the master' and his cat in the drawing-room together. 'The master' was reading at a small table, on which a lighted candle was placed. Suddenly the candle went out. My father, who was much interested in his book, relighted the candle, stroked the cat, who was looking at him pathetically he noticed, and continued his reading. A few minutes later, as the light became dim, he looked up just in time to see puss deliberately put out the candle with his paw, and then look appealingly toward him. This second and unmistakable hint was not disregarded, and puss was given the petting he craved. Father was full of this anecdote when all met at breakfast the next morning.

From *My Father as I Recall Him* by Mamie Dickens

The Invisible Cat

A cat proves difficult to dematerialise in H. G. Wells' celebrated science fiction.

'My first experiment was with a bit of white wool fabric. It was the strangest thing in the world to see it soft and white in the flicker of the flashes, and then to watch it fade like a wreath of smoke and vanish.

'I could scarcely believe I had done it. I put my hand into the emptiness and there was the thing as solid as ever. I felt it awkwardly, and threw it on the floor. I had a little trouble finding it again.

'And then came a curious experience. I heard a miaow behind me, and turning, saw a lean white cat, very dirty, on the cistern cover outside the window. A thought came into my head. "Everything ready for you," I said, and went to the window, opened it, and called softly. She came in, purring – the poor beast was starving – and I gave her some milk. All my food was in a cupboard in the corner of the room. After that she went smelling round the room, evidently with the idea of making herself at home. The invisible rag upset her a bit; you should have seen her spit at it! But I made her comfortable on the pillow of my truckle-bed, and I gave her butter to get her to wash.'

'And you processed her?'

'I processed her. But giving drugs to a cat is no joke, Kemp! And the process failed.'

'Failed?'

'In two particulars. These were the claws and the pigment stuff – what is it? At the back of the eye in a cat. You know?'

'*Tapetum.*'

'Yes, the *tapetum*. It didn't go. After I'd given the stuff to bleach the blood and done certain other things to her, I gave the beast opium, and put her and the pillow she was sleeping on, on the apparatus. And after all the rest had faded and vanished, there remained the two little ghosts of her eyes.'

'Odd.'

'I can't explain it. She was bandaged and clamped of course – so I had her safe, but she awoke while she was still misty, and miawled dismally, and someone came knocking. It was an old woman from downstairs, who suspected me of vivisecting – a drink-sodden old creature, with only a cat to care for in all the world. I whipped out some chloroform, applied it, and answered the door. "Did I hear a cat?" she asked. "My cat?" "Not here," said I, very politely. She was a little doubtful, and tried to peer past me into the room – strange enough to her, no doubt, bare walls, uncurtained windows, truckle-bed, with the gas-engine vibrating, and the seethe of the radiant points, and that faint stinging of chloroform in the air. She had to be satisfied at last, and went away again.'

'How long did it take?' asked Kemp.

'Three or four hours – the cat. The bones and sinews and the fat were the last to go, and the tips of the coloured hairs. And, as I say, the back part of the eye, tough, iridescent stuff it is, wouldn't go at all.

'It was night outside long before the business was over, and nothing was to be seen but the dim eyes and the claws. I stopped the gas-engine, felt for and stroked the beast, which was still insensible, released its fastenings, and then, being tired, left it sleeping on the invisible pillow and went to bed. I found it hard to sleep. I lay awake thinking weak, aimless stuff, going over the experiment again and again, or dreaming feverishly of things growing misty and vanishing about me until everything, the ground I stood on, vanished, and so I came to that sickly, falling nightmare one gets. About two the cat began miawling about the room. I tried to hush it by talking to it, and then I decided to turn it out. I remember the shock I had striking a light – there were just the round eyes shining green – and nothing round them. I would have given it milk, but I hadn't any. It wouldn't be quiet, it just sat down and miaowed at the door. I tried to catch it, with an idea of putting it out of the window, but it wouldn't be caught, it vanished. It kept on miaowing in different parts of the room. At last I opened the window and made a bustle. I suppose it went out at last. I never saw nor heard any more of it. Then – Heaven knows why – I fell thinking of my father's funeral again, and the dismal, windy hillside, until the day had come. I found sleep was hopeless, and, locking my door after me, wandered out into the morning streets.'

'You don't mean to say there's an Invisible Cat at large in the world?' said Kemp.

From *The Invisible Man* by H. G. Wells

The Cheshire Cat

In which Alice (in Wonderland) encounters a grin without a cat.

The cat only grinned when it saw Alice. It looked good-natured, she thought: still it had *very* long claws and a great many teeth, so she felt that it ought to be treated with respect.

'Cheshire Puss,' she began, rather timidly, as she did not at all know whether it would like the name: however, it only grinned a little wider. 'Come, it's pleased so far,' thought Alice, and she went on. 'Would you tell me, please, which way I ought to go from here?'

'That depends a good deal on where you want to get to,' said the Cat.

'I don't much care where –' said Alice.

'Then it doesn't matter which way you go,' said the Cat.

'– so long as I get *somewhere*,' Alice added as an explanation.

'Oh, you're sure to do that,' said the Cat. 'If you only walk long enough.'

Alice felt that this could not be denied, so she tried another question. 'What sort of people live about here?'

'In *that* direction,' the Cat said, waving its right paw round, 'lives a Hatter: and in *that* direction,' waving the other paw, 'lives a March Hare. Visit either you like: they're both mad.'

'But I don't want to go among mad people,' Alice remarked.

'Oh, you can't help that,' said the Cat: 'we're all mad here. I'm mad. You're mad.'

'How do you know I'm mad?' said Alice.

'You must be,' said the Cat, 'or you wouldn't have come here.'

Alice didn't think that proved it at all; however, she went on. 'And how do you know that you're mad?'

'To begin with,' said the Cat, 'a dog's not mad. You grant that?'

'I suppose so,' said Alice.

'Well, then,' the Cat went on, 'you see a dog growls when it's angry, and wags its tail when it's pleased. Now *I* growl when I'm pleased, and wag my tail when I'm angry. Therefore I'm mad.'

'*I* call it purring, not growling,' said Alice.

'Call it what you like,' said the Cat. 'Do you play croquet with the Queen to-day?'

'I should like it very much,' said Alice, 'but I haven't been invited yet.'

'You'll see me there,' said the Cat, and vanished.

Alice was not much surprised at this, she was getting so used to queer things happening. While she was looking at the place where it had been, it suddenly appeared again.

'By-the-bye, what became of the baby?' said the Cat. 'I'd nearly forgotten to ask.'

'It turned into a pig,' Alice quietly said, just as if it had come back in a natural way.

'I thought it would,' said the Cat, and vanished again.

Alice waited a little, half expecting to see it again, but it did not appear, and after a minute or two she walked on in the direction in which the March Hare was said to live. 'I've seen hatters before,' she said to herself; 'the March Hare will be much the most interesting, and perhaps, as this is May, it won't be raving mad – at least not so mad as it was in March.' As she said this, she looked up, and there was the Cat again, sitting on a branch of a tree.

'Did you say pig, or fig?' said the Cat.

'I said pig,' replied Alice; 'and I wish you wouldn't keep appearing and vanishing so suddenly: you make one quite giddy.'

'All right,' said the Cat; and this time it vanished quite slowly, beginning with the end of the tail, and ending with the grin, which remained some time after the rest of it had gone.

'Well! I've often seen a cat without a grin,' thought Alice; 'but a grin without a cat! It's the most curious thing I ever saw in all my life!'

From *Alice's Adventures in Wonderland* by Lewis Carroll

The Flying Cat

Once I was surprised to see a cat walking along the stony shore of the pond, for they rarely wander so far from home. The surprise was mutual. Nevertheless the most domestic cat, which has lain on a rug all her days, appears quite at home in the woods, and, by her sly and stealthy behavior, proves herself more native there than the regular inhabitants. Once, when berrying, I met with a cat with young kittens in the woods, quite wild, and they all, like their mother, had their backs up and were fiercely spitting at me. A few years before I lived in the woods there was what was called a 'winged cat' in one of the farm-houses in Lincoln nearest the pond, Mr Gilian Baker's. When I called to see her in June, 1842, she was gone a-hunting in the woods, as was her wont, (I am not sure whether it was a male or female, and so use the more common pronoun,) but her mistress told me that she came into the neighborhood a little more than a year before, in April, and was finally taken into their house; that she was of a dark brownish-gray color, with a white spot on her throat, and white feet, and had a large bushy tail like a fox; that in the winter the fur grew thick and flatted out along her sides, forming strips ten or twelve inches long by two and a half wide, and under her chin like a muff, the upper side loose, the under matted like felt, and in the spring these appendages dropped off. They gave me a pair of her 'wings,' which I keep still. There is no appearance of a membrane about them. Some thought it was a part flying-squirrel or some other wild animal, which is not impossible, for, according to naturalists, prolific hybrids have been produced by the union of the marten and domestic cat. This would have been the right kind of cat for me to keep, if I had kept any; for why should not a poet's cat be winged as well as his horse?

From *Walden, or Life in the Woods* by Henry David Thoreau

A Cat's Courage

Sunday, *January 27th*. – A little snow. A remarkable instance of a cat's affection for her young offered at the burning of a Music Hall lately. A tabby cat had four kittens in a basket behind the stage. When the fire began she was seen rushing wildly about, and at last forced her way down a smoky corridor and returned with a kitten in her mouth. This she did three times and then eluding those who attempted to stop her, she went for the fourth and was not seen again, but her burnt body was found beside her kitten.

There was another story in the paper a week or so since. A gentleman had a favourite cat whom he taught to sit at the dinner-table where it behaved very well. He was in the habit of putting any scraps he left on to the cat's plate. One day puss did not take his place punctually, but presently appeared with two mice, one of which it placed on its master's plate, the other on its own.

From *The Journal of Beatrix Potter from 1881 to 1897*

A Crushing Encounter

Montmorency adopts the between-the-legs position for his tail after a face-losing encounter with a disreputable tom, in Jerome K. Jerome's novel.

We were, as I have said, returning from a dip, and half-way up the High Street a cat darted out from one of the houses in front of us, and began to trot across the road. Montmorency gave a cry of joy – the cry of a stern warrior who sees his enemy given over to his hands – the sort of cry Cromwell might have uttered when the Scots came down the hill – and flew after his prey.

His victim was a large black tom. I never saw a larger cat, nor a more disreputable-looking cat. It had lost half its tail, one of its ears, and a fairly appreciable proportion of its nose. It was a long, sinewy-looking animal. It had a calm, contented air about it.

Montmorency went for that poor cat at the rate of twenty miles an hour; but the cat did not hurry up – did not seem to have grasped the idea that its life was in danger. It trotted quietly on until its would-be assassin was within a yard of it, and then it turned round and sat down in the middle of the road, and looked at Montmorency with a gentle, inquiring expression, that said:

'Yes! You want me?'

Montmorency does not lack pluck; but there was something about the look of that cat that might have chilled the heart of the boldest dog. He stopped abruptly, and looked back at Tom.

Neither spoke; but the conversation that one could imagine was clearly as follows:

THE CAT: 'Can I do anything for you?'

MONTMORENCY: 'No – no, thanks.'

THE CAT: 'Don't you mind speaking, if you really want anything, you know.'

MONTMORENCY (*backing down the High Street*): 'Oh no – not at all – certainly – don't you trouble. I – I am afraid I've made a mistake. I thought I knew you. Sorry I disturbed you.'

THE CAT: 'Not at all – quite a pleasure. Sure you don't want anything, now?'

MONTMORENCY (*still backing*): 'Not at all, thanks – not at all – very kind of you. Good morning.'

THE CAT: 'Good morning.'

Then the cat rose, and continued his trot; and Montmorency, fitting what he calls his tail carefully into its groove, came back to us, and took up an unimportant position in the rear.

To this day, if you say the word 'Cats!' to Montmorency, he will visibly shrink and look up piteously at you, as if to say:

'Please don't.'

From *Three Men in a Boat* by Jerome K. Jerome

The Test of a Suitor

Two young ladies elect a rectory cat as romantic oracle in Charlotte Brontë's third novel.

'I wonder we don't all make up our minds to remain single,' said Caroline. 'We should if we listened to the wisdom of experience. My uncle always speaks of marriage as a burden; and I believe whenever he hears of a man being married, he invariably regards him as a fool, or, at any rate, as doing a foolish thing.'

'But, Caroline, men are not all like your uncle: surely not – I hope not.'

She paused and mused.

'I suppose we each find an exception in the one we love, till we *are* married,' suggested Caroline.

'I suppose so: and this exception we believe to be of sterling materials; we fancy it like ourselves; we imagine a sense of harmony. We think his voice gives the softest, truest promise of a heart that will never harden against us: we read in his eyes that faithful feeling – affection. I don't think we should trust to what they call passion at all, Caroline. I believe it is a mere fire of dry sticks, blazing up and vanishing: but we watch him, and see him kind to animals, to little children, to poor people. He is kind to us likewise – good – considerate: he does not flatter women, but he is patient with them, and he seems to be easy in their presence, and to find their company genial. He likes them not only for vain and selfish reasons, but as *we* like him – because we like him. Then we observe that he is just – that he always speaks the truth – that he is conscientious. We feel joy and peace when he comes into a room: we feel sadness and trouble when he leaves it. We know that this man has been a kind son, that he is a kind brother: will any one dare to tell me that he will not be a kind husband?'

'My uncle would affirm it unhesitatingly. "He will be sick of you in a month," he would say.'

'Mrs Pryor would seriously intimate the same.'

'Mrs Yorke and Miss Mann would darkly suggest ditto.'

'If they are true oracles, it is good never to fall in love.'

'Very good, if you can avoid it.'

'I choose to doubt their truth.'

'I am afraid that proves you are already caught.'

'Not I: but if I were, do you know what soothsayers I would consult?'

'Let me hear.'

'Neither man nor woman, elderly nor young: – the little Irish beggar that comes barefoot to my door: the mouse that steals out of the cranny in the wainscot; the bird that in frost and snow pecks at my window for a crumb; the dog that licks my hand and sits beside my knee.'

'Did you ever see any one who was kind to such things?'

'Did you ever see any one whom such things seemed instinctively to follow, like, rely on?'

'We have a black cat and an old dog at the Rectory. I know somebody to whose knee that black cat loves to climb: against whose shoulder and cheeks it likes to purr. The old dog always come out of the kennel and wags his tail, and whines affectionately when somebody passes.'

'And what does that somebody do?'

'He quietly strokes the cat, and lets her sit while he conveniently can, and when he must disturb her by rising, he puts her softly down, and never flings her from him roughly; he always whistles to the dog and gives him a caress.'

'Does he? Is it not Robert?'

'But it is Robert.'

From *Shirley* by Charlotte Brontë

The Spinster's Sweet-Arts

Naäy – let ma stroäk tha down till I maäkes tha es smooth es silk,
But if I 'ed married tha, Robby, thou'd not 'a been worth thy milk,
Thou'd niver 'a cotch'd ony mice but 'a left me the work to do.
And 'a taäen to the bottle beside, so es all that I 'ears be true;
But I loovs tha to maäke thysen 'appy, an' soä purr awaäy, my dear,
Thou'ed wellnigh purr'd ma awaäy fro' my oän two 'oonderd a-year.

From 'The Spinster's Sweet-Arts' by Alfred Tennyson

Old Maids and Cat's Meat

The supply of food for cats and dogs is far greater than may be generally thought. 'Vy, sir,' said one of the dealers to me, 'can you tell me 'ow many people's in London?' On my replying, upwards of two millions; 'I don't know nothing vatever,' said my informant, 'about millions, but I think there's a cat to every ten people, aye, and more than that; and so, sir, you can reckon.

'I must know, for they all knows me, and I sarves about 200 cats and 70 dogs. Mine's a middling trade, but some does far better. Some cats has a hap'orth a day, some every other day; werry few can afford a penn'orth, but times is inferior. Dogs is better pay when you've a connection among 'em.'

The cat and dogs'-meat dealers, or 'carriers,' as they call themselves, generally purchase the meat at the knackers' (horse-slaughterers') yards.

The carriers then take the meat round town, wherever their 'walk' may lie. They sell it to the public at the rate of 2.½d. per lb., and in small pieces, on skewers, at a farthing, a halfpenny, and a penny each. Some carriers will set as much as a hundred-weight in a day, and about half a hundred-weight is the average quantity disposed of by the carriers in London. Some sell much cheaper than others.

But the trade is much worse now. There are so many at it, they say, that there is barely a living for any. A carrier assured me that he seldom went less than 30, and frequently 40 miles, through the streets every day. The best districts are among the houses of tradesmen, mechanics, and labourers. 'The coachmen in the mews at the back of the squares are very good customers. The work lays thicker there,' said my informant. Old maids are bad, though very plentiful, customers. They cheapen the carriers down so, that they can scarcely live at the business. 'They will pay one halfpenny and owe another, and forget that after a day or two.' The cats' meat dealers generally complain of their losses from bad debts.

One gentleman has as much as 4 lbs. of meat each morning for two Newfoundland dogs; and there was one woman – a black – who used to have as much as 16 pennyworth every day. This person used to get out on the roof of the house and throw it to the cats on the tiles. By this she brought so many stray cats round about the neighbourhood, that the parties in the vicinity complained; it was quite a nuisance. She *would* have the meat always brought to her before ten in the morning, or else she would send to a shop for it, and between ten and eleven in the morning the noise and cries of the hundreds of stray cats attracted to the spot was 'terrible to hear'. When the meat was thrown to the cats on the roof, the riot, and confusion, and fighting, was beyond description.

'A beer-shop man,' I was told, 'was obliged to keep five or six dogs to drive the cats from his walls.'

The generality of the dealers wear a shiny hat, black plush waistcoat and sleeves, a blue apron, corduroy trousers, and a blue and white spotted handkerchief round their necks. Some, indeed, will wear two and three handkerchiefs around their necks, this being fashionable among them.

From *Mayhew's London* by Henry Mayhew

Nancy's Cat

Anne Brontë contrasts a widow's relief at the return of her prodigal cat with the discomfiture of Agnes Grey in the presence of the pet's rescuer.

I took the opportunity of repairing to the widow's cottage, where I found her in some anxiety about her cat, which had been absent all day. I comforted her with as many anecdotes of that animal's roving propensities as I could recollect. 'I'm feared o' th' gamekeepers,' said she, 'that's all 'at I think on. If th' young gentlemen had been at home, I should a' thought they'd been setting their dogs at her, an' worried her, poor thing, as they did *many* a poor thing's cat; but I haven't that to be feared on now.' Nancy's eyes were better, but still far from well: she had been trying to make a Sunday shirt for her son, but told me she could only bear to do a little bit at it now and then, so that it progressed but slowly, though the poor lad wanted it sadly. So I proposed to help her a little, after I had read to her, for I had plenty of time that evening, and need not return till dusk. She thankfully accepted the offer.

'An' you'll be a bit o' company for me too, miss,' said she; 'I like as I feel lonesome without my cat.' But when I had finished reading, and done the half of a seam, with Nancy's capacious brass thimble fitted on to my finger by means of a roll of paper, I was disturbed by the entrance of Mr Weston, with the identical cat in his arms. I now saw that he could smile, and very pleasantly too.

'I've done you a piece of good service, Nancy,' he began: then seeing me, he acknowledged my presence by a slight bow. I should have been invisible to Hatfield, or any other gentleman of those parts. 'I've delivered your cat,' he continued, 'from the hands, or rather the gun, of Mr Murray's gamekeeper.'

'God bless you, sir!' cried the grateful old woman, ready to weep for joy as she received her favourite from his arms.

'Take care of it,' said he, 'and don't let it go near the rabbit warren, for the gamekeeper swears he'll shoot it if he sees it there again: he would have done so to-day, if I had not been in time to stop him. – I believe it is raining, Miss

Grey,' added he, more quietly, observing that I had put aside my work, and was preparing to depart. 'Don't let me disturb you – I shan't stay two minutes.'

'You'll *both* stay while this shower gets owered,' said Nancy, as she stirred the fire, and placed another chair beside it; 'what! there's room for all.'

'I can see better here, thank you, Nancy,' replied I, taking my work to the window, where she had the goodness to suffer me to remain unmolested, while she got a brush to remove the cat's hairs from Mr Weston's coat, carefully wiped the rain from his hat, and gave the cat its supper, busily talking all the time: now thanking her clerical friend for what he had done; now wondering how the cat had found out the warren; and now lamenting the probable consequences of such a discovery. He listened with a quiet, good-natured smile, and at length took a seat in compliance with her pressing invitations, but repeated that he did not mean to stay.

'I have another place to go to,' said he, 'and I see' (glancing at the book on the table) 'some one else has been reading to you.'

'Yes, sir; Miss Grey has been as kind as read me a chapter; an' now she's helping me with a shirt for our Bill – but I'm feared she'll be cold there. Won't you come to th' fire, miss?'

'No, thank you, Nancy, I'm quite warm. I must go as soon as this shower is over.'

'Oh, miss! You said you could stop while dusk!' cried the provoking old woman, and Mr Weston seized his hat.

'Nay, sir,' exclaimed she, 'pray don't go now, while it rains so fast.'

'But it strikes me I'm keeping your visitor away from the fire.'

'No, you're not, Mr Weston,' replied I, hoping there was no harm in a falsehood of that description.

'No, sure!' cried Nancy. 'What, there's lots o' room!'

'Miss Grey,' said he, half-jestingly, as if he felt it necessary to change the present subject, whether he had anything particular to say or not, 'I wish you would make my peace with the squire when you see him. He was by when I rescued Nancy's cat, and did not quite approve of the deed. I told him I thought he might better spare all his rabbits than she her cat, for which audacious assertion he treated me to some rather ungentlemanly language; and I fear I retorted a trifle too warmly.'

'Oh, lawful sir! I hope you didn't fall out wi' th' maister for sake o' my cat! he cannot bide answering again – can th' maister.'

'Oh! it's no matter, Nancy: I don't care about it, really; I said nothing *very* uncivil; and I suppose Mr Murray is accustomed to use rather strong language when he's heated.'

From *Agnes Grey* by Anne Brontë

Verses on a Cat

A cat in distress,
Nothing more, nor less;
Good folks, I must faithfully tell ye,
As I am a sinner,
It waits for some dinner,
To stuff out its own little belly.

You would not easily guess
All the modes of distress
Which torture the tenants of earth;
And the various evils,
Which, like so many devils,
Attend the poor souls from their birth.

Some living require,
And others desire
An old fellow out of the way;
And which is best
I leave to be guessed,
For I cannot pretend to say.

One wants society,
Another variety,
Others a tranquil life;
Some want food,
Others, as good,
Only want a wife.

But this poor little cat
Only wanted a rat,
To stuff out its own little maw;
And it were as good
Some people had such food,
To make them *hold their jaw*!

Percy Bysshe Shelley

A Modest Dinner

The poor Cat had a dreadful pain in his stomach, and could eat only thirty-five mullet in tomato sauce, and four helpings of tripe garnished with Parmesan cheese. Because he thought the tripe was a bit tasteless, he asked three times for more butter and more grated cheese!

From Pinocchio by Carlo Collodi

Fifty Dinners

Lewis Carroll enchantingly encapsulates a child's habit of passing on parental discipline to her toys or pets in this episode from *Through the Looking-Glass*.

One thing was certain, that the *white* kitten had had nothing to do with it: – it was the black kitten's fault entirely. For the white kitten had been having its face washed by the old cat for the last quarter of an hour (and bearing it pretty well, considering); so you see that it *couldn't* have had any hand in the mischief.

The way Dinah washed her children's faces was this: first she held the poor thing down by its ear with one paw, and then with the other paw she rubbed its face all over, the wrong way; beginning at the nose: and just now, as I said, she was hard at work on the white kitten, which was lying quite still and trying to purr – no doubt feeling that it was all meant for its good.

But the black kitten had been finished with earlier in the afternoon, and so, while Alice was sitting curled up in a corner of the great arm-chair, half talking to herself and half asleep, the kitten had been having a grand game of romps with the ball of worsted Alice had been trying to wind up, and had been rolling it up and down till it had all come undone again; and there it was, spread over the hearth-rug, all knots and tangles, with the kitten running after its own tail in the middle.

'Oh, you wicked wicked little thing!' cried Alice, catching up the kitten, and giving it a little kiss to make it understand that it was in disgrace. 'Really, Dinah ought to have taught you better manners! You *ought*, Dinah, you know you ought!' she added, looking reproachfully at the old cat, and speaking in as cross a voice as she could manage – and then she scrambled back into the arm-chair, taking the kitten and worsted with her, and began winding up the ball again. But she didn't get on very fast, as she was talking all the time, sometimes to the kitten, and sometimes to herself. Kitty sat very demurely on her knee, pretending to watch the progress of the winding, and now and then putting out one paw and gently touching the ball, as if it would be glad to help if it might.

'Do you know what to-morrow is, Kitty?' Alice began. 'You'd have guessed if you'd been up in the window with me – only Dinah was making you tidy, so you couldn't. I was watching the boys getting in sticks for the bonfire – and it wants plenty of sticks, Kitty! Only it got so cold, and it snowed so, they had to leave off. Never mind, Kitty, we'll go and see the bonfire to-morrow.' Here Alice wound two or three turns of the worsted round the kitten's neck, just to see how it would look: this led to a scramble, in which the ball rolled down upon the floor, and yards and yards of it got unwound again.

'Do you know, I was so angry, Kitty,' Alice went on, as soon as they were comfortably settled again, 'when I saw all the mischief you had been doing, I was very nearly opening the window, and putting you out into the snow! And you'd have deserved it, you little mischievous darling! What have you got to say for yourself? Now don't interrupt me!' she went on, holding up one finger. 'I'm going to tell you all your faults. Number one: you squeaked twice while Dinah was washing your face this morning. Now you can't deny it, Kitty, for I heard you! What's that you say?' (pretending that the kitten was speaking.) 'Her paw went into your eye? Well, that's *your* fault, for keeping your eyes open – if you'd shut them tight up, it wouldn't have happened. Now don't make any more excuses, but listen! Number two: you pulled Snowdrop away by the tail just as I had put down the saucer of milk before her! What, you were thirsty, were you? How do you know she wasn't thirsty too? Now for number three: you unwound every bit of the worsted while I wasn't looking!

'That's three faults, Kitty, and you've not been punished for any of them yet. You know I'm saving up all your punishments for Wednesday week – Suppose they had saved up all *my* punishments!' she went on, talking more to herself than the kitten. 'What *would* they do at the end of a year? I should be sent off to prison, I suppose, when the day came. Or – let me see – suppose each punishment was to be going without a dinner: then, when the miserable day came, I should have to go without fifty dinners at once! Well, I shouldn't mind *that* much! I'd far rather go without them than eat them!'

From *Through the Looking-Glass* by Lewis Carroll

Rather a Lengthy Business

A kitten completes this delightful picture of domestic contentment observed by Silas Marner.

Silas ate his dinner more silently than usual, soon laying down his knife and fork, and watching half abstractedly Eppie's play with Snap and the cat, by which her own dining was made rather a lengthy business. Yet it was a sight that might well arrest wandering thoughts: Eppie, with the rippling radiance of her hair and the whiteness of her rounded chin and throat set off by the dark-blue cotton gown, laughing merrily as the kitten held on with her four claws to one shoulder, like a design for a jug-handle, while Snap on the right hand and Puss on the other put up their paws towards a morsel which she held out of the reach of both – Snap occasionally desisting in order to remonstrate with the cat by a cogent worrying growl on the greediness and futility of her conduct; till Eppie relented, caressed them both, and divided the morsel between them.

From *Silas Marner* by George Eliot

Love and Mutton

A downy cove is our old tom cat,
Just turned thirty years old;
He eateth the lean, and leaveth the fat,
And won't touch his meals when too cold.
His food must be crumbled, and not decayed,
To pleasure his dainty whim,
But a turkey bone from the kitchen-maid
Is a very good meal for him.

Chorus:
Creeping over the tiles pit pat,
A downy cove is the old tom cat.

Whole joints have fled, and their bones decayed,
And dishes have broken been,
But old tom still follows the kitchen-maid,
And slyly licks up the cream.
Now, old tom cat, in his lonely days,
Shall joyously think of the past,
And a big leg of mutton, that never was touched,
Shall be food for our Tommy at last.

Fast creepeth he, though he hath no wings,
And a sly old dodger is he,
As under the garret window he sings –
Ain't you coming out tonight, love, to me?
Then slyly he creepeth the gutters all round,
And his old tail he joyously waves,
As his lady love from a garret he spies,
And he sings his amorous staves.

Music hall song

Love of Mutton

Maria told us the story of Anna Kilvert and the cat, and the Epiphany Star. It seems that when Aunt Sophia was dying Anna thought some mutton would do her good and went to fetch some. When she came back the nurse said, 'She can't eat mutton. She's dying.' Anna put the mutton down on the floor and rushed to the bed. At that moment Aunt Sophia died and Anna turned round to see the cat running away with the mutton and the Epiphany Star shining in through the window.

From the diary of Francis Kilvert

The Pobble Who Has No Toes

And all the sailors and the Admirals cried,
When they saw him nearing the further side, –
'He has gone to fish, for his Aunt Jobiska's
'Runcible Cat with crimson whiskers'.

From 'The Pobble Who Has No Toes', in *Laughable Lyrics* by Edward Lear

The Children of the Owl and the Pussy Cat

Lear died before he could complete his sequel to *The Owl and the Pussy-Cat*. The temptation for readers to fill in the incomplete lines is like that of picking a new scab to a small child.

Our mother was the Pussy-Cat, our father was the Owl,
And so we're partly little beasts and partly little fowl,
The brothers of our family have feathers and they hoot,
While all the sisters dress in fur and have long tails to boot.
   We all believe that little mice,
    For food are singularly nice.
Our mother died long years ago. She was a lovely cat,
Her tail was 5 feet long, and grey with stripes, but what of that?
In Sila forest on the East of far Calabria's shore
She tumbled from a lofty tree – none ever saw her more.
Our owly father long was ill from sorrow and surprise,
But with the feathers of his tail he wiped his weeping eyes.
And in the hollow of a tree in Sila's inmost maze
We made a happy home and there we pass our obvious days.

From Reggian Cosenza many owls about us flit
And bring us worldly news of which we do not care a bit.
We watch the sun each morning rise, beyond Tarento's strait;
We go out _____ before it gets too late;
And when the evening shades begin to lengthen from the trees
_____ as sure as bees is bees.
We wander up and down the shore _____
Or tumble over head and heels, but never, never more
Can see the far Gromboolian plains _____
Or weep as we could once have wept o'er many a vanished scene:
This is the way our father moans – he is so very green.

Our father still preserves his voice, and when he sees a star
He often sings _____ to that original guitar.

_____

_____

The pot in which our parents took the honey in their boat,
But all the money has been spent, beside the £5 note.
The owls who come and bring us news are often ____
Because we take no interest in poltix of the day.

From *Edward Lear* by Angus Davidson

The Demon Cat (an Irish legend)

There was a woman in Connemara, the wife of a fisherman; as he had always good luck, she had plenty of fish at all times stored away in the house ready for market. But, to her great annoyance, she found that a great cat used to come in at night and devour all the best and finest fish. So she kept a big stick by her, and determined to watch.

One day, as she and a woman were spinning together, the house suddenly became quite dark; and the door was burst open as if by the blast of the tempest, when in walked a huge black cat, who went straight up to the fire, then turned round and growled at them.

'Why, surely this is the devil,' said a young girl, who was by, sorting fish.

'I'll teach you how to call me names,' said the cat; and, jumping at her, he scratched her arm till the blood came. 'There, now,' he said, 'you will be more civil another time when a gentleman comes to see you.' And with that he walked over to the door and shut it close, to prevent any of them going out, for the poor young girl, while crying loudly from fright and pain, had made a desperate rush to get away.

Just then a man was going by, and hearing the cries, he pushed open the door and tried to get in; but the cat stood on the threshold, and would let no one pass. On this the man attacked him with his stick, and gave him a sound blow; the cat, however, was more than a match in the fight, for it flew at him and tore his face and hands so badly that the man at last took to his heels and ran away as fast as he could.

'Now, it's time for my dinner,' said the cat, going up to examine the fish that was laid out on the tables. 'I hope the fish is good to-day. Now, don't disturb me, nor make a fuss; I can help myself.' With that he jumped up, and began to devour all the best fish, while he growled at the woman.

'Away, out of this, you wicked beast,' she cried, giving it a blow with the tongs that would have broken its back, only it was a devil; 'out of this; no fish shall you have to-day.'

But the cat only grinned at her, and went on tearing and spoiling and devouring the fish, evidently not a bit the worse for the blow. On this, both the women attacked it with sticks, and struck hard blows enough to kill it, on which the cat glared at them, and spit fire; then making a leap, it tore their heads and arms till the blood came, and the frightened women rushed shrieking from the house.

But presently the mistress returned, carrying with her a bottle of holy water; and, looking in, she saw the cat still devouring the fish, and not minding. So she crept over quietly and threw holy water on it without a word. No sooner was this done than a dense black smoke filled the place, through which nothing was seen but the two red eyes of the cat, burning like coals of fire. Then the smoke gradually cleared away, and she saw the body of the creature burning slowly till it became shrivelled and black like a cinder, and finally disappeared. And from that time the fish remained untouched and safe from harm, for the power of the evil one was broken, and the demon cat was seen no more.

Lady Wilde

The Sphinx

In a dim corner of my room for longer than my fancy thinks
A beautiful and silent Sphinx has watched me through the
    shifting gloom.

Inviolate and immobile she does not rise she does not stir
For silver moons are naught to her and naught to her the suns
    that reel.

Red follows grey across the air, the waves of moonlight ebb and
    flow
But with the Dawn she does not go and in the night-time she is
    there.

Dawn follows Dawn and Nights grow old and all the while this
    curious cat
Lies couching on the Chinese mat with eyes of satin rimmed with
    gold.

Upon the mat she lies and leers and on the tawny throat of her
Flutters the soft and silky fur or ripples to her pointed ears.

Come forth, my lovely seneschal! so somnolent, so statuesque!
Come forth you exquisite grotesque! half woman and half animal!

Come forth my lovely languorous Sphinx! and put your head
    upon my knee!
And let me stroke your throat and see your body spotted like the
    Lynx!

And let me touch those curving claws of yellow ivory and grasp
The tail that like a monstrous Asp coils round your heavy velvet
    paws!

From 'The Sphinx' by Oscar Wilde

A Sort of Little Sphinx

Finally, as regards the canine tribe, it cannot be denied that there are good dogs, very good dogs; dogs that look up at you with the most lovable eyes. Personally I must confess that I have felt considerable esteem and affection for some of them. All the same, I share the opinion of the Orientals, who rather despise the dog as being tainted with filthy instincts, whilst they respect and fear the cat as a sort of little sphinx.

From 'Cats and Dogs' by Pierre Loti, transl. Fred Rothwell

8

CONTEMPORARY CAT STORIES

Cats are like women and women are like cats – they are both very ungrateful.

Damon Runyon, *Lillian*

The Cat and the Devil

James Joyce wrote this story for his grandson Stephen Joyce – to whom he was 'Nonno' – in 1936. It is typical of Joyce's sense of humour that he gave the devil a sympathetic character. The lord mayor is named after a celebrated mayor of Dublin whose name also crops up in Joyce's larger fiction.

Villa s/Mer
10 August 1936

My Dear Stevie,

I sent you a little cat filled with sweets a few days ago but perhaps you do not know the story about the cat of Beaugency. Beaugency is an old town on a bank of the Loire, France's longest river. It is also a very wide river, for France, at least. At Beaugency it is so wide that if you wanted to cross it from one bank to the other you would have to take at least one thousand steps.

Long ago the people of Beaugency, when they wanted to cross it, had to go in a boat for there was no bridge. And they could not make one for themselves or pay anyone else to make one. So what were they to do?

The Devil, who is always reading the newspapers, heard about this sad state of theirs so he dressed himself and came to call on the lord mayor of Beaugency, who was named Monsieur Alfred Byrne.

The lord mayor was fond of dressing himself too. He wore a scarlet robe and always had a great golden chain round his neck even when he was fast asleep in bed with his knees in his mouth.

The devil told the lord mayor what he had read in the newspaper and said he could make a bridge for the people of Beaugency so that they could cross the river as often as they wished. He said he could make as good a bridge as ever was made, and make it in one single night. The lord mayor asked him how much money he wanted for making such a bridge.

No money at all, said the devil, all I ask is that the first person who crosses the bridge shall belong to me.

Good, said the lord mayor.

The night came down, all the people in Beaugency went to bed and slept.

The morning came. And when they put their heads out of the windows they cried: O Loire, what a fine bridge! For they saw a fine stone bridge thrown across the wide river.

All the people ran down to the head of the bridge and looked across it. There was the devil, standing at the other side of the bridge, waiting for the first person who should cross it. But nobody dared to cross it for fear of the devil.

There was a sound of bugles – that was a sign for the people to be silent – and the lord mayor M. Alfred Byrne appeared in his great scarlet robe and wearing his heavy golden chain round his neck. He had a bucket of water in one hand and under his arm – the other arm – he carried a cat.

The devil stopped dancing when he saw him from the other side of the bridge and put up his long spyglass.

All the people whispered to one another and the cat looked up at the lord mayor because in the town of Beaugency it was allowed that a cat should look at a lord mayor. When he was tired of looking at the lord mayor (because even a cat gets tired of looking at a lord mayor) he began to play with the lord mayor's heavy golden chain.

When the lord mayor came to the head of the bridge every man held his breath and every woman held her tongue.

The lord mayor put the cat down on the bridge and, quick as a thought, splash! he emptied the whole bucket of water over it.

The cat who was now between the devil and the bucket of water made up his mind quite as quickly and ran with his ears back across the bridge and into the devil's arms.

The devil was as angry as the devil himself.

Messieurs les Balgentiens, he shouted across the bridge, *vous n'etes pas des belles gens du tout*! *Vous n'etes que des chats*! And he said to the cat: *Viens ici, mon petit chat*! *Tu as peur, mon petit chou-chat*? *Tu as froid, mon pau petit chou-chat*? *Viens ici, le diable t'emporte*! *On va se chauffer tous les deux.*

And off he went with the cat.

And since that time the people of that town are called 'les chats de Beaugency'.

But the bridge is there still and there are boys walking and riding and playing upon it.

I hope you will like this story.

Nonno.

P.S. The devil mostly speaks a language of his own called Bellysbabble which he makes up himself as he goes along but when he is very angry he can speak quite bad French very well though some who have heard him say that he has a strong Dublin accent.

James Joyce

A Nice Way to Go

S uddenly and simply it had come to him: he had had enough.
Later, he was able to fix the precise moment of that realization, the overhead kitchen light isolating him in a blank world while his hands, twisted by arthritis, fastidiously removed a milky, spear-shaped bone from the fish pie that Mrs Crawford had left for him to warm up for his supper. There was no surprise or shock. Yes, I've had enough, he repeated to himself as, slouched towards the table in his darned cardigan, the transistor radio beside him crackling with yet another news bulletin to which he did not listen, he dug his fork once again into the mush. I've had enough; I'd better do something about it.

There had been a whole sequence of happenings, some important and some trivial, that, a sinuously powerful river, had first carried him towards this decision and had then cast him up on it. He had retired and he and his wife and his already middle-aged spinster daughter had left a large house in Putney for this small basement flat not far from it. His wife had died with the clumsy abruptness with which she had been in the habit of breaking into a conversation or a television or wireless programme to put some question or to make some demand. A year or two later the spinster daughter, a medical librarian, had announced that she was going off to live with a fierce female friend, a gynaecologist, in a damp cottage in the New Forest. He and the Siamese cat had lived on in the basement flat, with occasional visits from the daughter and even more occasional ones from his son and his son's wife and children, and daily ones from brisk, brusque Mrs Crawford, who looked after far too many widowers and bachelors to have time for a chat or even for a gulped cup of tea or coffee.

The cat was old, her mask now tinged with silver and her movements careful and leisurely. She could no longer jump up on to the high brass bedstead but would stand beside it, tail erect, emitting a series of squeaks as of chalk on slate until, throwing down *The Times* crossword in exasperation – every night he went to sleep over it – he would stoop down and lift her up beside him. She smelled musty now, like clothes hung up too long in an untenanted room, and the threads of saliva from her half-open, nearly toothless mouth would smear the eiderdown and sometimes even the sheet. 'Oh, you filthy cat!' he would often exclaim aloud to her, rubbing with a handkerchief; but he felt a curious kinship between his own ageing body, with its aches and stiffnesses and insistence on relieving itself two and three times in the course of a single brief night, and the ageing body of the animal curled beside him.

Then, one night, she did not come to his bed; and when, at last missing her, he clambered, skinny and friable, down out of the warmth of the vast bed and made his way, cursing, into the kitchen and the sitting room, he could not find her. The food lay out for her, untouched, on the kitchen floor, the snippets of melts – he would cut them up carefully with a pair of scissors – now dry and curling up on the saucer like the shrivelled petals of some purple flower. The kitchen window was open on to the exiguous yard that was part of his domain; he must have forgotten to close it, as so often – 'You'll have a burglar in here one day,' Mrs Crawford would tell him, often adding: 'And then where will you be?' But the cat seldom now ventured, even in summer weather like this, out of the flat.

'Oh, damn you!' he muttered, as he unlocked and pulled open the door into the yard and then ventured out, narrow bare feet crinkling at the touch of stone, on to the first of the three steps. He called her name and whistled; ventured up to the next step; called again. Slowly his eyes grew accustomed to the thunder-laden darkness until at last he became aware of the two infinitely small, intensely glittering points of light in the dark shadow under the straggling elder. Again he called her name; but she did not stir. He walked over to her, one bare heel treading on something disgustingly soft and sticky, and stopped. A branch of the elder grazed his cheek. 'Oh, silly cat!' She gave a curious breathy squeak as he lifted her up. She seemed very light, almost insubstantial. He carried her back into his room, holding her to his chest with one hand while the other struggled to fasten kitchen window and door, and then placed her in her usual place on top of the part of the eiderdown that, in the past, had covered his wife's humped, snoring form. He leant over and switched off the bedside light and then put a hand over to the cat, running one of her ears through forefinger and middle finger. Something was amiss; and for a while he lay in the dark, the cat's ear resting between his fingers like a dead leaf, until he realized what it was. She was not purring.

When he awoke the next morning, with the habitual dizziness as he raised his head from the pillow and the habitual ache in his bones as he struggled off the bed, the cat had once more vanished. In dressing-gown and slippers this time, he searched for her as he had searched for her the night before; and once again it was in the yard that he found her, under the lanky elder tree. Her pale blue eyes, fixedly staring into some space behind him, were now two misty opals. A thread of saliva trailed from her chin. He carried her into the kitchen and poured out some cream for her from a carton almost empty. But she sat before it, where he had set her down, indifferently hunched. Soon, without his noticing her departure as he prepared for another day, she had slithered back into the garden, to take up her place under the elder.

Somewhere there was a cat basket and eventually he found it, its wicker thick with dust, under the bed in the room that had once been occupied by his daughter but was now so often empty. In the past the cat had always struggled against being placed inside it; but now, inert and again curiously insubstantial, she suffered him to pick her up and immure her.

The vet, an elderly woman who was herself like some rangy, famished cat, briskly palped the sides of the animal with long, bony fingers, and as she did so a viscous orange liquid, reeking of decay and death, spread over the slab. 'Tumour,' she grunted laconically. And then, 'Kidney failure.' The teenage girl, with the red scrubbed cheeks and raw hands, who acted as her assistant, swabbed at the mess, as though it were nothing worse than spilled tea.

The cat lay on his knees as the fatal injection was administered to her. His trousers felt warm and sodden but he did not care. He had similarly held his wife folded in his arms at the moment of her death.

He had walked out of the surgery with the sensation that something painlessly amputated from him had made him clumsy and lopsided. There was a void and though, briefly, as he went about his daily chores, shopping and preparing meals for himself and stooping over the sink, he could forget about it, he was never for long unaware of it. His son came to call on him with his garrulous wife and the void was there; he played chess with the bedridden old man in the flat on the second floor and between moves – the old man was always slow – the void persisted.

But one day, where the void had been, there was suddenly this terrible pain, as though something molten had been poured into it to harden to an intolerable weight of lead. He lay on his bed and groaned and the cold sweat trickled down his cheeks. The pain came back and that second time it was as though some filament running along his left arm had leapt into incandescence. Eventually he went to see the impatient young man, his blond hair reaching to the collar of his jacket, who had taken the place of the patient old man, a refugee from Hitler's Germany, who had once been his doctor. The young man told him that he had angina; but it need not be serious, if he were careful he had many more years ahead of him, there was no reason why he should not live to be seventy. What the young man had not bothered to note – it was all there in a folder before him – was that his patient was already seventy-one.

So that was how he came to his decision: I've had enough. And he came to it gently and simply, with neither surprise nor shock. He went to see his solicitor and he made a new will, leaving less of his money to his son and daughter than would eventually please them and more to the RSPCA. He began to tidy up the flat, discarding whatever would be useless to anyone else and tearing up the duplicates of income-tax returns years and years old (he had been an accountant by profession), receipted bills, photographs, letters. He made a fire in the yard of all this detritus, once so important to him and now so trivial, and watched as the photographs curled and darkened (yes, that was him in that extraordinary bathing costume that had a skirt reaching almost to his knees and that was his daughter in her school blazer and straw hat), as the income-tax returns took flame and then subsided to a crimson glow, as the letters (written to him in the trenches by the hospital nurse whom he had eventually married) were reduced to a grey dust. There was a wind that summer morning and everything consumed so easily.

He already had the pills, prescribed not for him (he had never had difficulty in sleeping) but for his wife. Some time soon he would swallow them, when this succession of brilliant, beautiful summer days had ended and he had ceased to enjoy the sensation of glad accomplishment derived from the order that he had created out of a lifetime's disorder.

It was his custom every evening before supper to go for a brief walk along the tow-path. He had walked there with his children and his wife on his returns from work; and then, later, he had walked there with his daughter and the dog, a mongrel, that she had taken away with her to the New Forest, where it had soon been run over – ironically, in a country lane by a car crammed with tipsy trippers. Now he walked there alone, a man who looked much younger than his years and whose walk was determinedly sprightly even though that impatient young doctor had warned him never to over-exert himself or be in a hurry.

That evening, in the late sunlight, the river was particularly beautiful, uncoiling lazily like some vast, shimmering snake. Some boys, trousers rolled up to their knees, were wading in it, intent on dredging something out of its depths. Their arms were black with sludge, even their cheeks were daubed with it. Beyond them an eight skimmed by, the cox's voice falsetto as he shrilled, 'In, out . . . In, out . . .' A dog scampered past, trailing some name-less horror – it looked like a putrescent length of tripe – from its slavering jaws. A valedictory sadness came over him, as he passed into the shade of the four beech trees and then out again into the sunshine, where, on the other side of the sagging fence, flat white figures moved lethargically over the baize of the cricket ground. His boy had played there, before he had married and got portly and rich and self-important.

He walked on, still at a sprightly pace, even though he was experiencing that disagreeable but now familiar tightness of the chest that made him from time to time halt and gulp for breath. The sun was warm on his face; the breeze was warm in his hair.

There were four houses here, their railings removed during the war and never put back, with plateaux of mangy lawn outside front doors that, because of flooding, were raised some feet above the tow-path. Many years before a prostitute had lived in one of them, until outraged neighbours had managed to drive her out. She used to sit, broodingly monumental, in a skimpy cotton frock, her face painted like a clown's and her hair an immense orange beehive about it, out on her lawn, in a deckchair, striped red and blue, on evenings such as this. He smiled to himself at the remembrance. His wife had joined the general outrage – so bad for the children to have to see that kind of thing going on under their noses. But if the children glanced at the huge, impassive woman, waiting for her custom on those waning summer evenings, it was only for a moment. She had never been of the slightest interest to them.

All at once he heard his cat miaow, and he halted, under a solitary beech tree smaller than the four that he had passed, that breathlessness now grown acute as he thought: 'This is some kind of hallucination.' He looked up, and there, high in the branches, she was gazing down at him, with a seemingly tranquil gaze out of her clear blue eyes, even though her miaowing, persistent now, reiterated over and over again on the same two notes, told him that she was terrified.

Then a voice said, from the other side of the tree, from the pock-marked plateau of grass on which the prostitute used to lie out in her deck-chair: 'I don't know how to get her down. I suppose I'd better send for the fire brigade, but they charge for that, don't they?'

'Is it – is it your cat then?' For he still believed it to be his.

'Yes. Silly little brute. She will go up there after birds and then she can't get down again. My husband used to climb up to fetch her. The other day I had to tip a boy to go up for me.'

She was a middle-aged woman, with the coarse straight blond hair, round, rosy-cheeked face and thick thighs and ankles of a Russian peasant woman. She had large white teeth, and he noticed, as she now smiled at him, that one of them, just at the corner of her mouth, was chipped.

'Is your husband not at home?'

'Oh, no.' She gave a loud, clear laugh, as though he had said something funny. 'He ran away months ago.'

The cat continued its plaintive miaowing; and now both of them peered up into the tree. Eventually he said:

'Perhaps I could get her down for you.'

'You?' Then, realizing that her incredulity might offend him, she said quickly: 'Oh, you wouldn't want to dirty your nice clothes.'

He was, in fact, wearing a pair of old grey flannels that had shrunk so that there was a gap between them and his canvas shoes, an open-necked shirt and the darned cardigan.

'I'll have a try,' he said.

'But do you think you ought to . . . ?'

He grabbed a branch of the tree and swung himself up, hearing her gasp out in involuntary panic, 'Oh, do be careful!' It was all so easy; nothing to it. He did not feel the smallest breathlessness or discomfort. He began to climb, his feet unerringly finding one hold after another. Once he looked down and through the leaves, flickering in the evening sunlight, he saw her round, upturned face, the eyes screwed up, below him. It gave him an extraordinary surge of pleasure. It looked so beautiful, wholesome and kind and beautiful, glimmering up out of the swirling green. And I don't feel giddy, he thought. Not in the least.

'Don't let her scratch you!' she called out. 'Be careful!'

The cat did scratch him, in brief terror, as he put out a hand, pleading, 'Good puss; come, puss, come, come.' But he hardly noticed as the talons, cruel and sharp, lacerated the side of his neck. Then all at once the cat was purring as he clutched her against him. He began the slow descent, pausing from moment to moment to look either down at that glimmering upturned face or out, over the tow-path, to the lazy, snake-like coils of the river.

'Shall I take her from you?' She put up a hand and he noticed how coarse and rough its palm was. He imagined her peeling potatoes, scrubbing floors and digging the garden. He passed the totally passive cat down to her and she cradled it against her ample breast, almost as though to suckle it there.

'That was splendid of you, I'm so grateful,' she began. And then, as he jumped down off the lowest branch and began to wipe his hands on the handkerchief he had pulled from his trouser pocket: 'Oh, but look what she's done to your neck! Oh, the naughty thing!'

Touching the long scratch with his fingers, so that their tips became smeared with blood, and then pressing the handkerchief, already darkened with grime, to the wound, he said that it was nothing, nothing at all. But she replied that of course it wasn't nothing, it could easily go septic, she must wash the place at once and put some iodine on it.

So that was how he entered the dilapidated, untidy house, so unlike the flat that he had left in such scrupulous order behind him; how he came to be sitting on the broken lavatory seat while she first washed the scratch and then, telling him, 'This will hurt, I'm afraid,' dabbed with a piece of iodine-soaked cottonwool; how eventually, as the eight returned up the river, they sipped at glasses of a warm, too-sweet sherry together out on the pockmarked plateau of grass.

'It's funny I've never seen you before,' he said. 'I walk along here almost every evening.'

'I've seen you, often.'

'Once, many years ago . . .' He broke off; he had been going to tell her of the statuesque prostitute sitting out on this same patch of grass as now they were doing.

'Yes?'

'I used to come here with my children,' he said. 'And with our dog. But that must have been long before you came to live here.'

'My husband insisted on buying this house. I never wanted it. And then when he did his bunk it was all he left me. Nothing else.'

'It must be valuable now. These houses facing the river . . .'

'Yes, I suppose it is. But it's damp and the rooms are too small and the rats come in from the river. That's why I got the cat. But she's no earthly use as a ratter.'

'Siamese never are. Mine felt she was far too grand to chase after vermin.'

They revealed little of themselves to each other; for much of the time they sat in silence, looking out at the peaceful river, with its occasional swan or boat or flotsam. She offered him another glass of sherry but he said that no, thank you, he should really be getting home. She said, well, then, another time, and he said yes, that would be nice, very nice, another time, of course.

He was awkward when he got up to go and the awkwardness seemed to communicate itself to her, so that, a woman not naturally shy, she became so for a moment. 'I do hope that scratch doesn't go septic,' she said, and unaccountably her plain, pleasant, round face began to redden.

'Oh, no. It's nothing.'

Out on the tow-path, he called over his shoulder: 'Next time I pass, I'll look out for you.'

'Yes, please.'

He sketched a brief wave and she waved back. She had picked up the cat again and once more she was cradling it against her ample breast as though to suckle it. The setting sun glinted on her thick, blonde hair. Though she must have been, oh, fifty or fifty-five, she suddenly looked young.

He walked back home, full of a calm, spacious happiness. He walked even more briskly than usual but he felt no breathlessness, no tightness, no pain. He thought of that round face glimpsed through the shivering foliage, with the eyes screwed up and the mouth slightly parted to reveal those large, white teeth. He thought of the thick, sturdy thighs and ankles as she had lain out in the deck-chair with the glass of that sweet, tacky sherry resting on her slightly pro-turberant stomach. He thought of the walk that he would take the next evening and of how, perhaps, she would be out there on the plateau before her house.

He warmed up the stew that Mrs Crawford had prepared for him and for once he ate every morsel of one of her over-lavish meals instead of putting at least half of it down the waste-disposal unit. Then he poured himself a whisky and, glass in hand, wandered out into the dank, narrow yard, while from the open window of the flat above pop music blared out. But for once the din did not annoy him. He walked over to the elder tree, and then, on an impulse he could not explain, he tipped up the glass and let a few drops of the whisky trickle down on to the spot where the cat had sat, hunched up in that last vigil of hers, awaiting her death.

He went back into the flat and, though it was still early – the sun had hardly set – he began to take off his clothes and prepare for bed. He wanted the morrow to come quickly so that, once again, he could walk along the tow-path, past the dogs and the boys wading out into the sludge and the skimming eights, and then perhaps, beyond the four giant beech trees, once again could meet . . .

In his pyjamas he opened the drawer of the bedside table and took out the glass tube with the twelve white tablets within it. For a long time he considered them; then he went into the bathroom, pulled out the plastic stopper and emptied them into the lavatory basin and flushed them away. Still holding the tube, he went back into his bedroom, lay down on the bed, outside the sheet, and closed his eyes. Leaves swirled and rippled and among them a round, peasant face gleamed up at him . . .

His son and his daughter, who had never greatly liked each other, had been dividing up the spoils. By an unspoken agreement the son had not brought his wife and the daughter had not brought her friend.

'When I first saw him like that – clutching that bottle – I felt sure he must have killed himself,' the son said. It was to him that Mrs Crawford, totally calm but for a faint exasperation at a disruption to her daily schedule, had telephoned.

'And Dr Hamilton must have had the same idea to have wanted a post-mortem, I suppose.'

'Oh, yes. He said as much.'

The son opened another drawer of the desk, as scrupulously tidy as the one before it. 'The way that everything has been put in perfect order . . . ! Like someone who has made all his preparations for a long journey ahead of him. He must have had some kind of premonition.'

'Poor Father.' And for a brief moment the daughter felt it. 'It wouldn't have been really surprising if he *had* done himself in. He had so little to live for.'

'Well, it was a nice way to go.'

The daughter sighed, deciding that it was she who was going to have that Stubbs print over the chimney-piece, whatever her brother said.

From *Hard Feelings* by Francis King

Lillian

What I always say is that Wilbur Willard is nothing but a very lucky guy, because what is it but luck that has him teetering along Forty-ninth Street one cold snowy morning when Lillian is mer-owing around the sidewalk looking for her mamma?

And what is it but luck that has Wilbur Willard all mulled up to a million, what with him having been sitting out a few glasses of Scotch with a friend by the name of Haggerty in an apartment over in Fifty-ninth Street? Because if Wilbur Willard is not mulled up he will see Lillian is nothing but a little black cat, and give her plenty of room, for everybody knows that black cats are terribly bad luck, even when they are only kittens.

But being mulled up like I tell you, things look very different to Wilbur Willard, and he does not see Lillian as a little black kitten scrabbling around in the snow. He sees a beautiful leopard; because a copper by the name of O'Hara, who is walking past about then, and who knows Wilbur Willard, hears him say:

'Oh, you beautiful leopard!'

The copper takes a quick peek himself, because he does not wish any leopards running around his beat, it being against the law, but all he sees, as he tells me afterwards, is this rumpot ham, Wilbur Willard, picking up a scrawny little black kitten and shoving it in his overcoat pocket, and he also hears Wilbur say:

'Your name is Lillian.'

Then Wilbur teeters on up to his room on the top floor of an old fleabag in Eighth Avenue that is called the Hotel de Brussels, where he lives quite a while, because the management does not mind actors, the management of the Hotel de Brussels being very broadminded, indeed.

There is some complaint this same morning from one of Wilbur's neighbours, an old burlesque doll by the name of Minnie Madigan, who is not working since Abraham Lincoln is assassinated, because she hears Wilbur going on in his room about a beautiful leopard, and calls up the clerk to say that a hotel which allows wild animals is not respectable. But the clerk looks in on Wilbur and finds him playing with nothing but a harmless-looking little black kitten, and nothing comes of the old doll's grouse, especially as nobody ever claims the Hotel de Brussels is respectable anyway, or at least not much.

Of course when Wilbur comes out from under the ether next afternoon he can see Lillian is not a leopard, and in fact Wilbur is quite astonished to find himself in bed with a little black kitten, because it seems Lillian is sleeping on Wilbur's chest to keep warm. At first Wilbur does not believe what he sees, and puts it down to Haggerty's Scotch, but finally he is convinced, and so he puts Lillian in his pocket, and takes her over to the Hot Box night club and gives her some milk, of which it seems Lillian is very fond.

Now where Lillian comes from in the first place of course nobody knows. The chances are somebody chucks her out of a window into the snow, because people are always chucking kittens, and one thing and another, out of windows in New York. In fact, if there is one thing this town has plenty of, it is kittens, which finally grow up to be cats, and go snooping around ash cans, and mer-owing on roofs, and keeping people from sleeping well.

Personally, I have no use for cats, including kittens, because I never seen one that has any too much sense, although I know a guy by the name of Pussy McGuire who makes a first-rate living doing nothing but stealing cats, and sometimes dogs, and selling them to old dolls who like such things for com-pany. But Pussy only steals Persian and Angora cats, which are very fine cats, and of course Lillian is no such cat as this. Lillian is nothing but a black cat, and nobody will give you a dime a dozen for black cats in this town, as they are generally regarded as very bad jinxes.

Furthermore, it comes out in a few weeks that Wilbur Willard can just as well name her Herman, or Sidney, as not, but Wilbur sticks to Lillian, because this is the name of his partner when he is in vaudeville years ago. He often tells me about Lillian Withington when he is mulled up, which is more often than somewhat, for Wilbur is a great hand for drinking Scotch, or rye, or bourbon, or gin, or whatever else there is around for drinking, except water. In fact, Wilbur Willard is a high-class drinking man, and it does no good telling him it is against the law to drink in this country, because it only makes him mad, and he says to the dickens with the law, only Wilbur Willard uses a much rougher word than dickens.

'She is like a beautiful leopard,' Wilbur says to me about Lillian Withington. 'Black-haired, and black-eyed, and all ripply, like a leopard I see in an animal act on the same bill at the Palace with us once. We are headliners then,' he says, 'Willard and Withington, the best singing and dancing act in the country.

'I pick her up in San Antonio, which is a spot in Texas,' Wilbur says. 'She is not long out of a convent, and I just lose my old partner, Mary McGee, who ups and dies on me of pneumonia down there. Lillian wishes to go on the stage, and joins out with me. A natural-born actress with a great voice. But like a leopard,' Wilbur says, 'Like a leopard. There is cat in her, no doubt of this, and cats and women are both ungrateful. I love Lillian Withington. I wish to marry her. But she is cold to me. She says she is not going to follow the stage all her life. She says she wishes money, and luxury, and a fine home, and of course a guy like me cannot give a doll such things.

'I wait on her hand and foot,' Wilbur says. 'I am her slave. There is nothing

I will not do for her. Then one day she walks in on me in Boston very cool and says she is quitting me. She says she is marrying a rich guy there. Well, naturally it busts up the act and I never have the heart to look for another partner, and then I get to belting that old black bottle around, and now what am I but a cabaret performer?'

Then sometimes he will bust out crying, and sometimes I will cry with him, although the way I look at it, Wilbur gets a pretty fair break, at that, in getting rid of a doll who wishes things he cannot give her. Many a guy in this town is tangled up with a doll who wishes things he cannot give her, but who keeps him tangled up just the same and busting himself trying to keep her quiet.

Wilbur makes pretty fair money as an entertainer in the Hot Box, though he spends most of it for Scotch, and he is not a bad entertainer, either. I often go to the Hot Box when I am feeling blue to hear him sing Melancholy Baby, and Moonshine Valley, and other sad songs which break my heart. Personally, I do not see why any doll cannot love Wilbur, especially if they listen to him sing such songs as Melancholy Baby when he is mulled up well, because he is a tall, nice-looking guy with long eyelashes, and sleepy brown eyes, and his voice has a low moaning sound that usually goes very big with the dolls. In fact, many a doll does do some pitching to Wilbur when he is singing in the Hot Box, but somehow Wilbur never gives them a tumble, which I suppose is because he is thinking only of Lillian Withington.

Well, after he gets Lillian, the black kitten, Wilbur seems to find a new interest in life, and Lillian turns out to be right cute, and not bad-looking after Wilbur gets her fed up well. She is blacker than a yard up a chimney, with not a white spot on her, and she grows so fast that by and by Wilbur cannot carry her in his pocket any more, so he puts a collar on her and leads her around. So Lillian becomes very well known on Broadway, what with Wilbur taking her to many places, and finally she does not even have to be led around by Willard, but follows him like a pooch. And in all the Roaring Forties there is no pooch that cares to have any truck with Lillian, for she will leap aboard them quicker than you can say scat, and scratch and bite them until they are very glad indeed to get away from her.

But of course the pooches in the Forties are mainly nothing but Chows, and Pekes, and Poms, or little woolly white poodles, which are led around by blonde dolls, and are not fit to take their own part against a smart cat. In fact, Wilbur Willard is finally not on speaking terms with any doll that owns a pooch between Times Square and Columbus Circle, and they are all hoping that both Wilbur and Lillian will go lay down and die somewhere. Furthermore, Wilbur has a couple of battles with guys who also belong to the dolls, but Wilbur is no boob in a battle if he is not mulled up too much and leg-weary.

After he is through entertaining people in the Hot Box, Wilbur generally goes around to any speakeasies which may still be open, and does a little off-hand drinking on top of what he already drinks down in the Hot Box, which is plenty, and although it is considered very risky in this town to mix Hot Box liquor with any other, it never seems to bother Wilbur. Along toward daylight he takes a couple of bottles of Scotch over to his room in the Hotel de Brussels and uses them for a nightcap, so by the time Wilbur Willard is ready to slide off to sleep he has plenty of liquor of one kind and another inside him, and he sleeps pretty good.

Of course nobody on Broadway blames Wilbur so very much for being such a rumpot, because they know about him loving Lillian Withington, and losing her, and it is considered a reasonable excuse in this town for a guy to do some drinking when he loses a doll, which is why there is so much drinking here, but it is a mystery to one and all how Wilbur stands all this liquor without croaking. The cemeteries are full of guys who do a lot less drinking than Wilbur, but he never even seems to feel extra tough, or if he does he keeps it to himself and does not go around saying it is the kind of liquor you get nowadays.

He costs some of the boys around Mindy's plenty of dough one winter, because he starts in doing most of his drinking after hours in Good Time Charley's speakeasy, and the boys lay a price of four to one against him lasting until spring, never figuring a guy can drink very much of Good Time Charley's liquor and keep on living. But Wilbur Willard does it just the same, so everybody says the guy is just naturally superhuman, and lets it go at that.

Sometimes Wilbur drops into Mindy's with Lillian following him on the look-out for pooches, or riding on his shoulder if the weather is bad, and the two of them will sit with us for hours chewing the rag about one thing and another. At such times Wilbur generally has a bottle on his hip and takes a shot now and then, but of course this does not come under the head of serious drinking with him. When Lillian is with Wilbur she always lies as close to him as she can get and anybody can see that she seems to be very fond of Wilbur, and that he is very fond of her, although he sometimes forgets himself and speaks of her as a beautiful leopard. But of course this is only a slip of the tongue, and anyway if Wilbur gets any pleasure out of thinking Lillian is a leopard, it is nobody's business but his own.

'I suppose she will run away from me some day,' Wilbur says, running his hand over Lillian's back until her fur crackles. 'Yes, although I give her plenty of liver and catnip, and one thing and another, and all my affection, she will probably give me the go-by. Cats are like women, and women are like cats. They are both very ungrateful.'

'They are both generally bad luck,' Big Nip, the crap shooter, says.

'Especially cats, and most especially black cats.'

Many other guys tell Wilbur about black cats being bad luck, and advise him to slip Lillian into the North River some night with a sinker on her, but Wilbur claims he already has all the bad luck in the world when he loses Lillian Withington, and that Lillian, the cat, cannot make it any worse, so he goes on taking extra good care of her, and Lillian goes on getting bigger and bigger until I commence thinking maybe there is some St Bernard in her.

Finally I commence to notice something funny about Lillian. Sometimes she will be acting very loving towards Wilbur, and then again she will be very unfriendly to him, and will spit at him, and snatch at him with her claws, very hostile. It seems to me that she is all right when Wilbur is mulled up, but is as sad and fretful as he is himself when he is only a little bit mulled. And when Lillian is sad and fretful she makes it very tough indeed on the pooches in the neighbourhood of the Brussels.

In fact, Lillian takes to pooch-hunting, sneaking off when Wilbur is getting his rest, and running pooches bow-legged, especially when she finds one that is not on a leash. A loose pooch is just naturally cherry pie for Lillian.

Well, of course this causes great indignation among the dolls who own the pooches, particularly when Lillian comes home one day carrying a Peke as big as she is herself by the scruff of the neck, and with a very excited blonde doll following her and yelling bloody murder outside Wilbur Willard's door when Lillian pops into Wilbur's room through a hole he cuts in the door for her, still lugging the Peke. But it seems that instead of being mad at Lillian and giving her a pasting for such goings on, Wilbur is somewhat pleased, because he happens to be still in a fog when Lillian arrives with the Peke, and is thinking of Lillian as a beautiful leopard.

'Why,' Wilbur says, 'this is devotion, indeed. My beautiful leopard goes off into the jungle and fetches me an antelope for dinner.'

Now of course there is no sense whatever to this, because a Peke is certainly not anything like an antelope, but the blonde doll outside Wilbur's door hears Wilbur mumble, and gets the idea that he is going to eat her Peke for dinner and the squawk she puts up is very terrible. There is plenty of trouble around the Brussels in cooling the blonde doll's rage over Lillian snagging her Peke, and what is more the blonde doll's ever-loving guy, who turns out to be a tough Ginney bootlegger by the name of Gregorio, shows up at the Hot Box the next night and wishes to put the slug on Wilbur Willard.

But Wilbur rounds him up with a few drinks and by singing Melancholy Baby to him, and before he leaves the Ginney gets very sentimental towards Wilbur, and Lillian, too, and wishes to give Wilbur five bucks to let Lillian grab the Peke again, if Lillian will promise not to bring it back. It seems

Gregorio does not really care for the Peke, and is only acting quarrelsome to please the blonde doll and make her think he loves her dearly.

But I can see Lillian is having different moods, and finally I ask Wilbur if he notices it.

'Yes,' he says, very sad, 'I do not seem to be holding her love. She is getting very fickle. A guy moves on to my floor at the Brussels the other day with a little boy, and Lillian becomes very fond of this kid at once. In fact, they are great friends. Ah, well,' Wilbur says, 'cats are like women. Their affection does not last.'

I happen to go over to the Brussels a few days later to explain to a guy by the name of Crutchy, who lives on the same floor as Wilbur Willard, that some of our citizens do not like his face and that it may be a good idea for him to leave town, especially if he insists on bringing ale into their territory, and I see Lillian out in the hall with a youngster which I judge is the kid Wilbur is talking about. This kid is maybe three years old, and very cute, what with black hair and black eyes, and he is mauling Lillian around the hall in a way that is most surprising, for Lillian is not such a cat as will stand for much mauling around, not even from Wilbur Willard.

I am wondering how anybody comes to take such a kid to a place like the Brussels, but I figure it is some actor's kid, and that maybe there is no mamma for it. Later I am talking to Wilbur about this, and he says:

'Well, if the kid's old man is an actor, he is not working at it. He sticks close to his room all the time, and he does not allow the kid to go anywhere but in the hall, and I feel sorry for the little guy, which is why I allow Lillian to play with him.'

Now it comes on a very cold spell, and a bunch of us are sitting in Mindy's along towards five o'clock in the morning when we hear fire engines going past. By and by in comes a guy by the name of Kansas, who is named Kansas because he comes from Kansas, and who is a gambler by trade.

'The old Brussels is on fire,' this guy Kansas says.

'She is always on fire,' Big Nig says, meaning there is always plenty of hot stuff going on around the Brussels.

About this time who walks in but Wilbur Willard, and anybody can see he is just naturally floating. The chances are he comes from Good Time Charley's, and is certainly carrying plenty of pressure. I never see Wilbur Willard mulled up more. He does not have Lillian with him, but then he never takes Lillian to Good Time Charley's because Charley hates cats.

'Hey, Wilbur,' Big Nig says, 'your joint, the Brussels, is on fire.'

'Well,' Wilbur says, 'I am a little firefly, and I need a light. Let us go where there is a fire.'

1 Elinor Glyn and friends: 'Elinor was a guest speaker and she wore, with fine panache, her huge Persian cat Candide, asleep, round her neck instead of a fox fur . . . "Great success!" commented Elinor in her diary.'

2a Colette and company: 'O, beautiful Fanchette,
your bad behaviour is so remarkably becoming to you!'

2b Brigid Brophy: 'Cats, who will eat out of my mother's hand melon, grapes,
pineapple . . . cats who would not ordinarily dream of eating any such thing
but who take it from my mother for the sheer pleasure of sharing her diet.'

3a Doris Lessing in 1956: '. . . days of tears, loneliness, knowledge of betrayal – and all for a small, thin, dying cat.'

3b Mervyn Peake with his wife Maeve Gilmore, and cat: '. . . a face of fur, peculiarly blanched in the dim light of the hall.'

4 Hemingway with his cat Christopher Columbus at Finca Vigia.
'Don't let him see you cry', Ernest Hemingway begged his wife
when their favourite cat was injured.

5 Mark Twain and kitten, Connecticut:
'Devil follow corpse, cat follow devil,
warts follow cat, I'm done with ye.'

6a Barbara Pym: 'When she is grooming her cat
she has to put on her spectacles to see the fleas,
gleaming red-brown among the combings . . .'

6b Antonia White: 'No one cares about me
except the poor puss-cat.'

7a Dora Carrington with Tiger in 1929:
'. . . the black cat in the wildest state of spring lust
careers about the garden after Ralph crying out to be raped.'

7b David Garnett:
'Can you explain how and why
cats make love to us?'

8 Edith Sitwell with Leo in 1962: 'When in Paris I bought a record
especially for my beloved cat, called "Baby don't be blue",
sung by a gentleman known as High Hatted Tragedian of Song.'

The Brussels is only a few blocks from Mindy's and there is nothing else to do just then, so some of us walk over to Eighth Avenue with Wilbur teetering along ahead of us. The old shack is certainly roaring away when we get in sight of it, and the firemen are tossing water into it, and the coppers have the fire lines out to keep the crowd back, although there is not much of a crowd at such an hour in the morning.

'Is it not beautiful?' Wilbur Willard says, looking up at the flames. 'Is it not like a fairy palace all lighted up this way?

You see, Wilbur does not realise the place is on fire, although guys and dolls are running out of it every which way, most of them half dressed, or not dressed at all, and the firemen are getting out the life nets in case anybody wishes to hop out of the windows.

'It is certainly beautiful,' Wilbur says, 'I must get Lillian so she can see this.'

And before anybody has time to think, there is Wilbur Willard walking into the front door of the Brussels as if nothing happens. The firemen and the coppers are so astonished all they can do is holler at Wilbur, but he pays no attention whatever. Well, naturally everybody figures Wilbur is a gone gosling, but in ten minutes he comes walking out of this same door through the fire and smoke as cool as you please, and he has Lillian in his arms.

'You know,' Wilbur says, coming over to where we are standing with our eyes popping out, 'I have to walk all the way up to my floor because the elevators seem to be out of commission. The service is getting terrible in this hotel. I will certainly make a strong complaint to the management about it as soon as I pay something on my account.'

Then what happens but Lillian lets out a big mer-row, and hops out of Wilbur's arms and skips past the coppers and the firemen with her back all humped up, and the next thing anybody knows she is tearing through the front door of the old hotel and making plenty of speed.

'Well, well,' Wilbur says, looking much surprised, 'there goes Lillian.'

And what does this daffy Wilbur Willard do but turn and go marching back into the Brussels again, and by this time the smoke is pouring out of the front doors so thick he is out of sight in a second. Naturally he takes the coppers and firemen by surprise, because they are not used to guys walking in and out of fires on them.

This time anybody standing around will lay you plenty of odds – two and a half and maybe three to one that Wilbur never shows up again, because the old Brussels is now just popping with fire and smoke from the lower windows, although there does not seem to be quite so much fire in the upper storey. Everybody seems to be out of the building, and even the firemen are fighting the blaze from the outside because the Brussels is so old and ramshackly there is no sense in them risking the floors.

I mean everybody is out of the place except Wilbur Willard and Lillian, and we figure they are getting a good frying somewhere inside, although Feet Samuels is around offering to take thirteen to five for a few small bets that Lillian comes out okay, because Feet claims that a cat has nine lives and that is a fair bet at the price.

Well, up comes a swell-looking doll all heated up about something and pushing and clawing her way through the crowd up to the ropes and scream-ing until you can hardly hear yourself think, and about this same minute every-body hears a voice going ai-lee-hi-hee-hoo, like a Swiss yodeller, which comes from the roof of the Brussels, and looking up what do we see but Wilbur Willard standing up there on the edge of the roof, high above the fire and smoke, and yodelling very loud.

Under one arm he has a big bundle of some kind, and under the other he has the little kid I see playing in the hall with Lillian. As he stands up there going ai-lee-hi-hee-hoo, the swell-dressed doll near us begins screaming louder than Wilbur is yodelling, and the firemen rush over under him with a life net.

Wilbur lets go another ai-lee-hi-hee-hoo, and down he comes all spraddled out, with the bundle and the kid, but he hits the net sitting down and bounces up and back again for a couple of minutes before he finally settles. In fact, Wilbur is enjoying the bouncing, and the chances are he will be bouncing yet if the firemen do not drop their hold on the net and let him fall to the ground.

Then Wilbur steps out of the net, and I can see the bundle is a rolled-up blanket with Lillian's eyes peeking out of one end. He still has the kid under the other arm with his head stuck out in front, and his legs stuck out behind, and it does not seem to be that Wilbur is handling the kid as careful as he is handling Lillian. He stands there looking at the firemen with a very sneering look, and finally he says:

'Do not think you can catch me in your net unless I wish to be caught. I am a butterfly, and very hard to overtake.'

Then all of a sudden the swell-dressed doll who is doing so much hollering, piles on top of Wilbur and grabs the kid from him and begins hugging and kissing it.

'Wilbur,' she says, 'God bless you, Wilbur, for saving my baby! Oh, thank you, Wilbur, thank you! My wretched husband kidnaps and runs away with him, and it is only a few hours ago that my detectives find out where he is.'

Wilbur gives the doll a funny look for about half a minute and starts to walk away, but Lillian comes wiggling out of the blanket, looking and smelling pretty much singed up, and the kid sees Lillian and begins hollering for her, so

Wilbur finally hands Lillian over to the kid. And not wishing to leave Lillian, Wilbur stands around somewhat confused, and the doll gets talking to him, and finally they go away together, and as they go Wilbur is carrying the kid, and the kid is carrying Lillian, and Lillian is not feeling so good from her burns.

Furthermore, Wilbur is probably more sober than he ever is before in years at this hour in the morning, but before they go I get a chance to talk some to Wilbur when he is still rambling somewhat, and I make out from what he says that the first time he goes to get Lillian he finds her in his room and does not see hide or hair of the little kid and does not even think of him, because he does not know what room the kid is in, anyway, having never noticed such a thing.

But the second time he goes up, Lillian is sniffing at the crack under the door of a room down the hall from Wilbur's and Wilbur says he seems to remember seeing a trickle of something like water coming out of the crack.

'And,' Wilbur says, 'as I am looking for a blanket for Lillian, and it will be a bother to go back to my room, I figure I will get one out of this room. I try the knob but the door is locked, so I kick it in, and walk in to find the room is full of smoke, and fire is shooting through the windows very lovely, and when I grab a blanket off the bed for Lillian, what is under the blanket but the kid?

'Well,' Wilbur says, 'the kid is squawking, and Lillian is mer-owing, and there is so much confusion generally that it makes me nervous, so I figure we better go up on the roof and let the stink blow off us, and look at the fire from there. It seems there is a guy stretched out on the floor of the room alongside an upset table between the door and the bed. He has a bottle in one hand, and he is dead. Well, naturally there is nothing to be gained by lugging a dead guy along, so I take Lillian and the kid and go up on the roof, and we just naturally fly off like humming birds. Now I must get a drink,' Wilbur says. 'I wonder if anybody has anything on their hip?'

Well, the papers are certainly full of Wilbur and Lillian the next day, especially Lillian, and they are both great heroes.

But Wilbur cannot stand publicity very long, because he never has no time to himself for his drinking, what with the scribes and the photographers hopping on him every few minutes wishing to hear his story, and to take more pictures of him and Lillian, so one night he disappears, and Lillian disappears with him.

About a year later it comes out that he marries his old doll, Lillian Withington-Harmon, and falls into a lot of dough, and what is more he cuts out the liquor and becomes quite a useful citizen one way and another. So everybody has to admit that black cats are not always bad luck, although I say Wilbur's case is a little exceptional because he does not start out knowing

Lillian is a black cat, but thinking she is a leopard.

I happen to run into Wilbur one day all dressed up in good clothes and jewellery and cutting quite a swell.

'Wilbur,' I say to him, 'I often think how remarkable it is the way Lillian suddenly gets such an attachment for the little kid and remembers about him being in the hotel and leads you back there a second time to the right room. If I do not see this come off with my own eyes, I will never believe a cat has brains enough to do such a thing, because I consider cats are extra dumb.'

'Brains nothing,' Wilbur says. 'Lillian does not have brains enough to grease a gimlet. And what is more she has no more attachment for the kid than a jack rabbit. The time has come,' Wilbur says, 'to expose Lillian. She gets a lot of credit which is never coming to her. I will now tell you about Lillian, and nobody knows this but me.

'You see,' Wilbur says, 'when Lillian is a little kitten I always put a little Scotch in her milk, partly to help make her good and strong, and partly because I am never no hand to drink alone, unless there is nobody with me. Well, at first Lillian does not care so much for this Scotch in her milk, but finally she takes a liking to it, and I keep making her toddy stronger until in the end she will lap up a good big snort without any milk for a chaser, and yell for more. In fact, I suddenly realize that Lillian becomes a rumpot, just like I am in those days, and simply must have her grog, and it is when she is good and rummed up that Lillian goes off snatching Pekes, and acting tough generally.

'Now,' Wilbur says, 'the time of the fire is about the time I get home every morning and give Lillian her schnapps. But when I go into the hotel and get her the first time I forget to Scotch her up, and the reason she runs back into the hotel is because she is looking for her shot. And the reason she is sniffing at the kid's door is not because the kid is in there but because the trickle that is coming through the crack under the door is nothing but Scotch running out of the bottle in the dead guy's hand. I never mention this before because I figure it may be a knock to a dead guy's memory,' Wilbur says. 'Drinking is certainly a disgusting thing, especially secret drinking.'

'But how is Lillian getting along these days?' I ask Wilbur Willard.

'I am greatly disappointed in Lillian,' he says. 'She refuses to reform when I do and the last I hear of her she takes up with Gregorio, the Ginney bootlegger, who keeps her well Scotched up all the time so she will lead his blonde doll's Peke a dog's life.'

Damon Runyon

9

THE
TWENTIETH
CENTURY

There's no cats i' the bible.

Mary Webb, *Gone to Earth*

The Nature of Cats

Quorum Porum*

In a dark Garden, by a dreadful Tree,
The Druid Toms were met. They numbered three:
Tab Tiger, Demon Black, and Ginger Hate.
Their forms were tense, their eyes were full of fate.
Save for the involuntary caudal thrill,
The horror was that they should sit so still.
An hour of ritual silence passed: then low
And marrow-freezing, Ginger moaned OROW,
Two horrid syllables of hellish lore,
Followed by deeper silence than before.
Another hour, the tabby's turn is come:
Rigid, he rapidly howls MUM MUM MUM,
Then reassumes his silence like a pall,
Clothed in negation, a dumb oracle.
At the third hour, the Black gasps out AH BLURK
Like a lost soul that founders in the mirk,
And the grim, ghastly, damned, and direful crew
Resumes its voiceless vigilance anew.
The fourth hour passes. Suddenly all three
Chant WEGGY WEGGY WEGGY mournfully,
Then stiffly rise, and melt into the shade,
Their Sabbath over, and their demons laid.

Ruth Pitter

*'Porum', genitive plural of 'Puss'.

Ode to a Fat Cat

Unhatch you April butterflies
For Maud is in a drawer.
Filling the air
With piles of overnourished fur.

Come crown the wonder of such startling size,
And tiny fish bones, spaced with violets, twine
To wreath the tips of those twin ears,
While down the graceful tabby-speckled spine
Lay bows in rows,
And round white paws
That out-vie Venus or the Himalayan snows.

Those strange and ornamental eyes
Stare with shifting sights,
Cavernous
Readily ravenous,
Lugubrious with subtle feline sighs.

And irresistible, the monster skittish pat
Of prima donna paw
Stretched from silky depths of flowing fur and fat,
Most exquisite!

And so I sing
To matchless Maud
Squatting in a drawer in Spring.

                                                Annabel Farjeon

To a Young Cat in the Orchard

Elegant creature with black shoulders bent,
Stalking the bird in song,
To what intent?
Tell what a wild source brims those empty eyes,
What well of shameless light,
Beyond the bounds of Hell or Paradise
Or wrong
Or right.

Frances Cornford

To Winky

You walk as a king scorning his subjects;
You flirt with me as a concubine in robes of silk.
Cat,
I am afraid of your poisonous beauty,

I have seen you torturing a mouse.
Yet when you lie purring in my lap
I forget everything but how soft you are,
And it is only when I feel your claws open upon my hand
That I remember –

Remember a puma lying out on a branch above my head
Years ago.

Shall I choke you, Cat,
Or kiss you?
Really I do not know.

From 'To Winky' by Amy Lowell

Cruel Clever Cat

Sally, having swallowed cheese,
Directs down holes the scented breeze,
Enticing thus with baited breath
Nice mice to an untimely death.

Geoffrey Taylor

Touch of Spring

Thin wind winds off the water,
earth lies locked in dead snow,
but sun slants in under the yew hedge,
and the ground there is bare,
with some green blades there,
and my cat knows,
sharpening her claws on the flesh-pink wood.

From *Tossing and Turning* by John Updike

Work-Shy

George Orwell's celebrated political satire reserved honourable mention for the cat's ability to disoblige with diplomacy.

But everyone worked according to his capacity. The hens and ducks, for instance, saved five bushels of corn at the harvest by gathering up the stray grains. Nobody stole, nobody grumbled over his rations, the quarrelling and biting and jealousy which had been normal features of life in the old days had almost disappeared. Nobody shirked – or almost nobody. Mollie, it was true, was not good at getting up in the morning, and had a way of leaving work early on the ground that there was a stone in her hoof. And the behaviour of the cat was somewhat peculiar. It was soon noticed that when there was work to be done the cat could never be found. She would vanish for hours on end, and then reappear at meal-times, or in the evening after work was over, as though nothing had happened. But she always made such excellent excuses, and purred so affectionately, that it was impossible not to believe in her good intentions.

From *Animal Farm* by George Orwell

The Galloping Cat

Oh I am a cat that likes to
Gallop about doing good
So
One day when I was
Galloping about doing good, I saw
A Figure in the path; I said:
Get off! (Be-
cause
I am a cat that likes to
Gallop about doing good)
But he did not move, instead
He raised his hand as if
To land me a cuff
So I made to dodge so as to
Prevent him bring it orf,
Un-for-tune-ately I slid
On a banana skin
Some Ass had left instead
Of putting in the bin. So
His hand caught me on the cheek
I tried
To lay his arm open from wrist to elbow
With my sharp teeth
Because I am
A cat that likes to gallop about doing good.
Would you believe it?
He wasn't there
My teeth met nothing but air,
But a Voice said: Poor cat,
(Meaning me) and a soft stroke
Came on me head
Since when
I have been bald.
I regard myself as
A martyr to doing good.
Also I heard a swoosh
As of wings, and saw
A halo shining at the height of

Mrs Gubbins's backyard fence.
So I thought: What's the good
Of galloping about doing good
When angels stand in the path
And do not do as they should
Such as having an arm to be bitten off
All the same I
Intend to go on being
A cat that likes to
Gallop about doing good
So
Now with my bald head I go,
Chopping the untidy flowers down, to and fro,
An' scooping up the grass to show
Underneath
The cinder path of wrath
Ha ha ha ha, ho,
Angels aren't the only ones who do not know
What's what and that
Galloping about doing good
Is a full-time job
That needs
An experienced eye of earthly
Sharpness, worth I dare say
(If you'll forgive a personal note)
A good deal more
Than all that skyey stuff
Of angels that make so bold as
To pity a cat like me that
Gallops about doing good.

                                        Stevie Smith

Cat

Dear creature by the fire a-purr,
  Strange idol, eminently bland,
Miraculous puss! As o'er your fur
  I trail a negligible hand,

And gaze into your gazing eyes,
  And wonder in a demi-dream,
What mystery it is that lies,
  Behind those slits that glare and gleam,

An exquisite enchantment falls
  About the portals of my sense;
Meandering through enormous halls,
  I breathe luxurious frankincense,

An ampler air, a warmer June
  Enfold me, and my wondering eye
Salutes a more imperial moon
  Throned in a more resplendent story

Than ever knew this northern shore.
  Oh, strange! For you are with me too,
And I who am a cat once more
  Follow the woman that was you

With tail erect and pompous march,
  The proudest puss that ever trod,
Through many a grove, 'neath many an arch,
  Impenetrable as a god.

Down many an alabaster flight
  Of broad and cedar-shaded stairs,
While over us the elaborate night
  Mysteriously gleams and glares.

                                Lytton Strachey

No Cat

'Sitting at the supper in a grand shining gown wi' roses on it,' said Hazel ecstatically, her voice rising to a kind of chant, 'with a white cloth on table like school-treat, and the old servant hopping to and agen like thrussels after worms.'

'Thrussel yourself!' muttered Andrew, peering in at the door. He retired again, remarking to the cat in a sour lugubrious voice, as he always did when ruffled: 'There's no cats i' the Bible.' He began to sing 'By the waters of Babylon.'

From *Gone to Earth* by Mary Webb

Without Violence

That cat who comes during sleep, quiet
On his cushioned claws, without violence,
Who enters the house with a low warm rattle
In his throat; that cat who has been said
To crawl into a baby's crib without brushing
The bars, to knit his paws on the pale
Flannel of the infant's nightdress, to settle
In sleep chin to chin with the dear one
And softly steal the child's breath
Without malice, as easily as pulling
A silk scarf completely through a gold ring;

The same cat who has been known to nudge
Through castle doors, to part tent flaps,
To creep to the breasts of brave men,
Ease between their blankets, to stretch
Full length on the satin bodices of lovely
Women, to nuzzle their cheeks with his great
Feline mane; it was that cat who leaped last night
Through the west window of father's bedroom,
Who chose to knead his night's rest on my father's
Shoulder, who slept well, breathing deeply,
Leaving just before dawn to saunter toward

The north, his magnificent tail and rump
Swaying with a listless and gorgeous grace.

From *The Expectations of Light* by Patiann Rogers

The Conscience of a Cat

A dog will often steal a bone,
But conscience lets him not alone,
And by his tail his guilt is known.

But cats consider theft a game
And, howsoever you may blame,
Refuse the slightest sign of shame.

When food mysteriously goes,
The chances are that Pussy knows
More than she leads you to suppose.

And hence there is no need for you,
If Puss declines a meal or two,
To feel her pulse or make ado.

Anon.

The Cat's Prayer

O my Master,
Do not expect me to be your slave, I have a thirst for freedom.
Do not probe my secret thoughts, I have a love of mystery.
Do not smother me with caresses, I have a preference for reserve.
Do not humiliate me, I have a sense of pride.
Do not, I beg, abandon me, I have a sure fidelity.
I'll return your love for me, I have a sense of true devotion.

Belgian traditional

The Prayer of the Cat

Lord,
I am the cat.
It is not, exactly, that I have something to ask of You!
No –
I ask nothing of anyone –
but,
if You have by some chance, in some celestial barn,
a little white mouse,
or a saucer of milk,
I know someone who would relish them.
Wouldn't You like someday
to put a curse on the whole race of dogs?
If so I should say,

                              AMEN

                    Carmen Bernos de Gasztold, transl. Rumer Godden

The Cat and the Moon

The cat went here and there
And the moon spun round like a top
And the nearest kin of the moon,
The creeping cat, looked up.
Black Minnaloushe stared at the moon,
For, wander and wail as he would,
The pure cold light in the sky
Troubled his animal blood.
Minnaloushe runs in the grass
Lifting his delicate feet.
Do you dance, Minnaloushe, do you dance?
When two close kindred meet,
What better than call a dance?
Maybe the moon may learn,
Tired of that courtly fashion
A new dance turn.
Minnaloushe creeps through the grass
From moonlit place to place,

The sacred moon overhead
Has taken a new phase.
Does Minnaloushe know that his pupils
Will pass from change to change,
And that from round to crescent,
From crescent to round they range?
Minnaloushe creeps through the grass
Alone, important and wise,
And lifts to the changing moon
His changing eyes.

W. B. Yeats

Potted Cat

As the cat
climbed over
the top of

the jamcloset
first the right
forefoot

carefully
then the hind
stepped down

into the pit of
the empty
flowerpot

William Carlos Williams

The Cat of the House

I muse
Over the hearth with my 'minishing eyes
Until after
the last coal dies.
Every tunnel of the mouse,
Every channel of the cricket,
I have smelt.
I have felt
The secret shifting of the mouldered rafter,
And heard
Every bird in the thicket . . .
I, born of a race of strange things,
Of deserts, great temples, great kings,
In the hot sands where the nightingale never sings!
Old he-gods of ingle and hearth,
Young she-gods of fur and silk –
Not mud of the earth –
Are the things I dream of.

Ford Madox Ford

Bernini's Cat

The tabby in front of
electric bars
having his chin scratched, feigns
St Teresa's ecstasy:
head back,
eyes closed,
mouth open. O
Heaven!

Gerda Mayer

Cat Love

Her Ally

Lyndall P. Hopkinson's poignant memoir of Antonia White includes a jealous recollection of her mother's apparent preference for the cat.

If ever Mother was out when I was at home, I used to take the opportunity to play the piano, since there was no fear of disturbing her. I had not been able to resist buying a piano score of *The Consul* and was dying to see if any of the arias that had been haunting me had easy accompaniments. I had found one I could sight-read, and was beginning to learn it, when Sue came in and sat beside me. We were in full throat in the middle of Magda's lilting aria 'Yes, yes, yesterday' when Mother burst into the room. She had mistaken the date of the meeting and made the journey to Roehampton in vain. Seeing us two sisters happily singing together was apparently more than she could bear.

She grabbed Domina, the over-fed cat who had never been out of doors – except for the time she fell out of the window – and set off down the stairs with Domina under her arm, murmuring, 'No one cares about me except the poor puss-cat.'

The flat door slammed behind her. We were sure she would come straight back, but she didn't. We went to look out of the window, just in time to see her small figure disappearing down Harrington Gardens with the fur bundle struggling in her arms. We looked at each other aghast: Was this serious? Might she be heading for the river as in the Tom days?

We telephoned the Glossops. 'Now don't you worry, Lynnie!' Silas reassured me. 'Tony isn't going to harm herself. She'll come home as soon as she realises what a damn fool she's being. The best thing is for you and Sue to come straight over and we'll have dinner as planned.'

Relieved that we need not worry, Sue went to run herself a bath and get changed, and I went back to playing the piano. Suddenly I heard footsteps on the stairs and called Sue. Mother walked past us looking demented. Her arms were bloody from scratches but she was reassuring the petrified cat she loved only it in the world. I plucked up all my courage to ask, 'But Mother, what's the matter?' She seemed not to hear and went over to a cupboard and began ferreting around until she found a cat-basket. She shoved the protesting

Domina into it and set off downstairs again, ignoring my second question, 'Where are you going, Mother?'

As she was about to go out of the flat door something made Mother look up suddenly. She turned round, and rushed back upstairs. She went straight to the bathroom which was above the stairs. We followed. The room was flooded and water was pouring over the edge of the bath-tub. As she turned off the taps, she bellowed, 'Susan, *your* doing I presume!'

The old Antonia was back in full force. The three of us spent the next ten minutes mopping up the bathroom floor while Domina yowled furiously from inside the basket. Then Antonia liberated her ally, made herself a cup of tea and went up to her work-room and shut the door without addressing a further word to us.

> From *Nothing to Forgive: A Daughter's Life of Antonia White* by Lyndall P.
> Hopkinson

Furry Love

The novelists David Garnett and Sylvia Townsend Warner were friends and correspondents for more than half a century and scarcely a letter was penned without reference to their cats.

Can you explain how and why cats make love to us? Tiber will come, if I am reading or writing or lying on my bed and will 'tease tow' with his claws. Then, coming closer, will gaze into my face, suddenly dig his pointed muzzle under my chin once or twice, retreat, roll on his side, inviting my hand, turn his head dreamily to one side, passive and luxurious. Then he will turn on me almost fiercely with a burst of purring, and so on, and so on.

But is this, as I think, reserved for human lovers? With a female cat I think he displays no such graces but is fiercely practical. It is more like the love that was shown him by his mother when he was a kitten. And naturally it is shown most strongly before and after I have fed him. But the luxury of his furry love is very beautiful.

> David Garnett, le Verger de Charry, 13 June 1973

Sylvia Townsend Warner responded to this query by return of post from Maiden Newton.

Dearest David, . . . Tiber makes love to you for the good reason that he loves you, and loves making love. Cats are passionate and voluptuous, they get satisfaction from mating but no pleasure (the females dislike it, and

this is wounding to the male), no voluptuousness; *and no appreciation.* Tiber
has the pleasure of being pleased and knowing he pleases in his love-making
with you. I am so glad you have each other. Does he roll on his head? Does he
fall asleep with an ownerly paw laid over you?

We had a dark grey cat (Norfolk bred, very Norfolk in character) called
Tom. He was reserved, domineering, voluptuous – much as I imagine Tiber to
be. When he was middle-aged he gave up nocturnal prowlings and slept on my
bed, against my feet. One evening I was reading in bed when I became aware
that Tom was staring at me. I put down my book, said nothing, watched.
Slowly, with a look of intense concentration, he got up and advanced on me,
like Tarquin with ravishing strides, poised himself, put out a front paw, and
stroked my cheek as I used to stroke his chops. A human caress from a cat. I
felt very meagre and ill-educated that I could not purr.

From *The Correspondence of Sylvia Townsend Warner and David Garnett*,
ed. Richard Garnett, 1994

The Most Ungenerous Cat in Christendom

In his essay on cats Gosse, quoting Paradis de Moncrif, relates the story of
'Mahomet who, being consulted one day on a point of piety, preferred to cut
off his sleeve on which his favourite pussy was asleep, rather than wake her
violently by rising.' Modern sartorial conditions would frustrate any such
operation, but it was a gesture with which Gosse would have sympathised. He
would deprecate interruptions which involved readjustments in his cat's
scheme of inertia. In his household there was none of the outrageous tyranny
exercised by favourite dogs, but the rights of a constitutional sovereignty were
assigned to the cat, and his sway accepted within legitimate limits.
Occasionally there was protest, as is evident from a letter written in 1915 to
John Drinkwater, who was ill at the time and who owned a cat named Punch.
'I hope you will take the greatest possible care of yourself, and obey Dr Punch,
whose expressed view I know to be that you should stay in bed and make warm
corners in the coverlid for him to fold his paws into. There I envy you, for
instead of seeing that pansy face smile and purr up at me, I have to endure the
fierce contempt and sneering malice of Caruso, without any question the most
ungenerous cat in Christendom. There is no doubt that he is a German at
heart, and he rules us on the system of "frightfulness." There is a theory that
the atrocious soul of Nietzsche has entered into him.'

From *The Life and Letters of Sir Edmund Gosse* by the Hon. Evan Charteris, K.C.

The Secretary

Raymond Chandler's 'staff' had no complaints about an episode of harrassment in the office, which the novelist revealed in this correspondence.

19 March 1945

To: Charles W. Morton

. . . A man named Engstead took some pictures of me for *Harper's Bazaar* a while ago (I never quite found out why) and one of me holding my secretary in my lap came out very well indeed. When I get the dozen I have ordered I'll send you one. The secretary, I should perhaps add, is a black Persian cat, 14 years old, and I call her that because she has been around me ever since I began to write, usually sitting on the paper I wanted to use or the copy I wanted to revise, sometimes leaning up against the typewriter and sometimes just quietly gazing out of the window from a corner of the desk as if to say, 'The stuff you're doing is a waste of time, bud'.

Her name is Taki (it was originally Take, but we got tired of explaining that this was a Japanese word meaning bamboo and should be pronounced in two syllables), and she has a memory such as no elephant ever tried to have. She is usually politely remote, but once in a while will get an argumentative spell and talk back for ten minutes at a time. I wish I knew what she is trying to say then, but I suspect it all adds up to a very sarcastic version of 'You can do better!'

I've been a cat lover all my life (have nothing against dogs except that they need such a lot of entertaining) and have never quite been able to understand them. Taki is a completely poised animal and always knows who likes cats, never goes near anybody that doesn't, always walks straight up to anyone, however lately arrived and completely unknown to her, who really does. . . . She has another curious trick (which may or may not be rare) of never killing anything. She brings 'em back alive and lets you take them away from her. She has brought into the house at various times such things as a dove, a blue parrakeet, and a large butterfly. The butterfly and the parrakeet were entirely unharmed and carried on just as though nothing had happened. The dove gave her a little trouble and had a small spot of blood on its breast, but we took it to a bird man and it was all right very soon. Just a bit humiliated. Mice bore her, but she catches them if they insist and then I have to kill them.

From *The World of Raymond Chandler*, ed. Miriam Gross

Making Way for Mr Thomas

Philip Wilson Steer's cat, Mr Thomas, appeared in his painting *The Muslin Dress* as a kitten playing with a girl's hat. He also ruled the artist's life.

'Old Pussy Steer', irreverently so-called in our household, had affinities with those pets, susceptible as he was no less to 'magic kindlings' of the senses than to chilly outer airs, and disposed to somnolence when at peace. The sleek, comfortable aloofness of the cats appealed to him, and their dignity, though he may not have imputed the condescension of the proud uncanny creatures to their Egyptian godhead. The reigning tom-cat, accordingly, was a third important member of the household, and Miss Hamilton has furnished a chronicle of the dynasty.

Steer enjoyed the quiet companionship of a cat and used to say that he liked them because they were not sycophants and provided their own boots. He made friends with strolling cats along the streets in Chelsea, talking to them in a special voice. As a child he had his special pussies, the 'Duchess', a tortoise-shell, and her daughter, the 'Countess'. His first attempt to handle oils at an early age was a portrait of the sleeping 'Duchess', and in letters while he was studying abroad were inquiries for his 'Mr Pop'.

It was not until he settled down at Cheyne Walk that he was able to keep a cat of his own in London. In *Hydrangeas* the girl on the sofa is playing with the first Mr Thomas, a black-and-white kitten, much beloved. After its death in 1906 a magnificent tabby was brought up from the country by his niece. This beautiful and sagacious creature ruled Steer for eighteen years. There never was such a cat! He could do no wrong and on the only occasion when he made a hole in his manners by jumping up on a mantelpiece and breaking a Sèvres vase he was forgiven.

When Steer began preparations for his annual outing this cat would become restive and distressed and afterwards mourn his absence, but upon the master's return after three months he was treated with hauteur for days. 'So you left me, did you? – Well then you can get on with it!' A chair was kept for him opposite Steer's. The great creature would leap noiselessly upon the table and contemplate anyone who sat in it with an expression of revolted patience till Steer would say, 'I am afraid you are sitting in Mr Thomas's chair.'

From *Life, Work and Setting of Philip Wilson Steer* by D. S. McColl

Confessions of a Cat Addict

By sheer inadvertence I have acquired the reputation of a cat- lover. Because I hate being photographed and will only endure it as long as I can give my attention to something other than the lens, I have once too often been photographed with a cat on my shoulder or in my arms. Cats walk through the back of televised interviews at my house. Cats are to be seen gazing sternly out of my windows at any intruders. Cats sit on my kitchen table, hang their tails in the sink, and lick the butter, to the intense disgust of casual visitors. A cat attempts to climb my legs whenever I stand still. A cat jumps into my lap if ever it finds me sitting down. It is therefore assumed that I love cats. It makes as much sense to say that I love cats as to say that a heroin addict loves heroin. Cats have been a bad habit of mine ever since my mother threw a bucket of water over the black and white kitten I had when I was ten because I made 'too much fuss over that damn cat'. Surely if I continually kiss and cuddle my cat, I love cats?

It is doubtless sheer perversity that makes me shudder at the thought of being included in any one of the mawkish tomes that appear each Christmas, celebrating the utter marvellousness and quiddity of the mog. If I were to make a cat book it would show the horribleness of cats, their cruelty, their jealousy, their territoriality, their utter lack of fine feeling, their abominable sex life. The proliferation of the domestic cat across the world is as much a disaster as the spread of any other human parasite. If cats had slime or scales instead of fur there would be no gainsaying their utter nastiness.

There are some people who are immune to the cuddlesomeness of the cat. They are the cat phobics who, unseduced by its throaty purr, disconcerted by its 'eyne of burning coal', see as clearly as Gower in *Pericles* what an awful creature the cat is. Shakespeare was almost certainly one of those listed by Shylock 'that are mad if they behold a cat' though I doubt he ever hung a cat in a basket and shot at it as Benedick has seen people do. The Shakespearean cat is no more than a rat-catcher, a Tib or a Tybalt, at best a 'harmless necessary creature', at worst (in *Cymbeline*) 'a creature vile of no esteem', in *Troilus and Cressida* classed with the fitchew and the toad. The mewing of the brindled cat boded nothing good in *Macbeth*. The worst that can be said of Goneril is that she is a grey cat.

From *Old Possum's Book of Practical Cats* then to Dr Greer's book of actual cats, with diagrams of the mayhem and slaughter accomplished by a single cat in a 24-hour period, a week, a month and a year, the last diagram showing *Felix triumphans* cleaning his paws and face atop a heap of dormice, tits, finches, butterflies, even shrews, toads, bats and moles, none of which he can eat. Behold a series of thrilling photographs of Felix with a shrilling rabbit, showing the various gastronomic approaches, the behind first approach, and the cut-the-scream-off approach in which the live rabbit has its face bitten off. Another gripping sequence will show Felix investigating a nest of robins, waiting until the nestlings are *à point*, and then polishing them all off in a single gourmet snack, while the robin parents, exhausted from feeding their young to this pitch of toothsomeness, scream dementedly from a nearby branch. You can feed a cat until he bulges; if he is one of my cats he will use up his expensive calories by hunting twice as hard. My cats try to eat most of the things they catch and are frequently forced to regurgitate long cylinders of fur, eyes, guts and teeth. Then they leap into my lap and kiss my nose, endowing me with a fishy blast of cannibal breath as a sign of their deep attachment. I am not deceived.

Those who take up their abode with me from time to time have often thought that it would be kind to indulge the human weakness that leads people to think that their animals are attached to them. I am always told how my red and white cat, Christopher, mopes when I am away. It is true that he climbs into my suitcase if ever I am packing and makes huge eyes at me, but his eyes are huge. He has no option but to make eyes at everybody. This is what he, a cat ransomed 10 years ago from Harrods zoo, was bred to do. He was also bred to talk. If asked a question he answers, usually in a querulous tone. His answers are inscrutable, of course, but a particularly sentimental person might be induced to entertain the notion that the cat was communicating. Under his red fox coat he is misshapen, with a tiny chest, a weak spine, and huge tail and paws, but he compensates for his inbred physical frailties by sheer imperiousness. Somehow he manages to take birds on the wing, possibly because, given his peculiar shape, he can hang-glide out of windows.

Just now the house is crammed with people, and everyone is busy. Fed up with dodging between their legs, Christopher took up his abode in the kitchen sideboard, where he sat, huge-eyed in the darkness, in self-imposed solitary confinement, emerging only to eat and relieve himself. Usually he sleeps with me. For three nights he lay in the cupboard, staring at the wall. I left him there. On the fourth night, I fetched him and brought him to bed with me. You would have sworn he was overjoyed. Not only did he purr every instant that he was not in deep sleep, he snuggled and sighed and stretched himself, tucking his head under my chin, incidentally dribbling all over my face and hair. My breath in his fur seemed to be the whole point of his existence. He may not have been happy, exactly, but he made a very good emblem of it, which is why his breed will set you back a few hundred quid even for parti-coloured runts like Christopher.

There is another cat at the Mills, a better cat than Christopher, a perfectly formed silver spotted British shorthair. Christopher was there when he was born on the hearth-rug of my London flat. Christopher mothered him when his own mother failed and has dominated him all his life. He is the kind of cat who respects other people's space, never climbs on a lap but looks on from a distance as you do whatever you are doing, with a slow cat smile if ever you catch his eye. Now he cannot put a forepaw to the ground. He has been in hospital twice but the savage pain does not abate. In the wild he would starve himself to death. He has brought Christopher a live rabbit most nights for eight years. Now that he is weak and ill Christopher howls at him as if he were a ghost. If he can reach him, he cuffs him hard, claws extended. I hate cats, if you want to know, especially when they are warm and silky and cute, and kiss and hug and smell of new-mown grass.

Germaine Greer

Pet Hate

A Case of Murder

They should not have left him there alone,
Alone that is except for the cat.
He was only nine, not old enough
To be left alone in a basement flat,
Alone, that is, except for the cat.
A dog would have been a different thing,
A big gruff dog with slashing jaws,
But a cat with round eyes mad as gold,
Plump as a cushion with tucked-in paws –
Better have left him with a fair-sized rat!
But what they did was leave him with a cat.
He hated that cat; he watched it sit,
A buzzing machine of soft black stuff,
He sat and watched and he hated it,
Snug in its fur, hot blood in a muff,
And its mad gold stare and the way it sat
Crooning dark warmth: he loathed all that.
So he took Daddy's stick and he hit the cat.
Then quick as a sudden crack in glass
It hissed, black flash, to a hiding place
In the dust and dark beneath the couch,
And he followed the grin on his new-made face,
A wide-eyed, frightened snarl of a grin,
And he took the stick and he thrust it in,
Hard and quick in the furry dark.
The black fur squealed and he felt his skin
Prickle with sparks of dry delight,
Then the cat again came into sight,
Shot for the door that wasn't quite shut,
But the boy, quick too, slammed fast the door:
The cat, half-through, was cracked like a nut
And the soft black thud was dumped on the floor.

Then the boy was suddenly terrified
And he bit his knuckles and cried and cried;
But he had to do something with the dead thing there.
His eyes squeezed beads of salty prayer
But the wound of fear gaped wide and raw;
He dared not touch the thing with his hands
So he fetched a spade and shovelled it
And dumped the load of heavy fur
In the spidery cupboard under the stair
Where it's been for years, and though it died
It's grown in that cupboard and its hot low purr
Grows slowly louder year by year:
There'll not be a corner for the boy to hide
When the cupboard swells and all sides split
And the huge black cat pads out of it.

Vernon Scannell

A Heavy Sentence

Henry James was not a man to be left alone with a cat, as this and the following anecdote verifies.

Settled in for the afternoon, surrounded by adoring ladies, the recluse of Rye sat complacent, holding my last new Persian kitten between his open palms, talking animatedly to the Beauty,* who could not talk but *looked*. He quite forgot the poor beast, which was too polite and too squeezed between the upper and the nether millstone of the great man's hands to remind him of its existence, and I dared not rescue it until the sentence on which Mr James was engaged was brought to a close – inside of half an hour.

Violet Hunt

From *The Legend of the Master: Henry James as Others Saw Him*
by Simon Newell-Smith

*Violet Hunt's niece.

The Turn of the Screw

On the whole [Henry James] liked animals, except cats, and owned a succession of dogs, although he was once heard at one of his own tea parties on the lawn at Lamb House to refer to a neighbour's albino Pekingese as 'a positive emetic'. On another occasion, when Henry received some visitors and the conversation flagged, for they were a little shy, one of them praised the canary, which at that time he kept in a cage in the drawing- room. 'Yes, yes,' said the Master, 'the little creature sings his song of adoration each morning with – er – the slightest modicum of encouragement from me'. But he hated cats and would always chase them out of the garden whenever he saw them. He once described to some friends how 'under the extreme provocation of its obscene caterwauling' he had killed one on his lawn. 'The act was followed by nausea and collapse.'

From *Henry James at Home* by H. Montgomery Hyde

Moore's Maladies

The novelist George Moore made plenty of enemies in Dublin, including his neighbour's cat, as W. B. Yeats recalls.

Sometimes Moore, instead of asking us to accept for true some monstrous invention, would press a spontaneous act into a deliberate comedy; starting in bad blood or blind passion, he would all in a moment see himself as others saw him. When he arrived in Dublin, all the doors in Upper Ely Place had been painted white by an agreement between the landlord and the tenants. Moore had his door painted green, and three Miss Beams – no, I have not got the name quite right – who lived next door protested to the landlord. Then began a correspondence between Moore and the landlord wherein Moore insisted on his position as an art critic, that the whole decoration of his house required a green door – I imagine that he had but wrapped the green flag around him – then the indignant young women bought a copy of *Esther Waters*, tore it up, put the fragments into a large envelope, wrote thereon: 'Too filthy to keep in the house,' dropped it into his letter-box. I was staying with Moore. I let myself in with a latch-key some night after twelve, and found a note on the hall-table asking me to put the door on the chain. As I was undressing, I heard Moore trying to get in; when I had opened the door and pointed to the note he said: 'Oh, I forgot. Every night I go out at eleven, at twelve, at one, and rattle my stick on the railings to make the Miss Beams' dogs bark.' Then I saw in the newspaper that the Miss Beams had hired organ-grinders to play under Moore's window when he was writing, that he had prosecuted the organ-grinders.

Moore had a large garden on the other side of the street, a blackbird sang there; he received his friends upon Saturday evening and made a moving speech upon the bird. 'I enjoy its song. If I were the bad man people say I am, could I enjoy its song?' He wrote every morning at an open window on the ground floor, and one morning saw the Miss Beams' cat cross the street, and thought, 'That cat will get my bird.' He went out and filled his pocket with stones, and whenever he saw the cat, threw a stone. Somebody, perhaps the typist, must have laughed, for the rest of the tale fills me with doubt. I was passing through Dublin just on my way to Coole; he came to my hotel. 'I remembered how early that cat got up. I thought it might get the blackbird if I was not there to protect it, so I set a trap. The Miss Beams wrote to the Society for the Prevention of Cruelty to Animals, and I am carrying on a correspondence with its secretary, cat versus bird.' (Perhaps, after all, the archives of the Society do contain that correspondence. The tale is not yet incredible.) I passed through Dublin again, perhaps on my way back. Moore came to see me in seeming great depression. 'Remember that trap?' – 'Yes.' – 'Remember that bird?' – 'Yes.' – 'I have caught the bird.'

From *Dramatis Personae* by W. B. Yeats

Moore's behaviour is curious as he had earlier, in London, formed a deep attachment to a cat of his own, but its demise managed to endow him with another adversary or two. In this incident, recalled by himself, he undertips his maid Jane, prior to his departure for Dublin

Your life is all pleasure and glory, but I shall have to look round for another place, I heard her say, as she pulled at the straps of my portmanteau, and her resentment against me increased when I put a sovereign into her hand. She cooked me excellent dinners, making life infinitely agreeable to me; a present of five pounds was certainly her due, and a sovereign was more than enough for the porter, whom I suspected of poisoning my cat – a large, grey, and affectionate animal upon whom Jane, without the aid of a doctor, had impressed the virtue of chastity so successfully that he never sought the she, but remained at home, a quiet, sober animal that did not drink milk, only water, and who, when thrown up to the ceiling, refrained from turning round, content to curl himself into a ball, convinced that my hands would receive him – an animal to whom I was so much attached that I had decided to bring him with me in a basket; but a few weeks before my departure he died of a stoppage in his entrails, brought about probably by a morsel of sponge fried in grease – a detestable and cruel way of poisoning cats often practised by porters. It was pitiful to watch the poor animal go to his pan and try to relieve himself, but he never succeeded in passing anything, and after the third day refused to try any more. We had recourse to a dose of castor oil, but it did not move him and after consultation we resolved to give an enema if he would allow us. The poor animal allowed us to do our will; he seemed to know that we were trying to help him, and received my caresses and my words with kindly looks while Jane administered the enema, saying that she didn't mind if the whole courtyard saw her do it, all she cared for was to save Jim's life. But the enema did not help him, and after it he neither ate nor drank, but lay down stoically to die. Death did not come to him for a long while; it seemed as if he would never drop off, and at last, unable to bear the sight of his sufferings any longer, Jane held his head in a pail of water, and after a few gasps the trial of life was over. It may have been that he died of the fur that he licked away, collecting in a ball in his entrails, and that there is not cause for me to regret the sovereign given to the porter when the great van drove up to my door to take away the bedroom and kitchen furniture.

From *Salve* by George Moore

A Successful Operation

In his autobiography, Aleister Crowley gives a chillingly dispassionate account of a practical experiment carried out in his teens.

There is one amazing incident; at the age of fourteen as near as I can remember. I must premise that I have always been exceptionally tender-hearted except to tyrants, for whom I think no tortures bad enough. In particular, I am uniformly kind to animals; no question of cruelty or sadism arises in the incident which I am about to narrate.

I had been told 'A cat has nine lives.' I deduced that it must be practically impossible to kill a cat. As usual, I became full of ambition to perform the feat. (Observe that I took my information unquestioningly *au pied de la lettre*.) Perhaps through some analogy with the story of Hercules and the hydra, I got it into my head that the nine lives of the cat must be taken more or less simultaneously. I therefore caught a cat, and having administered a large dose of arsenic I chloroformed it, hanged it above the gas jet, stabbed it, cut its throat, smashed its skull and, when it had been pretty thoroughly burnt, drowned it and threw it out of the window that the fall might remove the ninth life. In fact, the operation was successful; I had killed the cat. I remember that all the time I was genuinely sorry for the animal; I simply forced myself to carry out the experiment in the interest of pure science.

From *The Confessions of Aleister Crowley: An Autobiography*, ed. John Symonds and Kenneth Grant

Ceauşescu and the Cat

D r Theodor Ionescu was the bone surgeon at the Brancovenesc Hospital in Bucharest – as steeped in traditions and as much a part of the city as Bart's in London – who met Ceauşescu when he came to see the earthquake victims in 1977. The hospital treated 30,000 patients a year, handling 50,000 emergency outpatients a year, 200 to 300 emergency patients a day.

But it lay in the path of the Boulevard of Socialist Victory. The doctors in the hospital saw with mounting dismay the demolition of the homes around them, till in 1985 only the hospital stood like an isolated stump in the wasteland.

Dr Ionescu told me: 'One morning, it was a Sunday, without any announcement, he entered the hospital gate. With him was the mayor for this district of Bucharest and his dog, Corbu.' The doctor had heard that Corbu by that time enjoyed the rank of Colonel. 'Of course, there were many Securitate bodyguards around. Inside, there was a discussion about the future of the hospital. While this was going on, Colonel Corbu saw a cat.' The hospital, like many public buildings in Bucharest at the time, was infested with rats, partly because the regime was economising on rat poison. The doctors' response was to resort to nature: the hospital thronged with cats.

'The dog left its master for the cat. The cat skittered off with the dog barking after it. Eventually the dog caught the cat on a doorstep. There was a terrific fight. The dog caught the cat by the neck, but the cat scratched the dog's nose and made it bleed. Ceauşescu's reaction was very violent. He first shouted "Corbu" when it ran away after the cat. Then he started screaming at the bodyguards: "What are you doing standing there? Move!" Three of them ran to split up the dog and cat fighting. Of course, all three of them ended up being scratched to pieces. Corbu came back with blood on its nose. Ceauşescu hit the dog with his fist. It was a moment of despair, because his closest companion had left him for a cat.

'Ceauşescu was very furious. He turned around and left. The bodyguard who looked after the dog picked up Corbu and took him to Elias Hospital.' (This was one of the best hospitals in Bucharest, the preserve of the party's sick.) 'That afternoon a Securitate car came around, with three bodyguards, to look for the cat. The three Securitate men were very desperate to find the cat because they were afraid they would lose their jobs. So the whole hospital started to look for the cat. All the administration, all the nurses and the porters looked up and down, searched high and low. They caught lots of cats and brought them in front of the three Securitate men and the director of the hospital. But there were so many cats in the hospital. They couldn't find the right one. Cat after cat after cat was caught and shown to them – but it wasn't the right one. At 10.30 that night, having searched all afternoon and most of the evening, they found the right cat. They knew it was the right one because it had a tear on its skin where Corbu had bitten it. The carpenter of the hospital made a special cage. While he was doing so the cat was put in an emergency room and looked after by a special bodyguard. The cat was guarded all night and in the morning she was fed and watered. Usually,' the doctor said, 'we didn't feed the cats. Then the cat went in the special cage to the Institute of Veterinary Medicine. After two weeks we received a note from the Institute of Veterinary Medicine saying the cat had been checked for disease but was all right. In those two weeks Corbu was not allowed to go anywhere near Ceauşescu. But even though the cat was all right, we knew that this fight between the dog and the cat meant the end of the hospital.'

The bulldozers came when Ceauşescu was on a trip to North Korea. In three days they demolished the hospital, its wards, its gardens, its traditions and memories and an exquisite marble staircase. The staircase had been built by the hospital's founder, a nineteenth-century Romanian aristocrat called Grigore Constantin Brancoveanu, who had promoted something of a cultural renaissance in the country in the 1840s. The hospital had an inscription, set in marble, bearing the legend: 'Who endangers this hospital will be cast out from the love of God.'

From *The Life and Evil Times of Nicolae Ceauşescu* by John Sweeney

Cats and Couples

my cat and i

Girls are simply the prettiest things
My cat and i believe
And we're always saddened
When it's time for them to leave

We watch them titivating
(that often takes a while)
And though they keep us waiting
My cat & i just smile

We like to see them to the door
Say how sad it couldn't last
Then my cat and i go back inside
And talk about the past.

From *Watchwords* by Roger McGough

The Appointment

Yes, he said, darling, yes, of course you tried
To come, but you were kept. That's what I thought –
But something in his heart struggled and cried
Mortally, like a bird the cat has caught.

L. A. G. Strong

Hair Today, No Her Tomorrow

'I've been upstairs,' she said.
'Oh yes?' I said.
'I found a hair,' she said.
'A hair?' I said.
'In the bed,' she said.
'From a head?' I said.
'It's not mine,' she said.
'Was it black?' I said.
'It was,' she said.
'I'll explain,' I said.
'You swine,' she said.
'Not quite,' I said.
'I'm going,' she said.
'Please don't,' I said.
'I hate you!' she said.
'You do?' I said.
'Of course,' she said.
'But why?' I said.
'That black hair,' she said.
'A pity,' I said.

'Time for truth,' she said.
'For confessions?' I said.
'Me too,' she said.
'You what?' I said.
'Someone else,' she said.
'Oh dear,' I said.
'So there!' she said.
'Ah well,' I said.
'Guess who?' she said.
'Don't say,' I said.
'I will,' she said.
'You would,' I said.
'Your friend,' she said.
'Oh damn,' I said.
'And his friend,' she said.
'Him too?' I said.

'And the rest,' she said.
'Good God,' I said.

'What's that?' she said.
'What's what?' I said.
'That noise?' she said.
'Upstairs?' I said.
'Yes,' she said.
'The new cat,' I said.
'A cat?' she said.
'It's black,' I said.
'Black?' she said.
'Long-haired,' I said.
'Oh no,' she said.
'Oh yes,' I said.
'Oh shit!' she said.
'Goodbye,' I said.

'I lied,' she said.
'You lied?' I said.
'Of course,' she said.
'About my friend?' I said.
'Y-ess,' she said.
'And the others?' I said.
'Ugh,' she said.
'How odd,' I said.
'I'm forgiven?' she said.
'Of course,' I said.
'I'll stay?' she said.
'Please don't,' I said.
'But why?' she said.
'I lied,' I said.
'About what?' she said.
'The new cat,' I said.
'It's white,' I said.

From *Storm Damage* by Brian Patten

Taking the Cure

At a fashionable spa, the newly married Claudine employs her cat to provoke her snobbish friends.

Her white cat, on a lead, was asleep in a wicker chair. 'A chair that costs two sous, like a lady's,' Claudine had insisted. 'Not an iron one because Fanchette feels the cold in her behind!'

'I'm going to play a game!' she cried, suddenly inspired.

'You make me slightly apprehensive,' said her husband with his usual loving glance.

He was smoking fragrant Egyptian cigarettes and sat, for the most part, silent and detached as if he had transferred all his life to the woman he called his 'darling child'.

'A nice party game! I'm going to guess from your faces what diseases you've come here to cure, and, when I make a mistake, I'll pay a forfeit.'

'Pay me one straight away,' cried Marthe. 'I'm as fit as a fiddle.'

'Me too,' growled Maugis, whose face was purple under the panama pulled down as far as his moustache.

'Me too,' said Renaud quietly.

'So am I!' sighed Léon, pale and exhausted.

Claudine, enchantingly pretty in a white straw bonnet, tied under the chin with white tulle strings, menaced us with a pointed finger.

'Attention, all! You're going to see that every one of you has come here for pleasure . . . just like me!'

She picked up her little book again and distributed her diagnoses like so many bouquets.

'Marthe, for you "Acne and eczema"! For you, Renaud . . . let's see . . . ah! "furunculosis". Pretty, isn't it? It sounds like the name of a flower. In Annie, I divine "intermittent erysipelas" and in Léon "scrofulous anaemia" . . .'

'He won't thank you much for that,' broke in Renaud who saw a sickly smile on my brother-in-law's face . . .

'And in Maugis . . . Maugis . . . oh, bother, I can't find anything else . . . Ah! I've got it! In Maugis, I diagnose . . . "recurrent pruritus of the genital parts".'

There was an explosion of laughter! Marthe showed all her teeth and impudently directed her laugh straight at the furious Maugis who lifted his panama to pour out a stream of invectives against the brazen hussy. Renaud tried half-heartedly to impose silence, for a respectable group behind us had just taken flight with much scandalized clatter of overturned chairs.

'Pay no attention,' cried Claudine. 'Those people who've gone are just plain jealous,' (she picked up her book again) 'they've only got miserable little diseases not worth having . . . they're just . . . "chronic metritises", petty "aural catarrhs" or miserable twopenny-halfpenny "leucorrheas"!'

'What about you yourself, you poisonous little thing?' burst out Maugis. 'What the hell have you come here for, besides making yourself a thorough pest and disturbing everyone's peace?'

'Hush!' She leant forward, with an impressive mysterious air. 'Don't tell anyone. I've come here for the sake of Fanchette, who suffers from the same complaint as you.'

From *Claudine and Annie* by Colette, transl. Antonia White

A Disastrous Beginning

A cat-nap disturbed by human passion affords a suitably bizarre initiation for Gabriel García Márquez's lovers

The first thing Florentino Ariza observed in the living room was that the door to the only bedroom was open, and that the bed was huge and luxurious with a brocaded quilt and a headboard with brass foliage. That disturbed him. She must have realized it, for she crossed the living room and closed the bedroom door. Then she invited him to sit down on a flowered cretonne sofa where a sleeping cat was lying, and she placed her collection of albums on the coffee table. Florentino Ariza began to leaf through them in an unhurried way, thinking more about his next step than about what he was seeing, and then he looked up and saw that her eyes were full of tears. He advised her to cry to her heart's content, and to feel no shame, for there was no greater relief than weeping, but he suggested that she loosen her bodice first. He hurried to help her, because her bodice was tightly fastened in the back with a long closure of crossed laces. He did not have to unlace them all, for the bodice burst open from sheer internal pressure, and her astronomical bosom was able to breathe freely.

Florentino Ariza, who had never lost the timidity of a novice even in comfortable circumstances, risked a superficial caress on her neck with the tips of his fingers, and she writhed and moaned like a spoiled child and did not stop crying. Then he kissed her on the same spot, just as softly, and he could not kiss her a second time because she turned toward him with all her monumental body, eager and warm, and they rolled in an embrace on the floor. The cat on the sofa awoke with a screech and jumped on top of them. They groped like desperate virgins and found each other any way they could, wallowing in the torn albums, fully dressed, soaked with sweat, and more concerned with avoiding the furious claws of the cat than with the disastrous love they were making. But beginning the following night, their scratches still bleeding, they continued to make love for several years.

From *Love in the Time of Cholera* by Gabriel García Márquez

Uninvited Cats

A Phantom Army

In Mervyn Peake's *Gormenghast*, Doctor Prunesquallor has to cope with an unusual nocturnal visit.

But he was not destined to more than a few moments of relaxation, for feet were soon to be heard outside his window. Only two of them, it was true, but there was something in the weight and deliberation of the tread that reminded him of an army moving in perfect unison, a dread and measured sound. The rain had quietened and the sound of each foot as it struck the ground was alarmingly clear.

Prunesquallor could recognize that portentous gait among a million. But in the silence of the evening his mind flew to the phantom army it awakened in his leap-frogging brain. What was there in the clockwork stepping of an upright host to contract the throat and bring, as does the thought of a sliced lemon, that sharp astringency to throat and jaw? Why do the tears begin to gather? And the heart to thud?

He had no time to ponder the matter now, so at one and the same time he tossed a mop of grey thatch from his brow and an army-on-the-march from his mind.

Reaching the door before his bell could clang the servants into redundance he opened it, and to the massive figure who was about to whack the door with her fist –

'I welcome your Ladyship,' he said. His body inclined itself a little from the hips and his teeth flashed, while he wondered what, in the name of all that was heterodox, the Countess thought she was doing in visiting her physician at this time of night. She visited nobody, by day *or* night. That was one of the things about her. Nevertheless, here she was.

'Hold your horses.' Her voice was heavy, but not loud.

One of Doctor Prunesquallor's eyebrows shot to the top of his forehead. It was a peculiar remark to be greeted with. It might have been supposed that he was about to embrace her. The very notion appalled him.

But when she said: 'You can come in now,' not only did his other eyebrow fly up his forehead, but it set its counterpart atremble with the speed of its uprush.

To be told he could 'come in now' when he was already inside was weird enough; but the idea of being given permission to enter his own house by a guest was grotesque.

The slow, heavy, quiet authority in the voice made the situation even more embarrassing. She had entered his hall. 'I wish to see you,' she said, but her eyes were on the door which Prunesquallor was closing. When it had barely six inches to go before the night was locked out and the latch had clicked – 'Hold!' she said, in a rather deeper tone, 'hold hard!' And then, with her big lips pursed like a child's, she gave breath to a long whistle of peculiar sweetness. A tender and forlorn note to escape from so ponderous a being.

The doctor, as he turned to her, was a picture of perplexed inquiry, though his teeth were still shining gaily. But as he turned something caught the corner of his eye. Something white. Something that moved.

Between the space left by the all-but-closed door, and very close to the ground, Doctor Prunesquallor saw a face as round as a hunter's moon, as soft as fur. And this was no wonder, for it was a face of fur, peculiarly blanched in the dim light of the hall. No sooner had the Doctor reacted to this face than another took its place, and close upon it, silent as death, came a third, a fourth, a fifth . . . In single file there slid into the hall, so close upon each other's tails that they might have been a continuous entity, her ladyship's white clowder.

Prunesquallor, feeling a little dizzy, watched the undulating stream flow past his feet as he stood with his hand on the doorknob. Would they never end? He had watched them for over two minutes.

He turned to the Countess. She stood in coiling froth like a lighthouse. By the dim glow of the hall lamp her red hair threw out a sullen light.

Prunesquallor was perfectly happy again. For what had irked him was not the cats, but the obscure commands of the Countess. Their meaning was now self-evident. And yet, how peculiar to have enjoined a swarm of cats to hold their horses!

The very thought of it got hold of his eyebrows again, which had lowered themselves reluctantly while he waited for his chance to close the door, and they had leapt up his forehead as though a pistol had been cracked and a prize awaited the fastest.

'We're . . . all . . . here,' said the Countess. Prunesquallor turned to the door and saw that the stream had, indeed, run dry. He shut the door.

'Well, well, well, well!' he trilled, standing on his toes and fluttering his hands, as though he were about to take off like a fairy. 'How *delightful*! how very, very *delightful* that you should call, your Ladyship. God bless my ascetic soul! If you haven't whipped the old hermit out of his introspection. Ha, ha, ha, ha, ha! And here, as you put it, you all are. There's no doubt about that, is there?

What a party we will have! *Mew*-sical chairs and all! ha ha ha ha ha ha ha.'

The almost unbearable pitch of his laughter created an absolute stillness in the hall. The cats, sitting bolt upright, had their round eyes fixed on him.

From *Gormenghast* by Mervyn Peake

Expeditionary Cats

On 27 March 1911, from an archaeological dig at Carchemish on the Upper Euphrates, T. E. Lawrence wrote a letter full of good-humoured complaint to his friend E. T. Leeds, Assistant Keeper of the Department of Antiquities at the Ashmolean Museum, Oxford.

Then there are the cats: Father (who is only suffered, not encouraged); he comes in at the holes in the roof and walls by night, and offends lewdly in our beds. Then D.G.H. throws a boot towards it and hits Thompson, and plants it in the bath, or knocks the light down: and when he has got out and repaired damages he finds the cat in his bed when he lies down again. So much for Father. Mother is plaintive, and rather a bore: she wails aloud for food, usually about 2 a.m.: then she gets it, but in a tin: of late she receives sympathy, in spite of one very irregular night, when she woke me up with her claws over the face, and the rest of the expedition (who sleep together, with piled revolvers) by trying to escape my yells by jumping off the jam-tins through the window. She only knocked the tins down of course, and fell short in the wash-basin. Of late Mother has been in the family way, with Thompson a very gallant midwife. Her four kittens are David George (a tab), Gregori (a black), Haj Wahid (ginger),* and R. Campbell, a sort of Scots Grey. They make a ghastly noise in the Expeditionary bedroom half the night: I am a tolerable sleeper, but the others get up two or three times each, and draw beads on each other with revolvers.

From *The Letters of T. E. Lawrence*, sel. and ed. Malcolm Brown

*Named after Gregori, chief foreman, and Haj Wahid, expedition cook.

Questioning the Universe

A Manx cat treads on Virginia Woolf's thoughts.

If by good luck there had been an ash-tray handy, if one had not knocked the ash out of the window in default, if things had been a little different from what they were, one would not have seen, presumably, a cat without a tail. The sight of that abrupt and truncated animal padding softly across the quadrangle changed by some fluke of the subconscious intelligence the emotional light for me. It was as if some one had let fall a shade . . . Certainly, as I watched the Manx cat pause in the middle of the lawn as if it too questioned the universe, something seemed lacking, something seemed different. But what . . .?

From *A Room of One's Own* by Virginia Woolf

Stré-chi

While living in Italy Max Beerbohm kept in touch with his literary contemporaries by naming his pets after them. A kitten acquired in 1920 signally failed to live up to its namesake, as Beerbohm wrote to its 'Illustrissimo Eponymisto Inglese'.

'Dear Lytton Strachey, Some time in 1913, at this address, my wife and I acquired a young fox-terrier. We debated as to what to call him, and, as Henry James had just been having his 70th birthday, and as his books had given me more pleasure than those of any living man, I, rather priggishly perhaps, insisted that the dog should be known as James. But this was a name which Italian peasants, who are the only neighbours we have, of course would not be able to pronounce at all. So we were phonetic and called the name of the dog *Yah-mès*. And this did very well. By this name he was known far and wide – but not for long; for alas, he died of distemper. Now that we are re-established here, we haven't another dog; dogs aren't so necessary to one as they seem to be in England, and they have an odd and tactless way of making one feel that one *is* in England – perhaps because they don't gesticulate and don't speak one word of Italian and seem to expect to find rabbits among the olive-groves and to have bones of Welsh mutton thrown to them from the luncheon table. But the other day we were given a small kitten – charming in itself and somehow not distinctive of local colour. The old question arose: what shall we call it? Again I laid myself open to the charge of priggishness, perhaps. And again you will perhaps think I have taken a liberty. But – well, there it is: no book by a living man has given me so much pleasure – so much lasting pleasure in dipping and re-reading since I wrote to you – as your "Eminent Victorians". And the name of that kitten is, and the name of that cat will be: *Stré-chi* (or rather Stré-cci). I do hope you don't mind. I am sure you would be amused if you heard the passing-by peasants enticing it by your hardly recognisable name. We will re-christen it if you like.'

This letter was written from Villino Chiaro on 7 July 1920. Lytton, in his reply, expressed his sense of honour at this appellation, and two years later, in June 1922, Max took up the sequel to this story in another letter. 'The kitten of whom I told you last year is now a confirmed cat. He is much larger than he seemed likely to become, and is vigorous and vagrant, but not, I am sorry to say, either affectionate or intelligent. It is not known that he ever caught a mouse; he dislikes rain, but has no knowledge of how to avoid it if it falls; and if one caresses him he is very likely to scratch one. He is, however, very proud of his name, and sends his respectful regards to his Illustrissimo Eponymisto Inglese.'

From *Lytton Strachey* by Michael Holroyd

Kittens and Canaries

In 1903 George Bernard Shaw made a small loan to Francis Collison, a man whom he referred to as 'an occasional crony' and 'a bookseller-newsagent-philosopher-breeder of kittens'. In gratitude, Mr Collison sent Shaw a canary, with the offer of a kitten to follow. Shaw's response was not encouraging.

20th August 1903

Now I ask you, Mr Collison, as a sensible man, what the devil you suppose I want with a canary. I am a vegetarian, and can't eat it; and it is not big enough to eat me. But you are not a sensible man: you are a 'fancier'; and you believe that the height of earthly happiness is to be surrounded with pigeons & Persian cats & guinea pigs & rabbits, with a tub full of toads & newts under the counter. I once had a canary, a little green brute that flew in through the open window one day & would not go away. I hated it and it hated me. I bought it a cage – a thing I abhor – & gave it everything I could find at the seedsman's; but it was utterly miserable & did its best to make me miserable until some benevolent person stole it. I have been happy ever since until this day, when I have received from Woking the devastating news that you have inflicted another canary on me . . . And now, having taken advantage of my being away on my holiday to introduce this ornithological pest into my household, you want to send me a kitten as well. Why, man, the kitten will kill the canary when it grows up. Have you no common sense? . . . What did I ever do to . . . you that you should heap these injuries on me? Did my books ever do you any harm? did they disturb you with silly whistlings at your work, or bring forth litters of little books that you had to drown?

. . . My only hope is in the gardener's wife. She has one canary already; and perhaps, if I make her a present of the cage, she will consent to take the other if I offer her five shillings a week for the term of its natural life. I shall then hear it only when I walk in the garden; and at every trill I shall curse the name of F. Collison.

From *Dear Mr Shaw*, ed. Vivian Elliot

Delmore

Susan Cheever recalls how her father, John Cheever, invented a blackly comic role for an unwanted cat with half a tail.

Our family had a cat named Delmore Schwartz, and my father hated him. His descriptions of our household animals and their feelings, as well as his use of voices he attributed to them, were sometimes unusually revealing. His friends and family got letters from the Cheever dogs, complete with hilarious misspellings, describing the family goings-on from their point of view. Other letters almost always mentioned the dogs, whom he loved, or the cats, whom he didn't.

Delmore himself was the unwanted gift of my father's old friend Josie Herbst, who brought him with her when she came for lunch one day in 1960. Josie said the cat was a kitten named Blackie who had been owned by her friend Elizabeth Pollet, the former wife of Delmore Schwartz. My father suspected Josie of lying about the cat's age; he suspected her of unloading an aged, bad-tempered animal on her country friends. The evidence supported him. Blackie the kitten was a large animal with a worn coat and only half a tail. My father made up a past for the cat. Schwartz had locked him in a bathroom for months at a time; he had lost his tail in an accident with a refrigerator door. Blackie was renamed Delmore.

Josie had never made any money, and this kept the edge on her pro-labor 1930s politics. It was the responsibility of the rich to care for the poor, she felt. My father was rich, Delmore was poor. My father accepted this responsibility, but with reluctance. At first, Delmore was used as comic relief. At school in Woodstock, and later at college in Providence, Rhode Island, I got letters from my father about how he had washed the storm windows so well that Delmore had tried to jump through one and folded up like an accordion, or how Delmore had tried to leap from the bathtub to the windowsill and landed in the toilet. Other people's cats caught mice. Delmore sulkily coexisted with the mice and shrews that proliferated in the pantry and the kitchen cupboards. When he did catch a mouse, he was sure to leave it in the bathtub or in one of my father's shoes. Gradually Delmore became a scapegoat as well as a clown. It was Delmore who woke my parents with his angry shrieks at dawn, and who continued to yowl when my father went downstairs, presented him with a breakfast he refused to eat, and finally drop-kicked him out the kitchen door. It was Delmore who left mutilated bird carcasses on the front stairs when the Canfields came over for dinner from Bedford or when the Steegmullers arrived for lunch in their Rolls-Royce. It was Delmore who made a point of relieving himself in the darkest parts of the hallway so that you couldn't see it until you – or a guest – had stepped in it. He even turned up as the sinister black cat in *Bullet Park*. When Hammer's cat comes home smelling of perfume, Hammer follows the scent and the cat into trouble. In 1964, when my father telephoned me at college to say that Delmore was dead, his first words were, 'I want you to know that I didn't have anything to do with it.'

From *Home Before Dark* by Susan Cheever

A Furry Multitude

In pensive mood after the death of his fiancé, Brendan Archer finds The Majestic Hotel of J. G. Farrell's *Troubles* unnervingly *complet*.

On an impulse he went inside. It was very dark. The heavy curtains were still half-drawn as he had left them six months earlier, only allowing the faintest glimmer of light to penetrate. The bottles and glasses on the bar glowed in the shadows; there was a strong smell of cats and some silent movement in the darkness. Looking up, he was taken aback for a moment to see a pair of disembodied yellowish eyes glaring down at him from the ceiling. It was only when he had moved to the window to draw back the curtains that he realized that the room was boiling with cats.

They were everywhere he looked; nervously patrolling the carpet in every direction; piled together in easy chairs to form random masses of fur; curled up individually on the bar stools. They picked their way daintily between the bottles and glasses. Pointed timorous heads peered out at him from beneath chairs, tables and any other object capable of giving refuge. There was even a massive marmalade animal crouching high above him, piloting the spreading antlers of a stag's head fixed to the wall (this must be the owner of the glaring yellow eyes that had startled him a moment ago). He had a moment of revulsion at this furry multitude before the room abruptly dissolved in a shattering percussion of sneezes. A fine grey cascade of dust descended slowly around him. 'Well, I'll be damned, where the devil did this lot come from? All the cats in Kilnalough must be using the Majestic to breed in . . . and not all of them are wild either.' Indeed, led by the giant marmalade cat which from the stag's brow had launched itself heavily into the air to land on the back of a chair and thence to slither to the floor, they were moving towards him making the most fearful noise. In a moment he was up to his shins in a seething carpet of fur.

He moved brusquely, however, and the animals scattered and watched him in fear. The smell had become nauseating. He tried to open the window but the wooden frame must have swollen with the dampness; it was wedged tight, immovable. He was about to leave when his eye fell on the envelope which lay on the bar. It was the letter from Angela which Edward had handed to him on the day of her funeral; his name was written on the envelope in the precise handwriting which had once been so familiar. He thought of it lying here, Angela's final message to him, through the long months he had been away, the cats multiplying around it, the seasons revolving. Uneasily he opened it . . . but he did not read it. It was much too long. He put it in his pocket and picked his way sadly through the cats to the door.

From *Troubles* by J. G. Farrell

Cats About Town

Greebo

To Nanny Ogg Greebo was still the cute little kitten that chased balls of wool around the floor.

To the rest of the world he was an enormous tomcat, a parcel of incredibly indestructible life forces in a skin that looked less like a fur than a piece of bread that had been left in a damp place for a fortnight. Strangers often took pity on him because his ears were non-existent and his face looked as though a bear had camped on it. They could not know that this was because Greebo, as a matter of feline pride, would attempt to fight or rape absolutely anything, up to and including a four-horse logging wagon. Ferocious dogs would whine and hide under the stairs when Greebo sauntered down the street. Foxes kept away from the village. Wolves made a detour.

'He's an old softy really,' said Nanny.

Greebo turned upon Granny Weatherwax a yellow-eyed stare of self-satisfied malevolence, such as cats always reserve for people who don't like them, and purred. Greebo was possibly the only cat who could snigger in purr.

Greebo later undergoes a startling transformation when the witches take him to the Ball.

The witches landed in an alleyway a few minutes ahead of the coach.

'I don't hold with this,' said Granny. 'It's the sort of thing Lily does. You can't expect me to like this. Think of that wolf!'

Nanny lifted Greebo out of his nest among the bristles.

'But Greebo's nearly human anyway,' she said.

'Hah!'

'And it'll only be temp'ry, even with the three of us doing it,' she said. 'Anyway, it'll be int'resting to see if it works.'

'Yes, but it's *wrong*,' said Granny.

'Not for these parts, it seems,' said Nanny.

'Besides,' said Magrat virtuously, 'it can't be bad if *we're* doing it. We're the good ones.'

'Oh yes, so we is,' said Granny, 'and there was me forgetting it for a minute there.'

Nanny stood back. Greebo, aware that something was expected of him, sat up.

'You must admit we can't think of anything better, Granny,' said Magrat.

Granny hesitated. But under all the revulsion was the little treacherous flame of fascination with the idea. Besides, she and Greebo had hated one another cordially for years. Almost human, eh? Give him a taste of it, then, and see how he likes it . . . She felt a bit ashamed of the thought. But not much.

'Oh, *all* right.'

They concentrated.

As Lily knew, changing the shape of an object is one of the hardest magics there is. But it's easier if the object is alive. After all, a living thing already knows what shape it is. All you have to do is change its mind.

Greebo yawned and stretched. To his amazement he went on stretching.

Through the pathways of his feline brain surged a tide of belief. He suddenly believed he was human. He wasn't simply under the *impression* that he was human; he believed it implicitly. The sheer force of the unshakeable belief flowed out into his morphic field, overriding its objections, rewriting the very blueprint of his self.

Fresh instructions surged back.

If he was human, he didn't need all this fur. And he ought to be bigger . . .

The witches watched, fascinated.

'I *never* thought we'd do it,' said Granny.

. . . no points on the ears, the whiskers were too long . . .

. . . he needed more muscle, all these bones were the wrong shape, these legs ought to be longer . . .

And then it was finished.

Greebo unfolded himself and stood up, a little unsteadily.

Nanny stared, her mouth open.

Then her eyes moved downwards.

'Cor,' she said.

'I think,' said Granny Weatherwax, 'that we'd better imagine some clothes on him *right now*.'

That was easy enough. When Greebo had been clothed to her satisfaction Granny nodded and stood back.

'Magrat, you can open your eyes,' she said.

'I hadn't got them closed.'

'Well, you should have had.'

Greebo turned slowly, a faint, lazy smile on his scarred face. As a human, his nose was broken and a black patch covered his bad eye. But the other one glittered like the sins of angels, and his smile was the downfall of saints. Female ones, anyway.

Perhaps it was pheromones, or the way his muscles rippled under his black leather shirt. Greebo broadcast a kind of greasy diabolic sexuality in the megawatt range. Just looking at him was enough to set dark wings fluttering in the crimson night.

'Uh, Greebo,' said Nanny.

He opened his mouth. Incisors glittered.

'Wrowwwwl,' he said.

From Witches Abroad by Terry Pratchett

Gilding the Whiskers

The cat Behemoth prepares for a ball.

'A llow me to introduce to you . . .' Woland began, then interrupted himself. 'No, really, he looks too ridiculous! Just look what he's done to himself while he was under the bed!'

The cat, covered in dust and standing on its hind legs, bowed to Margarita. Round its neck it was now wearing a made-up white bow tie on an elastic band, with a pair of ladies' mother-of-pearl binoculars hanging on a cord. It had also gilded its whiskers.

'What have you done?' exclaimed Woland. 'Why have you gilded your whiskers? And what on earth do you want with a white tie when you haven't even got any trousers?'

'Trousers don't suit cats, messire,' replied the cat with great dignity. 'Why don't you tell me to wear boots? Cats always wear boots in fairy tales. But have you ever seen a cat going to a ball without a tie? I don't want to make myself look ridiculous. One likes to look as smart as one can. And that also applies to my opera-glasses, messire!'

'But your whiskers? . . .'

'I don't see why,' the cat objected coldly, 'Azazello and Koroviev are allowed to cover themselves in powder and why powder is better than gilt. I just powdered my whiskers, that's all. It would be a different matter if I'd shaved myself! A clean-shaven cat is something monstrous, that I agree. But I see . . .' – here the cat's voice trembled with pique – '. . . that this is a conspiracy to be rude about my appearance. Clearly I am faced with a problem – shall I go to the ball or not? What do you say, messire?'

Outraged, the cat had so inflated itself that it looked about to explode at any second.

'Ah, the rogue, the sly rogue,' said Woland shaking his head. 'Whenever he's losing a game he starts a spiel like a quack-doctor at a fair. Sit down and stop all this hot air.'

'Very well,' replied the cat, sitting down, 'but I must object. My remarks are by no means all hot air, as you so vulgarly put it, but a series of highly appo- site syllogisms which would be appreciated by such connoisseurs as Sextus Empiricus, Martian Capella, even, who knows, Aristotle himself.'

From *The Master and Margarita* by Mikhail Bulgakov, transl. Michael Glenny

Great Success!

In her youth Elinor Glyn collected tiger skins and the inclusion of one in her infa- mous 1907 novel *Three Weeks* gave rise to the comic verse, 'Would you like to sin/ With Elinor Glyn/ On a Tiger Skin/ Or would you prefer to err/ With her/ On some other fur.' The 'other fur' in Glyn's life belonged to the Persian cats, which she began collecting in middle age and which she used to no less spectacular effect, at this public appearance she made in her seventies.

The most enjoyable purely literary event that she attended was a literary lunch at the Dorchester Hotel in March 1939. Elinor was a guest speaker and she wore, with fine panache, her huge Persian cat Candide, asleep, round her neck instead of a fox fur. During the speeches Candide would open a bale- ful and somewhat desiccatting eye upon the speaker and then go to sleep again. 'Great success!' commented Elinor in her diary.

From *Elinor Glyn* by Anthony Glyn, 1955

Advertising with a Dasch!

Orlando, the Marmalade Cat, has recently returned to fashion and is sufficiently eccentric to merit his place in posterity. Here Orlando hits on a novel and daring scheme to promote his hospital.

It was so long since any patients had come to the hospital that it had been quite forgotten. Orlando thought of a fine scheme to advertise it.

First he needed a pair of dachshunds, and these he found at the Lost Dogs' Home.

'How much do they cost?' he asked the kennel man.

'We sell 'em by the yard, sir. Eight and sixpence a yard,' was the answer. 'There be one yard and seventeen sixteenths all told, sir.'   They measured rather more, really, but the lady dog managed to shorten herself, for she was afraid that Orlando would find their full length too expensive and only buy one dog; it would break her heart to be parted from her husband.

'I will take them both,' said Orlando.

'Shall I fold them up or will you take them flat, sir?'

'Just as they are, please,' replied Orlando, and he rode them home like a circus rider. Spick and Span, as the dogs were called, were overjoyed to have found a home, and already loved their new master.

Orlando made a tiny stretcher to which he harnessed Spick and Span. He explained to the kittens their important part in this scheme. 'Blanche, you will lie on the stretcher with your eyes closed and a thermometer in your mouth. Spick and Span will parade you through the main streets of the town. People will think you are pale from a very serious illness and some will follow you home to make sure that you are going to a really good hospital.'

When all was ready Orlando spread a newspaper over the whole arrangement, with holes for the Dogs' noses and tails to keep it in place.

'You will keep this on,' Orlando explained, 'until you reach the centre of the town, for nobody must see you coming out of the hospital as well as going in. That would give the game away. Now off you go!'

There was an anxious moment when a man in the street remarked to his friend: 'Odd! There isn't a breath of wind yet that old newspaper is being blown along as if by a regular gale.' Spick and Span, however ran quickly out of sight and Blanche folded the paper and put it under the pillow for further use.

Blanche arrived home followed by an anxious group of people who waited near the hospital hoping for news of the little patient.

'The scheme is working well,' whispered Orlando. 'Now Tinkle, you must wear this patch over one eye and get on to the stretcher. People will think you have been fighting and are black with bruises. They will certainly follow you to see that you get the right treatment. Au revoir!' and Orlando fixed the newspaper over them.

Tinkle had an adventure on his journey. An old man who collects wastepaper in the streets tweaked the newspaper off the stretcher, thinking it was rubbish. Spick and Span, however, reached the main street in a flash, before anyone had seen them, and all was well.

A number of people followed Tinkle, all very concerned as to his welfare.

Then Pansy got into the stretcher, bandaged all over to look as though she had been in a bad accident.

She, too, collected quite a crowd.

The people waiting outside the hospital thought it must be a very good one, as there were so many stretcher cases going in. Bit by bit they remembered that they suffered from some ailment or hurt, and one by one they all went in for treatment.

Orlando hung a stethoscope round his neck with which to listen to 99ses, fixed a light-reflector on his forehead to shine on the Arrs in throats, and a special kind of wrist-watch on his tail with which to count pulses. But where was he to put his thermometer and fountain pen? He had no pockets in his fur like the kangaroo. Grace saved the situation by cutting the thermometer pocket from the white coat that had been left behind by the last doctor, and she tied it on to Orlando.

Grace folded a white handkerchief round her head and hung keys and scissors from her waist.

They looked exactly like a doctor and a matron.

The waiting room was full and still more patients were arriving.   Orlando held his stethoscope ready, and Tinkle shouted 'Bags I me first! Bags I me first!' and Orlando listened to his 99ses, which were strong and healthy.

Orlando prescribed bed for some patients, medicines and holidays for others. But there were some who puzzled him very much; though not ill in any way, they felt too limp and tired to work, too sad and timid to play.

'They look to me,' thought Orlando, 'as though they have never had enough of what they fancy. I will give them everything they want, to make them gay and happy.'

From *Orlando Becomes a Doctor* by Kathleen Hale

Corker

An insatiable feline collector, Irish playwright and novelist Hugh Leonard still finds time to covet his neighbour's cat.

The most remarkable of our three 'walk-ons' was not our cat at all. A stray, he had been found wandering in Cork and so was given the name of Corker. It suited him, for he was the most self-possessed cat I have known. Indeed, I first laid eyes on him sitting on a barstool. That is not clumsy syntax. I mean that Corker was on a barstool next but one to mine. He wore a collar, and attached to it was a dangling lead. He was immersed in a contemplation of the row of beer pumps. It would not have surprised me if he had produced an *Evening Herald* and started doing the crossword.

His straight man (again, I cannot perpetrate the solecism of 'owner') recognized me by sight, thereby honouring the adage that more people know Tom-fool than Tom-fool knows. His name was Michael Andrews, and his business was the selling of out-of-the-way books. He was a bachelor and a loner; apart from an aged mother who lived in Devon, Corker was his only kin, and perhaps kith as well. Michael had no sooner introduced himself then he paid his dues with a long and ripely funny anecdote about an aeroplane trip across the Mediterranean ('Turn left for Malta, right for Gib'). Meanwhile, Corker deigned to refresh himself from an ashtray filled with water. People came to stare; he ignored them; his sang-froid was awesome. At closing time, I was allowed to peer into Michael's car: on the rear seat there was a litter tray, food and drink, and a cat basket, blanketed and snug. Apart from there being no tablet of mint chocolate on the pillow, it was the ideal home from home.

Corker was a one-off; the kind of prodigy that makes one sick if he happens to belong to someone else. Early each evening, Michael would drive him to Sorrento Point, where the bays of Dublin and Killiney meet. There as the cat vanished into the tanglewood of an untamed parkland, his straight man went home for dinner or to pay business calls. Two or three hours later, Michael would return and call Corker by name, and without fail a small grey ghost would drop down from a branch.

If, in the course of his overnight travels, Michael encountered a toffee-nosed hotelier who declared cats to be *non grata* in his establishment, Corker would be sternly commanded to spend the night in the car. All cats know when a voice has a wink and a nudge in it, and so he would instead make for the shrubbery and wait. As soon as Basil Fawlty had retired for the night, a voice would whisper from an open first-floor window, and with one leap the outcast was over the sill and enjoying the much-touted h. and c., c.h., Scand. duv. and int. sprung matt.

Michael's total devotion to Corker was touching and, for me, a little worrying. My own affections run so deep that out of a sense of self-preservation, I like to have an extra cat in hand for a rainy day. And the rain could not have come down more heavily when at last the unthinkable happened and Corker went missing.

It is easy to find a lost cat here in our town, where it could not walk the length of Castle Street without being asked its name, what it had for dinner, and wasn't the Dalkey Players' latest a howl. But Corker had disappeared in one of the immense suburbs of south London, where every redbricked house is a clone of the next, and people do not look at each other, never mind at cats. Michael was distraught. For days he tramped about, peering into pocket-handkerchief gardens; he wrote out a hundred 'Lost' notices and pinned them to trees.

As I told him afterwards, he should have had more faith in his friend's genius. When all hope was gone, there came a ring and a meow at the door, and

Corker walked in, followed by a uniformed member of London's finest. That prodigy among cats had probably grown tired of sitting in a tree, waiting to be found. At any rate, he finally took the remedy into his own paws, walked into the nearest police station and gave himself up.

From *Rover and Other Cats* by Hugh Leonard

Kittens

Anxious Lines on a New Kitten

Is this small ball of fur a noedipus,
Or just a budding feline Oedipus?
Will he, with lavish milk by me supplied,
Quickly forget his new-left mother's side?
Or, complex-fixed, become a – groedipus?

Pendennis Castle

Browned Off

I must say it's a little hard,
Father left me here on guard,
Detailed to watch this flipping hole
While he goes for his evening stroll.

I mustn't doze, I mustn't stir
Or let out just a single purr.
A youngster *should* respect his pa,
But this is going rather far . . . .

Of all the soul-destroying chores –
Watching a hole that is not yours.

Jane Anthony

The Pussies' Tea-Party

Last winter I had a visit of a week or two from my youngest niece, of nine years old. Wishing to have some small jollification before she went home, I thought it would be nice to have a pussies' tea-party, and as the prospect delighted her, we set to work to talk it over in earnest. No time was to be lost, for it was to be the next afternoon. So we sat down and seriously considered the items of the bill of fare. After some consultation, we decided that the basis of it should be fish, so we sent for some fresh herrings, and they were boiled and held in readiness.

Meanwhile my little companion proposed to issue cards of invitation, and said that she would write them herself. I asked if she could do them in the proper way, and as she was sure she could, I offered no further suggestions, and waited to see what would appear. So she found some scraps of writing-paper and wrote the invitations, and we went round together and presented them to the pussies, who duly purred their acceptance. They were all indoors, as it was wintry weather.

Next day, early in the afternoon, we prepared the feast. The invited guests were four grown pussies and two kittens, so we got ready four large and two small saucers. First a thick strip of fish was laid right across each saucer; an equal strip of cold rice pudding met it transversely, forming a cross-shaped figure that left four spaces in the angles. Thick cream was poured into these spaces, and the solid portion was decorated with tiny balls of butter, one rather larger in the middle, and two smaller on each of the rays. A reserve of fish and cream was to be at hand to replenish the portions most quickly exhausted.

In the middle of the sitting-room we placed a small, rather low, round table; and four stools were ranged round for the bigger pussies. As the hour for the feast drew near, much was the wondering as to how the guests would behave. They were to sit on the stools with their fore-paws on the edge of the table-cloth. We decided not to have flowers, because it would have overcrowded the space, as the two kittens were to be allowed to sit on the table.

At last the hour came, and meanwhile the excitement had grown intense. Five grown-ups were present, all as keenly interested as the little girl. The pussies were brought and placed on their stools, and the kittens, Chloe and Brindle, were put up to their saucers upon the table. To our great delight they all took in the situation at once; there was only a little hesitation on Maggie's part; she thought it was not manners to put her paws on the tablecloth; but this was soon overcome, and they all set to work as if they were quite accustomed to tea-parties and knew that nice behaviour was expected.

It was good to watch the pleasure of my little niece. I had expected that she would rush about and scream with delight, but she stood perfectly silent and still, with hands half raised, mouth a little open, and big eager eyes drinking in the scene, as if she thought it would vanish if she made a movement. Meanwhile the small guests were steadily eating away at their portions. Pinkieboy, as became the oldest and heaviest, finished his first, and after licking his saucer quite clean, and then his own lips, he looked round and clearly said, 'That was very good, and please I should like a little more, especially fish and cream.'

When they had all done there was a grand purring and washing of paws and faces before they got off their stools and as they dispersed to find cosy sleeping-places, as wise pussies do after a comfortable meal, we all thought that our little party had been brilliantly successful, and had even some thoughts of sending a report of it to the *Morning Post*.

From *Home and Garden* by Gertrude Jekyll

Lullaby for the Cat

Minnow, go to sleep and dream,
  Close your great big eyes;
Round your bed Events prepare
  The pleasantest surprise.

Darling Minnow, drop that frown,
  Just cooperate,
Not a kitten shall be drowned
  In the Marxist State.

Joy and Love will both be yours,
  Minnow, don't be glum.
Happy days are coming soon –
  Sleep, and let them come . . .

Elizabeth Bishop

The Naming of Curdy

Antonia White's sentimental side was reserved almost exclusively for her cats and was absolved by charm in her cat novel, *Minka and Curdy*.

Everything about him seemed to be round except his defiant little pointed tail. He had a round innocent pansy face, round blue eyes and a plump barrel of a body. His round paws (already far larger than Minka's oval ones) were absurdly too big for him. He kept stumbling over them like someone wearing shoes several sizes too large. His purr, on the other hand, was several sizes too small. Compared to Minka's, it was a mere whisper. He couldn't manage it very well either; it kept fading out and having to be wound up again. And after Minka's imperious yowl, his mew was a faint squeak. But his colouring was glorious. He was pure marmalade, without a single white hair, beautifully marked with deep orange stripes on a background of tawny gold. He was such a perfect sun-kitten that Mrs Bell almost christened him Phoebus on the spot. Yet somehow, she *knew* that was not his right name.

* * *

At that moment, the front-door bell rang.

'Bother!' said Mrs Grey. 'I'll have to answer it. But I'll send whoever it is away. We must get the kitten thoroughly used to you before you take him back tomorrow and we don't want other people bewildering him.'

She ran out into the passage so quickly that she forgot to shut the kitchen door. Mrs Bell heard the front door open. The next moment there was a heavy scampering noise in the passage. Then, to her horror, into the kitchen bounded an enormous black DOG! She nearly screamed. She was stooping down to snatch up the kitten when the most extraordinary thing happened. She felt the kitten's tiny back arch under her hand and heard a small, but businesslike snarl. In the same second, she realised there was no other sound in the kitchen. She looked round and there was the big black dog, sitting on its haunches and looking almost as frightened as she felt herself. She was so surprised that she took her hand off the kitten's back and stood staring at both of them. The kitten arched its back, fluffed up its baby fur and bristled its infant whiskers. And out of its open pink mouth came the most menacing swears. The huge black dog, who could have made one mouthful of it, did not attempt to advance; instead, it cowered on its haunches and even shifted back a little. It was the marmalade kitten who took a step forward, still hissing and swearing. And as Mrs Bell stood holding her breath, the great black Labrador stood up, turned round and slunk out of the kitchen with its tail between its legs.

'You little wonder!' she said, picking it up and cuddling it. The kitten relaxed and snuggled up to her. Though it had been so astonishingly brave, it was obviously relieved not to have to be be any more.

Mrs Grey and her friend who owned the black Labrador came into the kitchen.

'We saw it all from the passage,' said Mrs Grey.

'I knew Paula wouldn't *hurt* it,' said Paula's mistress. 'She's used to cats and very good-natured. But I was terrified she would frighten the poor little thing.'

'Poor little thing nothing,' said Mrs Grey. 'That kitten's as brave as a lion.'

'He certainly is,' said Paula's mistress. 'Paula, you great coward, letting yourself be put to flight by a baby one-twentieth your size. Come in and make friends.'

But Paula preferred to stay outside and Mrs Bell was secretly relieved when her owner, after having stroked and admired the marmalade kitten, took her home. The kitten had had quite enough excitement for one day.

Mrs Grey made some tea and she and Mrs Bell took the tray into the drawing-room and had tea in front of a lovely blazing wood fire. The November evening was getting chilly and the wind from the sea blew down the cobbled streets of Rye. But inside, with the curtains drawn and the fire flickering on their faces as they made themselves hot buttered toast, nothing could have been cosier. The marmalade kitten curled up on Mrs Bell's lap and went to sleep.

'What are you going to call him?' asked Mrs Grey. 'A kitten of such noble spirit should have a very special name. I have never seen anything so brave as the way he faced up to Paula.'

'Yes, indeed,' said Mrs Bell, feeling very proud of her new kitten's spirit. 'I think I shall call him Cœur-de-Lion after King Richard the lion-hearted. I believe *he* had red-gold hair too.' She ran a finger over the fluffy coat that felt so warm and silky after the cool chiffon texture of Minka's. And how soft and pudgy his body seemed after her firm, compact one.

'I think that is a splendid name,' said Mrs Grey. 'Though perhaps Cœur-de-Lion is a little overwhelming for such a tiny thing, also difficult to call in a hurry.'

'It will be his official name,' explained Mrs Bell. 'I shall call him Curdy for short.'

From *Minka and Curdy* by Antonia White

Roosevelt to the Rescue

A president describes to his daughter a fine example of philanthropy without responsibility.

White House, June 24 1906

Darling Ethel,

To-day as I was marching to church, with Sloane some 25 yards behind, I suddenly saw two terriers racing to attack a kitten which was walking down the sidewalk. I bounced forward with my umbrella, and after some active work put to flight the dogs while Sloane captured the kitten, which was a friendly, helpless little thing, evidently too well accustomed to being taken care of to know how to shift for itself. I inquired of all the bystanders and of people on the neighboring porches to know if they knew who owned it; but as they all disclaimed, with many grins, any knowledge of it, I marched ahead with it in my arms for about half a block. Then I saw a very nice colored woman and little colored girl looking out of the window of a small house with on the door a dressmaker's advertisement, and I turned and walked up the steps and asked if they did not want the kitten. They said they did, and the little girl welcomed it lovingly; so I felt I had gotten it a home and continued toward church.

From *Theodore Roosevelt's Letters to His Children*, ed. Joseph Bucklin Bishop

The First Kill

Hardly larger than a powder-puff, he crouches on the rug and watches a fleck of lint. His little blue eyes are bright, and presently his haunches tense and tremble. The tiny body shivers in an ague of excitement. He pounces, a little clumsily perhaps, and pinions the fleeting lint-fleck with his paws. In the fractional second of that lunge, the ten small needles of his claws have shot from their sheaths of flesh and muscle. It is a good game; but it is not an idle one. It is the kitten's introduction into the ancient ritual of the kill. Those queer little stiff-legged rushes and prancings are the heritage of an old death-dance, and those jerkings of his hind legs, as he rolls on his back, are the preparation for that day when – in desperate conflict with a bigger beast than himself – he will win the fight by the time-old feline technique of disembowlment. Even now, in his early infancy, he is wholly and inalienably a cat.

From *Our Enemy the Cat* by Alan Devor

The Last Protest

Confront a child, a puppy, and a kitten with sudden danger; the child will turn instinctively for assistance, the puppy will grovel in abject submission to the impending visitation, the kitten will brace its tiny body for a frantic resistance. And disassociate the luxury-loving cat from the atmosphere of social comfort in which it usually contrives to move, and observe it critically under the adverse conditions of civilization – that civilization which can impel a man to the degradation of clothing himself in tawdry ribald garments and capering mountebank dances in the street for the earning of the few coins that keep him on the respectable, or non-criminal, side of society. The cat of the slums and alleys, starved, outcast, harried, still keeps amid the prowlings of its adversity the bold, free, panther-tread with which it paced of yore the temple courts of Thebes, still displays the self-reliant watchfulness which man has never taught it to lay aside. And when its shifts and clever managings have not sufficed to stave off inexorable fate, when its enemies have proved too strong or too many for its defensive powers, it dies fighting to the last, quivering with the choking rage of mastered resistance, and voicing in its death-yell that agony of bitter remonstrance which human animals, too, have flung at the powers that may be; the last protest against a destiny that might have made them happy – and has not.

From *The Square Egg* by Hector Hugh Munro (Saki)

Siamese at Sea

Olivia Manning's most unforgettable cats were two kittens she never met.

Siamese cats were rare in the seaport town where I grew up. Few people had ever heard of them. My father had never forgotten two Siamese kittens he had known in the Orient a long time before. He was much older than us – having lost his first wife tragically, he did not remarry until he was over fifty – and his memories stretched so far back, they were more like the memories of a grandfather. He had joined the Royal Navy in the days of sail and, when very young, was sent to the Far East. Somewhere, among all those places that came into his stories – Hangchow, Kowloon, Borneo, the Celebes – someone presented a pair of Siamese cats to his ship. They were wild little creatures that chased one another up the rigging, leaping like flying foxes from rope to rope, then rushing down to roll on the deck in mock battles. When they were exhausted, they slept in each other's arms. They were the delight of the sailors.

Cats are sea-going animals. Sailors love them, often having little else to love. My father, who always had the family cat on his knee, often spoke of those Siamese kittens. He remembered them as being of unimaginable delicacy with large, alert ears and brilliant, watchful eyes; their thin, delicate, nervous limbs always aquiver with excitement about life as it was and wonder at life to come. He said they seemed scarcely to belong to earth.

During all his years of travelling round and about the world, the kittens remained in his memory, yet they had been on the ship for only a few weeks.

One day the admiral's wife came on board and she, too, was amused by the kittens. She told the Captain she simply must have one of them and at once it was passed down to the leading seaman that the men were required to present – quite voluntarily, of course – a kitten to the Admiral's wife. So one kitten was taken away and the other was left to play alone. A day or two later a message came to the ship that the kitten ashore was pining for its companion and could the second kitten be sent to join it? So both kittens left the ship and the sailors could no longer watch in wonder as they leapt overhead and fought their mock battles round the deck. For all I know they fared much better in the admiral's house than they ever could have done among shipboard rough and tumble, but the story filled me with rage against authority and I felt their loss much as did the sailors. Not that I ever did lose them, for in my imagination they still play among the rigging against the flamingo and persimmon colours of a tropical sunset.

From *Extraordinary Cats* by Olivia Manning

Caterwauling

Spring Lust

A letter from Dora Carrington

[*April 29th, 1922*] To Lytton Strachey

oh why are you not here to enjoy
the loveliness

oF The Mill House,
Tidmarsh,
Pangbourne?

Really today saturday its beauty
is unparelled.

are out

also

never

before

seen at

Tidmarsh

fly laden with honey

little

gambol about in the green orchard

*and the Black cat in the
wildess state of spring Lust*

*Careers about the garden after
Ralph crying out be raped!*

*Really she is
unabashed in
her attentions*

*old Marmaduke feels the weight
of his winter overcoat & rather
fretfully lies in the sun on
the footpath*

From *Carrington, Letters and Extracts from her Diaries* ed. David Garnett

Fanchette

Your behaviour is quite disgraceful: two or three times a year I catch you on the garden walls, wearing a crazy, ridiculous expression, with a swarm of tom-cats round you. I even know your favourite, you perverse Fanchette – he's a dirty-grey Tom, long and lean, with half his fur gone. He's got ears like a rabbit's and coarse, plebeian limbs. How can you make a *mésalliance* with this low-born animal, and make it so often? But, even at those demented seasons, as soon as you catch sight of me, your natural face returns for a moment, and you give me a friendly mew which says something like: 'You see what I'm up to. Don't despise me too much, nature has her urgent demands. But I'll soon come home again and I'll lick myself for ages to purify myself of this dissolute life.' O, beautiful Fanchette, your bad behaviour is so remarkably becoming to you!

From *Claudine at School* by Colette

A Lesson in Loving

'Cats scream,' I said, remembering something from the farm. 'They will scream like anything when a tomcat is doing it to them.'
'Wouldn't you?' said Naomi.

From *Lives of Girls and Women* by Alice Munro

Cat-Goddesses

A perverse habit of cat-goddesses –
Even the blackest of them, black as coals
Save for a new moon blazing on each breast,
With coral tongues and beryl eyes like lamps,
Long-legged, pacing three by three in nines –
This obstinate habit is to yield themselves,
In verisimilar love-ecstasies,
To tatter-eared and slinking alley-toms
No less below the common run of cats
Than they above it; which they do for spite,
To provoke jealousy – not the least abashed
By such gross-headed, rabbit-coloured litters
As soon they shall be happy to desert.

Robert Graves

Family Cats

The Matron Cat's Song

So once again the trouble's o'er
  And here I sit and sing;
Forgetful of my paramour
  And the pickle I was in;
Lord, lord, it is a trying time
  We bear when we're expecting,
When folk reproach us for the crime
  And frown with glance correcting.

So purra wurra, purra wurra, pronkum pronkum:
  Purra wurra pronkum, pronkum purr.

How much I feared my kits would be
  Slain in the hour of birth!
And so I sought a sanctuary
  Which causes me some mirth;
The surly cook, who hates all cats,
  Hath here a little closet,
And here we nest among her hats –
  Lord save me when she knows it!

Hey purra wurra, etc.

Four kits have I of aspect fair,
  Though usually but three;
Two female tabs, a charming pair,
  Who much resemble me;
Lord, lord, to think upon the sport
  Which doth await the hussies,
They'll be no better than they ought
  Nor worse than other pussies.

O purra wurra, etc.

Yet as becomes a mother fond
  I dote upon my boys,
And think they will excel beyond
  All other toms in noise;
How harsh their manly pelts will be,
  How stern and fixed each feature –
If they escape that cruelty
  Which man doth work on nature!

Ah purra wurra, etc.

Those eyes which now are sealed fast
  Nine days against the light
Shall ere few months are overpast
  Like stars illume the night;
Those voices that with feeble squall
  Demand my whole attention,
Shall earn with rousing caterwaul
  Dishonourable mention.

Then purra wurra, etc.

But then, alas, I shall not care
  How flighty they may be,
For ere they're grown I'll have to bear
  Another four, or three;
And after all, they are the best
  While the whole crew reposes
With fast-shut eyes, weak limbs at rest,
  And little wrinkled noses.

So purra wurra, purra wurra, pronkum pronkum:
  Purra wurra pronkum, pronkum ryestraw:
Pronkum ryestraw, pronkum ryestraw,
  Pur-ra – wur-ra – pronkum
Pronk . . . Foof.

(She sleeps.)

From *A Mad Lady's Garland* by Ruth Pitter

An Abandoned Family

Part of a letter written by Colette to the poet and short-story writer Francis Jammes in April 1906.

The day before yesterday I found on the fortifications a beautiful striped cat whom some abominable pig had abandoned in the cold with three kittens. I took all four up in my skirt and brought them home. And now they are secure. But my God, what desperate gratitude that cat expressed! Before such looks, one blushes, one says, 'That's too much, I don't deserve that . . .'

From *Letters from Colette*, sel. and transl. Robert Phelps

A Charming Family Party

In 1925 Vita Sackville-West found herself at the centre of a confusing pet-swap situation, as she wrote to Virginia Woolf.

My spaniel has seven puppies. My cat has five kittens. The spaniel steals the kittens, and, carrying them very carefully in her mouth, puts them into the puppies' basket. She then goes out for a stroll, and the cat in search of her progeny curls up in the basket and suckles the puppies. The spaniel returns, chases out the cat, curls up in the basket, and suckles the kittens. I find myself quite unable to cope with this situation. The kittens will bark and the puppies will mew, – that's what will happen. But at present it makes a charming family party – such a warm soft young heap.

From *The Letters of Vita Sackville-West to Virginia Woolf*, ed. Louise de Salvo and Mitchell A. Leaska

A Bereaved Mother

Lafcadio Hearn, the half-Irish, half-Greek nineteenth-century journalist, who became a naturalised Japanese citizen after his marriage to a Japanese woman in 1890, wrote this beautiful and moving account of a cat's grieving for her dead kittens.

Very much do I love cats; and I suppose that I could write a large book about the different cats which I have kept, in various climes and times on both sides of the world. But this is not a Book of Cats; and I am writing about Tama for merely psychological reasons. She has been uttering, in her sleep beside my chair, a peculiar cry that touched me in a particular way. It is the cry that a cat makes only for her kittens – a soft trilling coo – a pure caress of tone. And I perceive that her attitude, as she lies there on her side, is the attitude of a cat holding something – something freshly caught: the forepaws are stretched out as to grasp, and the pearly talons are playing.

Tama could not clearly remember that her kittens were dead. She knew that she ought to have had kittens; and she looked everywhere and called everywhere for them, long after they had been buried in the garden. She complained a great deal to her friends; and she made me open all the cupboards and closets – over and over again – to prove to her that the kittens were not in the house. At last she was able to convince herself that it was useless to look for them any more. But she plays with them in dreams, and coos to them, and catches for them small shadowy things – perhaps even brings to them, through some dim window of memory, a sandal of ghostly straw . . .

From *Kotto* by Lafcadio Hearn

Cats Eating and Eaten

Bustopher Jones

Bustopher Jones is *not* skin and bones –
In fact, he's remarkably fat.
He doesn't haunt pubs – he has eight or nine clubs,
For he's the St James's Street Cat!
He's the Cat we all greet as he walks down the street
In his coat of fastidious black:
No commonplace mousers have such well-cut trousers
Or such an impeccable back.
In the whole of St James's the smartest of names is
The name of this Brummell of Cats;
And we're all of us proud to be nodded or bowed to
By Bustopher Jones in white spats!

His visits are occasional to the *Senior Educational*
And it is against the rules
For any one Cat to belong both to that
And the *Joint Superior Schools*.
For a similar reason, when game is in season
He is found, not at *Fox's*, but *Blimp's*;
But he's frequently seen at the gay *Stage and Screen*
Which is famous for winkles and shrimps.
In the season of venison he gives his ben'son
To the *Pothunter's* succulent bones;
And just before noon's not a moment too soon
To drop in for a drink at the *Drones*.
When he's seen in a hurry there's probably curry
At the *Siamese* – or at the *Glutton*;
If he looks full of gloom then he's lunched at the *Tomb*
On cabbage, rice pudding and mutton.

So, much in this way, passes Bustopher's day –
At one club or another he's found.

It can cause no surprise that under our eyes
He has grown unmistakably round.
He's a twenty-five pounder, or I am a bounder,
And he's putting on weight every day:
But he's so well preserved because he's observed
All his life a routine, so he'll say.
And (to put it in rhyme) 'I shall last out my time'
Is the word of this stoutest of Cats.
It must and it shall be Spring in Pall Mall
While Bustopher Jones wears white spats!

From *Old Possum's Book of Practical Cats* by T. S. Eliot

In Time for Tea

Thomas Hardy enjoyed a curious social life while working on *The Dynasts*.

He worked upon it for several years, but we are given hardly a glimpse of him in this connection, quietly purposeful among his books and at his writing-table. In 1900, when Professor W. L. Phelps called on him, there was no invitation into the study, although kindness and hospitality shone. These qualities were enjoyed not only by human visitors. The place was a paradise of cats. 'Are all these your own cats?' 'Oh, dear, no, some of them are, and some are cats who come regularly to have tea, and some are still other cats, not invited by us, but who seem to find out about this time of day that tea will be going.'

From *Thomas Hardy* by Edmund Blunden

Eating out of Her Hand

Whenever I see a reference to that most poetically named of operas 'The Lady Macbeth of Mtsensk', I think of my mother. My mother is the Lady Macbeth of (at the moment) SW5 – a woman born to utter 'Infirm of purpose! Give me the daggers.'

Not that she is likely to commit murder, which is against her principles. But if she did she would carry it through resolutely, and get away with it. Judge and jury would, in one of her own favourite expressions, eat out of her hand. (Her fondness for the expression may reflect the remarkable way she has with cats, who will eat out of my mother's hand melon, grapes, pineapple or whatever she happens to be eating herself while they are on her lap – I am not speaking of those cats whose idiosyncrasy it is to like fruit, but of cats who would not ordinarily dream of eating any such thing but who take it from my mother for the sheer pleasure of sharing her diet.)

From *Don't Never Forget* by Brigid Brophy

Salute to Fruit

The novelist Margaret Mitchell's precocious engagement with her kittens when she was a child, and their uncharacteristic compliance, suggests that the character of Scarlett O'Hara in *Gone with the Wind* did not come off the bushes.

In the tall pine tree in the sideyard where she and Stephens had built a tree-house, she rigged up a wicker elevator for hauling Piedy's progeny up to her perch – much to the animals' annoyance, according to Stephens. After Piedy died, Hypatia and Lowpatia joined the household. The latter won fame for a special trick: 'Margaret taught him to stand up and salute with his right paw beside his ear. When he performed this in a proper military manner, he was rewarded by being fed cantaloup, his favourite delicacy.'

From *Southern Daughter: The Life of Margaret Mitchell*
by Darden Ashbury Pyron

Milk for the Cat

When the tea is brought at five o'clock,
  And all the neat curtains are drawn with care,
The little black cat with bright green eyes
  Is suddenly purring there.

At first she pretends, having nothing to do,
  She has come in merely to blink by the grate;
But, though tea may be late or the milk may be sour,
  She is never late.

And presently her agate eyes
  Take a soft large milky haze,
And her independent, casual glance
  Becomes a stiff, hard gaze.

Then she stamps her claws or lifts her ears,
  Or twists her tail or begins to stir,
Till suddenly all her lithe body becomes
  One breathing, trembling purr.

The children eat and wriggle and laugh,
  The two old ladies stroke their silk;
But the cat is grown small and thin with desire,
  Transformed to a creeping lust for milk.

The white saucer like some full moon descends
  At last from the clouds of the table above;
She sighs and dreams and thrills and glows,
  Transfigured with love.

She nestles over the shining rim,
  Buries her chin in the creamy sea;
Her tail hangs loose; each drowsy paw
  Is doubled under each bending knee.

A long, dim ecstasy holds her life;
  Her world is an infinite shapeless white
Till her tongue has curled the last holy drop,
  Then she sinks back into the night,

Draws and dips her body to heap
  Her sleepy nerves in the great arm-chair,
Lies defeated and buried deep
  Three or four hours unconscious there.

Harold Monroe

Eating the Elephant-Cat

In a Canton eating-house, Colin Thubron encountered a gastronomic challenge.

In the rowdy, proletarian Wild Game Restaurant, I interrogated the waitress for anything I could bear to eat. But she incanted remorselessly from the menu: Steamed Cat, Braised Guinea Pig (whole) with Mashed Shrimps, Grainy Dog Meat with Chilli and Scallion in Soya Sauce, Shredded Cat Thick

Soup, Fried Grainy Mud-puppy ('It's a fish,' she said) with Olive Kernels, Braised Python with Mushrooms. . . .

If I wanted the Steamed Mountain Turtle, she said, I'd have to wait an hour. And Bear's Paws, she regretted, were off.

I vacillated. I had turned suddenly vegetarian. I played for time by ordering python broth, then glanced furtively round at the main courses on nearby tables, hoping for escape; but their occupants were bent over opaque stews where dappled fragments floated anonymously. Around us the windows were glazed with pretty pictures of the animals concerned: deer and cats wearing necklaces.

The waitress tried to be helpful. 'What about Dog Meat Ready to be Cooked Earthen Pot over Charcoal Stove on Table?'

I guessed in desperation: 'It's too expensive.'

'Then I recommend Braised Wildcat.'

'Well. . . .' I glanced at a domestic tabby squatting on the veranda beside me. The waitress followed my gaze. 'It's not *that*.'

She tried to explain it. It had nothing to do with real cats, she said. She wrote down the Chinese character for it, which I couldn't read. In the end, hoping that it was a fancy name for something innocuous, I heard myself say: 'One braised wildcat, please.'

But the soup was a meal in itself. It came in a python-sized bowl, and beneath its brown liquid lurked a sediment of what appeared to be muscular white chicken meat. It tasted fishy. The darker flecks might have been skin. I excused myself by reflecting that pythons (although I had never known one) were less endearing than lambs, which I had eaten often.

The tabby had squirmed under my table. It looked scrawny but dangerously edible. In fact I had the impression that almost everything here was in peril. When somebody brought a warm flannel for my hands, I was half prepared to munch it. What else was nutritional, I wondered? The mosquitoes? The curtains? It occurred to me that should I fall from the fourth-floor stair-well. . . .

The cat was still under my table when its braised compatriot arrived. I lifted the lid to reveal a mahogany-coloured flotsam of mushrooms and indistinguishable flesh. A pair of fragile ribs floated accusingly on the surface. I ate the mushrooms first, with relief, but even they were suffused by the dark, gamey tang of whatever-it-was. The meat was full of delicate, friable bones. I did not know if my faint nausea arose from the thing's richness or from my mind. Several times my chopsticks hit rounded, meat-encircled fragments, like miniature rolling-pins, which resembled legs. I smuggled them to the cat under the table, as a melancholy atonement.

'You don't like your wildcat?' The waitress was peering into the bowl, disappointed.

'I'm rather full.' I smiled feebly, picking the python out of my teeth. But she seemed to understand my diffidence, and stooped down to sketch me an exonerating picture of the whatever-it-was. She drew what looked like the illustration of an Edward Lear limerick: a lugubrious, four-legged ellipse, with a face either cross or upset. But it was too late: I had already eaten it. And when later I showed an English-speaking Cantonese the word which she had written, he translated it 'elephant-cat' or 'cat-fox', and shook his head, nonplussed.

Under my table, the tabby's country cousin had been reduced to a puddle of broth.

From *Behind the Wall* by Colin Thubron

Musical Cats

A Russian Idyll

Music was not the chief attraction for the numerous cats that made their home with the composer Alyeksandr Borodin and his wife, Yekatyerina.

Several tom-cats that found a home in Borodin's apartment paraded across the dinner-table, sticking their noses into plates, unceremoniously leaping to the diners' backs. These tom-cats basked in Yekatyerina Sergeyevna's protection; various details of their biography were related. One tabby was called *Rybolov* ('Fisherman'), because, in the winter, he contrived to catch small fish with his paw through the ice-holes; the other was called *Dlinyeñki* ('Longy') and he was in the habit of fetching homeless kittens by the neck to Borodin's apartment; these the Borodins would harbour, later finding homes for them. Then there were other, and less remarkable specimens of the genus felis. You might sit at their tea-table, – and behold! Tommy marches along the board and makes for your plate; you shoo him off, but Yekatyerina Sergeyevna invariably takes his part and tells some incident from his biography. Meantime, zip! another cat has bounded at Alyeksandr Porfiryevich's neck and, twining himself about it, has fallen to warming that neck without pity. 'Listen, dear Sir, this is too much of a good thing!' says Borodin, but without stirring; and the cat lolls blissfully on.

From *My Musical Life* by N. A. Rimsky-Korsakov

The Cat and the Bagpipes

A cat came dancing out of a barn
With a pair of bagpipes under her arm;
She could sing nothing but, Fiddle cum fee,
The mouse has married the bumble-bee.
Pipe, cat; dance, mouse;
We'll have a wedding at our good house.

Nursery rhyme

The Singing Cat

It was a little captive cat
  Upon a crowded train
His mistress takes him from his box
  To ease his fretful pain.

She holds him tight upon her knee
  The graceful animal
And all the people look at him
  He is so beautiful.

But oh he pricks and oh he prods
  And turns upon her knee
Then lifteth up his innocent voice
  In plaintive melody.

He lifteth up his innocent voice
  He lifteth up, he singeth
And to each human countenance
  A smile of grace he bringeth.

He lifteth up his innocent paw
  Upon her breast he clingeth
And everybody cries, Behold
  The cat, the cat that singeth.

He lifteth up his innocent voice
  He lifteth up, he singeth
And all the people warm themselves
  In the love his beauty bringeth.

From *Selected Poems* by Stevie Smith

Try It on the Cat

When in Paris I bought a record especially for my beloved cat, called 'Baby don't be blue', sung by a gentleman known as High Hatted Tragedian of Song . . .

The words, as I remember them, were as follows:

> O baby don't say you're through,
> Baby I'm so blue . . .
> Baby . . .

My cat had a passion for this song and so I had no difficulty in recognizing it when I heard the familiar strains apparently emerging from the compartment next to mine on the train bearing me across America. This was followed by the first part of Grieg's Piano Concerto, by the March from *Zampa*, a waltz that was played a great deal at seaside hotels during my childhood, and the Priests' March from *Attila* . . .

After which there was a loud click as though somebody had removed their false teeth and on again with 'Baby I'm so Blue' . . . This began, as I remember, at seven in the morning and continued until midnight. Knowing that the woman next door had a child with her that doubtless had to be amused, I bore with this concert for the first day uncomplainingly. But when, punctually at seven next morning, it began again, this was too much. I removed my shoe and hammered with all my force on the dividing wall of our two compartments. Then I sent for the porter. He came in with a look of surprise on his face and went at once to a screen at the rear of the compartment. The concert, it seemed, had been self-inflicted . . .

At one of our recitals, my brother was asked, 'How can you tell good poetry from bad?'

'In the same way as you can tell fish . . . if it's fresh it's good, if it's stale it's bad, and if you're not certain, try it on the cat.'

From *Taken Care Of: An Autobiography* by Edith Sitwell

Chattie

Mrs Humphrey Ward almost certainly based this entrancing feline character on her own beloved pet Persian.

Chattie jumped up on the window-sill, with her usual stealthy aplomb, and rubbed herself against the girl's face.

'Oh, Chattie!' cried Rose, throwing her arms round the cat, 'if Catherine 'll *only* marry Mr Elsmere, my dear, and be happy ever afterwards, and set me free to live my own life a bit, I'll be *so* good, you won't know me, Chattie. And you shall have a new collar, my beauty, and cream till you die of it.'

And springing up she dragged in the cat, and snatching a scarlet anemone from a bunch on the table, stood opposite Chattie, who stood slowly waving her magnificent tail from side to side, and glaring as though it were not at all to her taste to be hustled and bustled in this way.

'Now, Chattie, listen! Will she?'

A leaf of the flower dropped on Chattie's nose.

'Won't she? Will she? Won't she? Will— Tiresome flower, why did Nature give it such a beggarly few petals? If I'd had a daisy it would have all come right. Come, Chattie, waltz; and let's forget this wicked world!'

And, snatching up her violin, the girl broke into a Strauss waltz, dancing to it the while, her cotton skirts flying, her pretty feet twinkling, till her eyes glowed, and her cheeks blazed with a double intoxication – the intoxication of movement, and the intoxication of sound – the cat meanwhile following her with little mincing perplexed steps, as though not knowing what to make of her.

From *Robert Elsmere* by Mrs Humphrey Ward

Cat Hygiene

Desolating a Cat

Colette offers a scathing reproach to the writer Renée Hamon in this extract from a letter written from paris in December 1941.

But whoever taught you to desolate a cat, to reduce him to despair, by pressing his nose in his own excrement? You not only dirty him, you poison him, literally, by clogging his nostrils and mouth! How horrible. And for the animal, what torture! Having him injected would be more merciful than a life in which you oblige him – because he cannot understand the reasons for your abominable behavior – to dread the time when he must do his business. Can his distended stomach be due to this treatment?

From *Letters from Colette*, sel. and transl. Robert Phelps

Spotless!

The previous vicar's wife couldn't have presided at Bingo – but this vicar's mother does, rather grimly as if a duty.

When she is grooming her cat she has to put on her spectacles to see the fleas, gleaming red-brown among the combings. 'I must say, she keeps Pussy *spotless*.'

Part of a letter from Barbara Pym to Philip Larkin, 16 February 1964.
Taken from: *A Very Private Eye, Barbara Pym*, Hazel Holt and Hilary Pym eds.

The Wrong Box

A cat's accident offered a moment of light relief to Anne Frank and her family during their grim incarceration in an attic in Nazi-occupied Amsterdam.

Wednesday, 10th May, 1944

Dear Kitty,

We were sitting in the attic doing some French yesterday afternoon when I suddenly heard water pattering down behind me. I asked Peter what it could be, but he didn't even reply, simply tore up to the loft, where the source of the disaster was, and pushed Mouschi, who, because of the wet earth box, had sat down beside it, roughly back to the right place. A great din and disturbance followed, and Mouschi, who had finished by that time, dashed downstairs.

Mouschi, seeking the convenience of something similar to his box, had chosen some wood shavings. The pool had trickled down from the loft into the attic immediately and, unfortunately, landed just beside and in the barrel of potatoes. The ceiling was dripping, and as the attic floor is not free from holes either, several yellow drips came through the ceiling into the dining-room between a pile of stockings and some books, which were lying on the table. I was doubled up with laughter, it really was a scream. There was Mouschi crouching under a chair, Peter with water, bleaching powder and floorcloth, and Van Danan trying to soothe everyone. The calamity was soon over, but it's a well known fact that cats' puddles positively stink. The potatoes proved this only too clearly and also the wood shavings, that Daddy collected in a bucket to be burned. Poor Mouschi! How were you to know that peat is unobtainable?

Yours, Anne

From *The Diary of Anne Frank*, transl. B. M. Moyaart-Doubleday

Cat Language

Double Dutch

That crafty cat, a buff-black Siamese,
Sniffing through wild wood, sagely, silently goes –
Prick ears, lank legs, alertly twitching nose –
And on her secret errand reads with ease
A language no man knows.

Walter de la Mare

A Linguistic Kitten

H. P. Lovecraft believed that his cat Nigger-Man was trying to tell him something. He may have been protesting about his racist appellation.

What a boy he was! I watched him grow from a tiny black handful to one of the most fascinating & understanding creatures I've ever seen. He used to talk in a genuine language of varied intonations – a special tone for every different meaning. There was even a special 'prr'p' for the smell of roast chestnuts, on which he doted. He used to play ball with me – kicking a large rubber sphere back at me from half across the room with all four feet as he lay on the floor. And on summer evenings in the twilight he would prove his kinship to the elfin things of shadow by racing across the lawn on nameless errands, darting into the blackness of the shrubbery now & then, & occasionally leaping at me from ambush & then bounding away again into invisibility before I could catch him.

From Lovecraft: A Biography by L. Sprague du Camp

Mrkgnao!

James Joyce's genius for the expression of human nature lay in his characters' internalised dialogue with women, children – and even cats.

Mr Leopold Bloom ate with relish the inner organs of beasts and fowls. He liked thick giblet soup, nutty gizzards, a stuffed roast heart, liverslices fried with crustcrumbs, fried hencods' roes. Most of all he liked grilled mutton kidneys which gave to his palate a fine tang of faintly scented urine.

Kidneys were in his mind as he moved about the kitchen softly, righting her breakfast things on the humpy tray. Gelid light and air were in the kitchen but out of doors gentle summer morning everywhere. Made him feel a bit peckish.

The coals were reddening.

Another slice of bread and butter: three, four: right. She didn't like her plate full. Right. He turned from the tray, lifted the kettle off the hob and set it sideways on the fire. It sat there, dull and squat, its spout stuck out. Cup of tea soon. Good. Mouth dry.

The cat walked stiffly round a leg of the table with tail on high.

—Mkgnao!

—O, there you are, Mr Bloom said, turning from the fire.

The cat mewed in answer and stalked again stiffly round a leg of the table, mewing. Just how she stalks over my writingtable. Prr. Scratch my head. Prr.

Mr Bloom watched curiously, kindly the lithe black form. Clean to see: the gloss of her sleek hide, the white button under the butt of her tail, the green flashing eyes. He bent down to her, his hands on his knees.

—Milk for the pussens, he said.

—Mrkgnao! the cat cried.

They call them stupid. They understand what we say better than we understand them. She understands all she wants to. Vindictive too. Cruel. Her nature. Curious mice never squeal. Seem to like it. Wonder what I look like to her. Height of a tower? No, she can jump me.

—Afraid of the chickens she is, he said mockingly. Afraid of the chook-chooks. I never saw such a stupid pussens as the pussens.

—Mrkrgnao! the cat said loudly.

She blinked up out of her avid shameclosing eyes, mewing plaintively and long, showing him her milkwhite teeth. He watched the dark eyeslits narrowing with greed till her eyes were green stones. Then he went to the dresser, took the jug Hanlon's milkman had just filled for him, poured warmbubbled milk on a saucer and set it slowly on the floor.

—Gurrhr! she cried, running to lap.

He watched the bristles shining wirily in the weak light as she tipped three times and licked lightly. Wonder is it true if you clip them they can't mouse after. Why? They shine in the dark, perhaps, the tips. Or kind of feelers in the dark, perhaps.

From *Ulysses* by James Joyce

Advice to a Siamese Cat

Compton Mackenzie empathizes with a thoroughbred's ennui.

Those who are considering the introduction of a Siamese cat to their house will do well to remember that Siamese are much more restless than Persian, half-Persian and ordinary cats. Siamese always have a perfectly clear idea of what they want whether it be a particular chair, a particular dish or a particular room. Therefore people who belong to Siamese cats must make up their minds to do a good deal of waiting upon them. Perhaps the characteristic of cats that many of their lovers find most attractive is their tranquillity. I fear that this tranquillity cannot be claimed for Siamese unless like children they are asleep. They compete with pot-holers and mountaineers in causing immense trouble to other people to extricate them from difficult situations. They are merciless to upholstery. They delight in making one get up from one's chair to let them into a room and then a few minutes later making one get up again to let them out of the room the arrangements of which have failed to suit the mood of the moment. I insist upon this aspect of the Siamese because few things depress me more than the sight of a Siamese cat whose lot has been cast with people unable to understand what it asks from life. Siamese cats are unable to indulge in the self-pity which allays with gentle massage a chip on the shoulder: they are just lonely and dull.

An old friend of mine once decided that he must have a Siamese cat, but neither he nor his wife nor his children have the faintest notion of how to treat a Siamese cat. I knew any advice from me to them would be idle. So I offered it to the cat.

Self. You're not happy here, are you?
Cat. Oh, I'm happy enough. I'm well fed. I have plenty of comfortable chairs. The house was cold at first but since this business they call central heating was put in I'm no longer chilly.
Self. But you're bored.
Cat. You've said it. I'm bored. Damnably bored.

Self. Yes, I felt that.

Cat. These people are perfectly kind. I've been living with them now for nearly four years. But they are doggy people, and I think they ought to have a dog.

Self. Would you like that?

Cat. No, I shouldn't but it would give me an excuse to leave them if they brought a dog here.

Self. Where would you go?

Cat. There's a woman living about a mile from here whom I visit occasionally. I think it would be a kindness to go and stay with her because she is undoubtedly lonely. I can tell that by the way she talks to me. I'm at my wits' end here for intelligent conversion.

I took an early opportunity of asking my old friend why he did not keep a dog. He told me that there was nothing he would like better but that he was worried about the cat's reaction. A few weeks later however, a golden Labrador puppy arrived, and my friend wrote to tell me that the cat had left them next day and gone to live with an old maid in the neighbourhood. The next time I went to stay with my friend I called on the cat. I asked him if he was happy and was glad to hear that he was.

'But do tell her not to waste milk on me and also to see that there is plenty of water available.'

From 'No Cats About the House' by Compton Mackenzie

A Conversation with a Cat

Hilaire Belloc was once unwise enough to bare his soul to a cat picked up casually in a bar.

The other day I went into the bar of a railway station and, taking a glass of beer, I sat down at a little table by myself to meditate upon the necessary but tragic isolation of the human soul. I began my meditation by consoling myself with the truth that something in common runs through all nature, but I went on to consider that this cut no ice, and that the heart needed something more. I might by long research have discovered some third term a little less hackneyed than these two, when fate, or some fostering star, sent me a tawny, silky, long-haired cat.

If it be true that nations have the cats they deserve, then the English people deserve well in cats, for there are none so prosperous or so friendly in the world. But even for an English cat this cat was exceptionally friendly and fine – especially friendly. It leapt at one graceful bound into my lap, nestled there, put out an engaging right front paw to touch my arm with a pretty timidity by way of introduction, rolled up at me an eye of bright but innocent affection, and then smiled a secret smile of approval.

No man could be so timid after such an approach as not to make some manner of response. So did I. I even took the liberty of stroking Amathea (for by that name did I receive this vision), and though I began this gesture in a respectful fashion, after the best models of polite deportment with strangers, I was soon lending it some warmth, for I was touched to find that I had a friend; yes, even here, at the ends of the tubes in S.W.99. I proceeded (as is right) from caress to speech, and said, 'Amathea, most beautiful of cats, why have you deigned to single me out for so much favour? Did you recognize in me a friend to all that breathes, or were you yourself suffering from loneliness (though I take it you are near your own dear home), or is there pity in the hearts of animals as there is in the hearts of some humans? What, then, was your motive? Or am I, indeed, foolish to ask, and not rather to take whatever good comes to me in whatever way from the gods?'

To these questions Amathea answered with a loud purring noise, expressing with closed eyes of ecstasy her delight in the encounter.

'I am more than flattered, Amathea,' said I, by way of answer; 'I am consoled. I did not know that there was in the world anything breathing and moving, let alone so tawny-perfect, who would give companionship for its own sake and seek out, through deep feeling, some one companion out of all living kind. If you do not address me in words I know the reason and I commend it; for in words lie the seeds of all dissension, and love at its most profound is silent. At least, I read that in a book, Amathea; yes, only the other day. But I confess that the book told me nothing of those gestures which are better than words, or of that caress which I continue to bestow upon you with all the gratitude of my poor heart.'

To this Amathea made a slight gesture of acknowledgement – not disdainful – wagging her head a little, and then settling it down in deep content.

'Oh, beautiful-haired Amathea, many have praised you before you found me to praise you, and many will praise you, some in your own tongue, when I am no longer held in the bonds of your presence. But none will praise you more sincerely. For there is not a man living who knows better than I that the four charms of a cat lie in its closed eyes, its long and lovely hair, its silence, and even its affected love.'

But at the word affected Amathea raised her head, looked up at me tenderly, once more put forth her paw to touch my arm, and then settled down again to a purring beautitude.

'You are secure,' said I sadly; 'mortality is not before you. There is in your complacency no foreknowledge of death nor even of separation. And for that reason, Cat, I welcome you the more. For if there has been given to your kind this repose in common living, why, then, we men also may find it by following your example and not considering too much what may be to come and not remembering too much what has been and will never return. Also, I thank you, for this, Amathea, my sweet Euplokamos' (for I was becoming a little familiar through an acquaintance of a full five minutes and from the absence of all recalcitrance), 'that you have reminded me of my youth, and in a sort of shadowy way, a momentary way, have restored it to me. For there is an age, a blessed youthful age (O my Cat) even with the miserable race of men, when all things are consonant with the life of the body, when sleep is regular and long and deep, when enmities are either unknown or a subject for rejoicing and when the whole of being is lapped in hope as you are now lapped on my lap, Amathea. Yes, we also, we of the doomed race, know peace. But whereas you possess it from blind kittenhood to that last dark day so mercifully short with you, we grasp it only for a very little while. But I would not sadden you by the mortal plaint. That would be treason indeed, and a vile return for your goodness. What! When you have chosen me out of seven London millions upon whom to confer the tender solace of the heart, when you have proclaimed yourself so suddenly to be my dear, shall I introduce you to the sufferings of those of whom you know nothing save that they feed you, house you and pass you by? At least you do not take us for gods, as do the dogs, and the more am I humbly beholden to you for this little service of recognition – and something more.'

Amathea slowly raised herself upon her four feet, arched her back, yawned, looked up at me with a smile sweeter than ever and then went round and round, preparing for herself a new couch upon my coat, whereon she settled and began once more to purr in settled ecstasy.

Already had I made sure that a rooted and anchored affection had come to me from out the emptiness and nothingness of the world and was to feed my soul henceforward; already had I changed the mood of long years and felt a conversion towards the life of things, an appreciation, a cousinship with the created light – and all that through one new link of loving kindness – when whatever it is that dashes the cup of bliss from the lips of mortal man (Tupper) up and dashed it good and hard. It was the Ancient Enemy who put the fatal sentence into my heart, for we are the playthings of the greater powers, and surely some of them are evil.

'You will never leave me, Amathea,' I said; 'I will respect your sleep and we will sit here together through all uncounted time, I holding you in my arms and you dreaming of the fields of paradise. Nor shall anything part us, Amathea; you are my cat and I am your human. Now and onwards into the fullness of peace.'

Then it was that Amathea lifted herself once more, and with delicate, discreet, unweighted movement of perfect limbs leapt lightly to the floor as lovely as a wave. She walked slowly away from me without so much as looking back over her shoulder; she had another purpose in her mind; and as she so gracefully and so majestically neared the door which she was seeking, a short, unpleasant man standing at the bar said 'Puss, Puss, Puss!' and stooped to scratch her gently behind the ear. With what a wealth of singular affection, pure and profound, did she not gaze up at him, and then rub herself against his leg in token and external expression of a sacramental friendship that should never die.

From 'A Conversation with a Cat' by Hilaire Belloc

Sporting Cats

Teaching Flavio Ping-Pong

One does not think of cats as sporting creatures, but ping-pong appears to be a popular occupation. Here the cat Flavio enjoys a sporting interlude under the indulgent eye of his master, George Rose.

He rose and went to the window. The yellow cat deliberately stretched himself, yawned, and followed; and proceeded to carry out a wonderful scheme of feints and ambuscades in regard to a ping-pong ball which was kept for his proper diversion. The man looked on almost lovingly. Flavio at length captured the ball, took it between his forepaws, and posed with all the majesty of a lion of Trafalgar Square. Anon he uttered a little low gurgle of endearment, fixing the great eloquent mystery of amber and black and velvet eyes, tardy, grave, upon his human friend. No notice was vouchsafed. Flavio got up; and gently rubbed his head against the nearest hand.

'My boy!' the man murmured; and he lifted the little cat on to his shoulder.

From *Hadrian the Seventh* by Frederick Rolfe (Baron Corvo)

Teaching Bluebell Ping-Pong

To teach a cat to play ping-pong you have first to win the confidence and approval of the cat. Bluebell was the second cat I had undertaken to teach; I found her more amenable than the first, which had been a male.

Ping-pong with a cat is a simplified and more individualistic form of the proper game. You play it close to the ground, and you imagine the net.

Gaining a cat's confidence is different from gaining the confidence of any other animal. Food is not the simple answer. You have to be prepared to play with it for as long as two hours on end. To gain the initial interest of a cat, I always place a piece of paper over my head and face and utter miaows and other cat noises. This is irresistible to most cats, who come nosing up to see what is going on behind the paper. The next phase involves soft whispering alternately with the whistling of high-pitched tunes.

I thought *Bluebells of Scotland* would be appropriate to Bluebell. She was enchanted. It made her purr and rise on her hind legs to paw my shoulder as I crouched on the patio whistling to her in the early afternoons.

After that I began daily to play with her, sometimes throwing the ping-pong ball in the air. She often leapt beautifully and caught it in her forepaws. By the second week in June I had so far won her confidence and approval as to be able to make fierce growling noises at her. She liked these very much, and would crouch menacingly before me, springing suddenly at me in a mock attack. Sometimes I would stalk her, one slow step after another, bent double, and with glaring eyes. She loved this wildly, making flying leaps at my downthrust head.

'You'll get a nasty scratch one day,' said Robinson.

'Oh, I understand cats,' I said.

'She understands cats,' said Jimmie unnecessarily.

Robinson walked away.

Having worked round Bluebell to a stage where she would let me do nearly anything with her and play rough-house as I pleased, I got an old carton out of Robinson's storehouse and set it on end against the patio wall. Bluebell immediately sat herself inside this little three-walled house. Then the first ping-pong lesson began. I knelt down two yards away from her and placed the ball in front of me. She crouched in readiness as if it were an ordinary ball game. With my middle finger and thumb I pinged the ball into Bluebell's box. It bounced against the walls. The cat sprang at it and batted it back. I sent it over again to Bluebell. This time she caught it in her forepaws and curled up on the ground, biting it and kicking it with her silver hind pads. However, for a first lesson her style was not bad. Within a week Bluebell had got the ping-pong idea. Four times out of ten she would send the ball back to me, sometimes batting it with her hind leg most comically, so that even Miguel had to laugh. On the other occasions she would appropriate the ball for herself, either dribbling it right across the patio, or patting it under her body and then sitting on it. Sometimes she would pat the ball only a little way in front of her, waiting for me, with her huge green eyes, to come and retrieve it.

The cat quickly discovered that the setting up of her carton on the patio was the start of the ping-pong game, and she was always waiting for me at that spot after lunch. She was an encouraging pupil, an enthusiast. One day when she was doing particularly well, and I was encouraging her with my lion growl to her great excitement, I heard Robinson's voice from the back of the house.

'Bluebell! Pussy-puss Bluebell. Nice puss. Come on!'

Her ear twitched very slightly in response, but she was at the ball and patting it over to me, it seemed in one movement. I cracked it back, and she forth again.

'Bluebell! – Where's the cat?' said Robinson, appearing on the patio just as I was growling more. 'There's a mouse in the storehouse. Do you *mind?*' he said to me.

The cat had her eyes on my hand which held the ball. I picked her up and handed her to Robinson. Bluebell struggled to free herself and go for the ball. I thought this funny and giggled accordingly. But Bluebell was borne reluctant away by solemn Robinson, with Miguel following like a righteous little retainer.

From *Robinson* by Muriel Spark

The Moonlighter

A Fisherman's tale boasts an unlikely hero in Eric Cross's evocation of rural Ireland.

Jerry, my saint, had a cat, which he called the 'Moonlighter'. He was very fond of it, and he would talk to it, and the cat would understand it. Certainly that cat had sense. Tell me the cat that has not. Jerry used to tell a story himself about how sensible the 'Moonlighter' was. I don't know if it was true, but I will tell it to you as it was told to me by Jerry himself.

Jerry was a great poacher, and one time, when the salmon were running up the river in the spawning season, Jerry and the 'Moonlighter' went out for a night's sport. Jerry was a great artist at getting a salmon out of a river. There was none better.

Jerry took one bank of the river and the 'Moonlighter' took the other. Jerry did fairly well at the game himself, and after a while he counted up and found that he had put out eleven.

He called over to the 'Moonlighter', 'How are things going with you, saint? I have eleven myself.'

The cat turned round and counted his own share of the night's work, and he found that he had eleven, too. What did he do but in with him to the river and out again with another salmon in his arms, making twelve and one the better of Jerry. I tell you, that cat was no mean scholar.

When the 'Moonlighter' died, Jerry was heartbroken. He thought that he was his only friend in the world. He waked him for two nights and two days. It was a right proper wake, too. There was tobacco and pipes and whiskey, and the 'Moonlighter' was laid out on Jerry's own bed. Then he buried him in a box, and put up a headstone to him.

From *The Tailor and Ansty* by Eric Cross

Addict Cats

One of the Boys

Lancelot Mulliner has almost had his spirit broken by Webster, the archbishop's puritanical cat, until Webster is confronted with a different kind of broken spirit.

For some minutes Lancelot Mulliner remained where he was, stunned. Then, insistently, there came to him the recollection that he had not had that drink. He rushed to the cupboard and produced the bottle. He uncorked it, and was pouring out a lavish stream, when a movement on the floor below him attracted his attention.

Webster was standing there, looking up at him. And in his eyes was that familiar expression of quiet rebuke.

'Scarcely what I have been accustomed to at the Deanery,' he seemed to be saying.

Lancelot stood paralysed. The feeling of being bound hand and foot, of being caught in a snare from which there was no escape, had become more poignant than ever. The bottle fell from his nerveless fingers and rolled across the floor, spilling its contents in an amber river, but he was too heavy in spirit to notice it. With a gesture such as Job might have made on discovering a new boil, he crossed to the window and stood looking moodily out.

Then, turning with a sigh, he looked at Webster again – and, looking, stood spellbound.

The spectacle which he beheld was of a kind to stun a stronger man than Lancelot Mulliner. At first, he shrank from believing his eyes. Then, slowly, came the realization that what he saw was no mere figment of a disordered imagination. This unbelievable thing was actually happening.

Webster sat crouched upon the floor beside the widening pool of whisky. But it was not horror and disgust that had caused him to crouch. He was crouched because, crouching, he could get nearer to the stuff and obtain crisper action. His tongue was moving in and out like a piston.

And then abruptly, for one fleeting instant, he stopped lapping and glanced up at Lancelot, and across his face there flitted a quick smile – so genial, so intimate, so full of jovial camaraderie, that the young man found himself automatically smiling back, and not only smiling but winking. And in answer to that wink Webster winked too – a whole-hearted, roguish wink that said as plainly as if he had spoken the words:

'How long has this been going on?'

Then with a slight hiccough he turned back to the task of getting his drink before it soaked into the floor.

Into the murky soul of Lancelot Mulliner there poured a sudden flood of sunshine. It was as if a great burden had been lifted from his shoulders. The intolerable obsession of the last two weeks had ceased to oppress him, and he felt a free man. At the eleventh hour the reprieve had come. Webster, that seeming pillar of austere virtue, was one of the boys, after all. Never again would Lancelot quail beneath his eye. He had the goods on him.

Webster, like the stag at eve, had now drunk his fill. He had left the pool of alcohol and was walking round in slow, meditative circles. From time to time he mewed tentatively, as if he were trying to say 'British Constitution'. His failure to articulate the syllables appeared to tickle him, for at the end of each attempt he would utter a slow, amused chuckle. It was about this moment that he suddenly broke into a rhythmic dance, not unlike the old Saraband.

It was an interesting spectacle, and at any other time Lancelot would have watched it raptly. But now he was busy at his desk, writing a brief note to Mrs Carberry-Pirbright, the burden of which was that if she thought he was coming within a mile of her foul house that night or any other night she had vastly underrated the dodging powers of Lancelot Mulliner.

And what of Webster? The Demon Rum now had him in an iron grip. A lifetime of abstinence had rendered him a ready victim to the fatal fluid. He had now reached the stage when geniality gives way to belligerence. The rather foolish smile had gone from his face, and in its stead there lowered a fighting frown. For a few moments he stood on his hind legs, looking about him for a suitable adversary: then, losing all vestiges of self-control, he ran five times round the room at a high rate of speed and, falling foul of a small footstool, attacked it with the utmost ferocity, sparing neither tooth nor claw.

From 'The Story of Webster' by P. G. Wodehouse

Soup's On

A man and his cat drown their sorrows in Robert Heinlein's futuristic fantasy.

. . . the SANS SOUCI Bar Grill, the sign said. I went in, picked a booth halfway back, placed the overnight bag I was carrying carefully on the seat, slid in by it, and waited for the waiter.

The overnight bag said, 'Waarrrh?'

I said, 'Take it easy, Pete.'

'Naaow!'

'Nonsense, you just went. Pipe down, the waiter is coming.'

Pete shut up. I looked up as the waiter leaned over the table, and said to him, 'A double shot of your bar Scotch, a glass of plain water, and a split of ginger ale.'

The waiter looked upset. 'Ginger ale, sir? With Scotch?'

'Do you have it or don't you?'

'Why, yes, of course. But—'

'Then fetch it. I'm not going to drink it; I just want to sneer at it. And bring a saucer too.'

'As you say, sir.' He polished the table top. 'How about a small steak, sir? Or the scallops are very good today.'

'Look, mate, I'll tip you for the scallops if you'll promise not to serve them. All I need is what I ordered . . . and don't forget the saucer.'

He shut up and went away. I told Pete again to take it easy, the Marines had landed. The waiter returned, his pride appeased by carrying the split of ginger ale on the saucer. I had him open it while I mixed the Scotch with the water. 'Would you like another glass for the ginger ale, sir?'

'I'm a real buckaroo; I drink it out of the bottle.'

He shut up and let me pay him and tip him, not forgetting a tip for the scallops. When he had gone I poured ginger ale into the saucer and tapped on the top of the overnight bag. 'Soup's on, Pete.'

It was unzipped; I never zipped it with him inside. He spread it with his paws, poked his head out, looked around quickly, then levitated his forequarters and placed his front feet on the edge of the table. I raised my glass and we looked at each other. 'Here's to the female race, Pete – find 'em and forget 'em!'

He nodded; it matched his own philosophy perfectly. He bent his head daintily and started lapping up ginger ale. 'If you can, that is,' I added, and took a deep swig. Pete did not answer. Forgetting a female was no effort to him; he was the natural-born bachelor type.

From *The Door into Summer* by Robert Heinlein

The Mandarin

The amiable Mandarin leads a sedentary existence, until Skip and Marvell spike her dinner.

Marvell stood swaying at the kitchen door. 'O.K.,' he said, closing it noise-lessly behind him and joining Skip by the cooker. Marvell handed Skip something small. At their feet The Mandarin purred stertorously as it worked its way through a large bowl of Kat.

'Right,' said Marvell. 'Dump it in its fuckin food. Give it fuckin all of it.'

Skip crouched, chuckling.

'Is it eating it?'

'It . . . Sure,' said Skip.

'Fuckin cats. Kick the shit out of them one minute, feed them the next, they think you're fuckin God. O.K.?'

'O.K.'

'Right. C'mon. Let's go watch the preview.'

'Whose cat was it, Mar? D'you know?'

'Leave the door open. So it can get out. Celia's, I think. Yeah, it – I think it belonged to Celia.'

'Look!' she cried. 'Here's my friend The Mandarin.'

Celia turned and smiled into her husband's green eyes. Those present looked up blearily.

'*Isn't* she in a good mood!'

She did seem to be. The Mandarin came jumping in from the kitchen. It spun round. Its tail hairbrushed and its body went tense. It leapt hissing in the air. Its body flattened out like a hunter. It ran galvanically round the room, on sofas, chairs, walls. It cuffed a champagne cork along the carpet. It lay on its back and indolently feinted at the air. It chased its tail. It ground and flexed its claws on the skirting-board. It went into a series of soft little springs. It nosed about the floor in impossible caution. Its eyes closed. It edged into the lap–like convexity of a cushion. It curled up and –

'It curled up and then we all like flashed that it was dead,' Roxeanne explained.

Andy knelt over The Mandarin's body. He raised its kittenish head – the creased eyelids, the folded–back, lupine ears. When he let go it fell at once into its dead posture.

'It just freaked,' said Marvell.

'Yeah.'

Andy crossed the room and gripped Celia's trembling shoulder. Quentin, in whose arms her head was buried, looked up hushedly at his friend.

'It was very old,' he said.

'Yeah.'

From *Dead Babies* by Martin Amis

Predatory Cats

Monmouth

'I am delighted to hear it,' said Mrs Jaraby, in reply to some statement of her husband's about the meeting.

Mr Jaraby poured himself tea, moving his teeth about with his tongue. Food was wedged somewhere. When he had released it he said:

'You are not. You say you are delighted but in fact you take no interest in the matter at all.'

Mrs Jaraby watched her husband's cat stalking a bird in the garden. The room they sat in smelt of the cat. Its hairs clung to the cushions. The surface of a small table had been savaged by its claws.

'I was being civil,' said Mrs Jaraby.

'Turtle came in late. He kept us cooling our heels. He claimed to have been in the company of a charwoman.'

'Well, well.' She believed he kept the cat only because she disliked it. Once a week he cooked fish for it in the kitchen, and she was forced on that day to leave the house and go to a cinema.

'He seems twice his years. And I thought was looking remarkably unhealthy. He has a dicky heart, poor fellow.'

'Which one seemed twice his years? It is something I would like to see. He would be a hundred and forty.'

'Be careful now: you are deliberately provoking me.'

'I am merely curious. How does this ancient look? Is he withered like a dead leaf, crooked and crackling?'

'You are picking up my remarks and trying to make a nonsense out of them. Are you unwell that you behave in this way? Don't say we are going to have illness in the house.'

'I am less well than I would be if the cat were not here. Your Monmouth has just disembowelled a bird on the lawn.'

'Ha, ha. So now you claim illness because we keep a pet. Are you psychic that you know what happens on the lawn?'

'A normal pet I might welcome. But a cat the size of a tiger I draw the line at. I know what happens on the lawn because I can observe the lawn through the window from where I sit.'

'My dear woman, you are too clever by half. I have said it before and I can only repeat it.' Mr Jaraby took a long draught of tea and leaned back in his armchair, pleased that once again he had established the truth of his wife's contrariness.

In the garden the cat fluffed through the sticky feathers, seeking a last mouthful. The late evening sun cooled the glow of antirrhinums and delphiniums, and bronzed the stones of the tiny rockery. The cat strode to the centre of the grass, its body slung high on black rods of legs, its huge furry tail extended in line with its back. A rat had once leapt at its left eye and bitten it from its head: there remained only a dark shell, a gap like a cave, with a hint of redness about it.

From *The Old Boys* by William Trevor

A Hunting Cat

Stevie Smith describes the following incident with the same detached fascination as her subject might have observed its prey.

I will now tell you about a hunting cat I once observed. As I put this hunting cat scene in a novel I once wrote, I will if I may lift it straight from that novel as then it was fresh to me and if I told it over again it would not be. It was a hot day in summer, and I was swimming at the seaside with a cousin, not my elderly old lady cousin this time, but a boy cousin and a dear one, his name was Caz. So this is how it goes:

'We were now swimming above a sandbank some half mile or so out from the shore. Presently the sandbank broke surface and we climbed out and stood up on it. All around us was nothing but the sea and the sand and the hot still air. Look, I said, what is this coming? (It was a piece of wreckage that was turning round in the current by the sandbank and coming towards us.) Why, I said, it is a cat. And there sure enough, standing spitting upon the wooden spar was a young cat. We must get it in, said Caz, and stretched out to get it. But I saw that the cat was not spitting for the thought of its plight – so far from land, so likely to be drowned – but for a large sea-beetle that was marooned upon the spar with the cat, and that the cat was stalking and spitting at. First it backed from the beetle with its body arched and its tail stiff, then, lowering its belly to the spar, it crawled slowly towards the beetle, placing its paws carefully and with the claws well out. Why look, said Caz, its jaws are chattering. The chatter of the teeth of the hunting cat could now be heard as the spar came swinging in to the sandbank. Caz made a grab for the spar, but the young cat, its eyes dark with anger, pounced upon his hand and tore it right across. Caz let go with a start and the piece of wreckage swung off at right angles and was already far away upon the current. We could not have taken it with us, I said, that cat is fighting mad, he does not wish to be rescued, with his baleful eye and his angry teeth chattering at the hunt, he does not wish for security.

From *Me Again* by Stevie Smith

Cat

Cat watches the lamp, concave
half-bow, but
the bug has gone to sleep,
a dancing dwarf from the land of ghosts.

The bug had black shining wings,
lined with emeralds,
closely-clipped into
place, its legs jointed wire.

Cat, lie in my lap, fat,
your jerky purr
not once calming you, or
causing your head to lower.

John Newlove

Mister Minkles

There was a time when kitchens in the afternoon held their distance. Cooks and kitchenmaids used to tidy up the kitchen at Durraghglass, perhaps take a little rest from their duties until it was time to make the Sally Lunn for drawing-room tea. Not any more, naturally. Times change.

In the big kitchen, where Jasper now ruled, nothing was ever tidied up, stored, or thrown away. Cats were the scavengers. Cardboard wine cases that had carried more groceries than wine to the house were piled and heaped and thrown in corners. Cats had their kittens in them – mostly born to be drowned. Jasper's great tiger cat, Mister Minkles, was the sire of them all. Strangely, he was clean for a tom cat. No dog ever had a more loving heart. Jasper returned his love and respected him as a person. Now he sat with majesty at the centre of the white deal dresser – sat on the breadboard. Behind him tier on tier of chipped and unchipped dinner services (Mason's ironware mostly), rose upward to the hook-studded ceiling, barren now of hams, and covered in dust thick as ashes.

* * *

Jasper's cat, having eaten as much as he was able of the pigeon, returned to the breadboard where he sat at his ease, making the noises of a sated tiger. 'All right, sit there if it gives you the smallest pleasure,' Jasper spoke in a different voice from the nipped-in tone of patient or impatient dislike provoked from him by his sisters. His love for that fierce cat and his predecessors set free in him a benison of indulgence, objectless since little Mummie's death. Seated on the breadboard within the wreath of carved wheatears, Mister Minkles not only supplied an object for Jasper's affection and carefulness, he embodied his enduring defiance of those sisters with their clinical, dainty ideas. They were afraid of Mister Minkles, afraid for themselves as well as for their dogs.

From *Time After Time* by Molly Keane

Close Encounters of the Furred Kind

Hazel the rabbit saves offends a cat's dignity in Richard Adams' tale of war on the warrens.

Boxwood was about to reply when suddenly Pipkin spoke from the floor. 'Hazel, there's a cat in the yard outside!'

'We're not afraid of cats,' said Hazel to Boxwood, 'as long as we're in the open.' Trying to appear unhurried, he went back to the floor by way of the straw-bale and crossed over to the door. Pipkin was looking through the hinge. He was plainly frightened.

'I think it's smelt us, Hazel,' he said. 'I'm afraid it knows where we are.'

'Don't stay there, then,' said Hazel. 'Follow me close and run when I do.' Without waiting to look out through the hinge, he went round the half-open door of the shed and stopped on the threshold.

The cat, a tabby with white chest and paws, was at the farther end of the little yard, walking slowly and deliberately along the side of a pile of logs. When Hazel appeared in the doorway it saw him at once and stood stock-still, with staring eyes and twitching tail. Hazel hopped slowly across the threshold and stopped again. Already sunlight was slanting across the yard and in the stillness the flies buzzed about a patch of dung a few feet away. There was a smell of straw and dust and hawthorn.

'You look hungry,' said Hazel to the cat. 'Rats getting too clever, I suppose?'

The cat made no reply. Hazel sat blinking in the sunshine. The cat crouched almost flat on the ground, thrusting its head forward between its front paws. Close behind, Pipkin fidgeted and Hazel, never taking his eyes from the cat, could sense that he was trembling.

'Don't be frightened, Hlao-roo,' he whispered. 'I'll get you away, but you must wait till it comes for us. Keep still.'

The cat began to lash its tail. Its hindquarters lifted and wagged from side to side in mounting excitement.

'Can you run?' said Hazel. 'I think not. Why, you pop-eyed, back-door saucer-scraper –'

The cat flung itself across the yard and the two rabbits leapt into flight with great thrusts of their hind legs. The cat came very fast indeed and although both of them had been braced ready to move on the instant, they were barely out of the yard in time. Racing up the side of the long barn, they heard the Labrador barking in excitement as it ran to the full extent of its rope. A man's voice shouted to it. From the cover of the hedge beside the lane they turned and looked back. The cat had stopped short and was licking one paw with a pretence of nonchalance.

'They hate to look silly,' said Hazel. 'It won't give us any more trouble.'

From *Watership Down* by Richard Adams

Cat Superstitions

The Cat's Revenge

Bernard Shaw's father was dogged by a feline curse which condemned him to a lifetime's unseriousness.

The story of George Carr Shaw's life was simple. He would tell you it had evolved as the retribution for an injury he had once done a cat. He had found this cat, brought it home with him, fed it. But next day he had let his dog chase it and kill it. In his imagination this cat now had its revenge, seeing to it that he would have neither luck nor money. He was permanently unsuccessful because of this cat; unskilled, unsober, and unserious too. It was no less than natural justice: he knew that. His genius for poverty established this lesson beyond doubt. His fate was to become 'a futile person'.

From *The Search for Love, Bernard Shaw, Volume I (1856–1898)*
by Michael Holroyd

The Return of the Sea-cat

The legendary fiend that almost scuppered St Brendan's voyage was also sighted in Flann O'Brien's unserious novel of Irish life.

The following day the Old-Grey-Fellow returned to us with his hunting-bag. We welcomed him tenderly and we all sat down to potatoes. When everybody within the house, both porcine and human, was replenished with potatoes, I took the Old-Fellow aside and whispered in his ear. I stated that my health was not too good after the events of the preceding night.

– Is it boozing you were at, oh young little son, he said, or was it night-hunting?

– In truth, no sir! I replied, but a great thing on legs was chasing me. I don't know any word of Gaelic for it but it was not to my good, without a doubt. I don't know how I managed to escape from it but I'm here today and it's a great victory for me. 'Twould be a shameful thing if I was lost from this life and I in the flower of my youth because my likes will not be there again.

– Were you in Donegal at that time, my soul? said he.

– I was.

A ruminative cloud gathered over the face of the Old–Grey–Fellow.

– Could you put down on paper, said he, the shape and appearance of this savage thing for me?

The memory of the previous night was so firmly fixed in my mind that I made little delay in drawing an image of the creature when I had procured paper. It was thus:

The Old–Fellow looked closely at the picture* and a shadow crept over his visage.

– If that's how it is, son, said he fearfully, it's good news that you're alive today and in your health among us. What you met last night was the Sea–cat! The Sea–cat!!

The blood drained from my face when I heard that evil name being mentioned by the Old–Fellow.

– It seems, said he, that he was after coming out of the sea to carry out some mischievous work in the Rosses because he had often been in that area in the past, attacking the paupers and scattering death and ill–luck liberally among them. His name is always in the people's mouths there.

– The Sea–cat . . . ? said I. My feet were not too staunch beneath me while I stood there.

– The same cat.

– Is it the way, said I weakly, that no one else saw the Sea–cat before this?

– 'Tis my idea that they did, said he slowly, but no account of it was got from them. They did not live!

From *The Poor Mouth* by Flann O'Brien

---

*The good reader will kindly notice the close resemblance between the Sea–cat, as delineated by O'Coonassa, and the pleasant little land which is our own. Many things in life are unintelligible to us but it is not without importance that the Sea–cat and Ireland bear the same shape and that both have all the same bad destiny, hard times and ill–luck attending on them which have come upon us.

A Bowl of Blood

Fursey and his 'familiar' Albert pay a visit to a sorcerer, in Mervyn Wall's satire of tenth-century monastic Ireland.

The only evidence that the occupant was other than a highly respectable sexton was a manuscript with cabalistic signs which lay on the table between two rushlights, and a huge brindled cat sitting on the hearth who, when Fursey caught her eye, grinned at him furiously.

The sexton pulled a stool up to the table and seated himself opposite Fursey. He folded the manuscript carefully and put it aside.

'Very fine weather we're having for this time of the year,' he remarked affably.

Fursey agreed that it was.

'Forgive me,' said the sexton, 'I have neglected to make the usual introductions. This is Tibbikins, my familiar.'

'I'm pleased to make your acquaintance,' muttered Fursey hoarsely.

The cat nodded cheerily and favoured Fursey with another grin. Albert lumbered over to the hearth, and the two familiars began a conversation in low tones.

'I judge from the fact that you have Albert attached to you, that you are now of the profession,' continued the sexton, 'but I am unaware of the name by which you are called.'

'My name is Fursey.'

'You are a monk?'

'No. A widower.'

'Ah yes,' the sexton nodded sympathetically. 'I watched the marriage ceremony on the road below this afternoon. Very unfortunate business, your wife's demise; but, if I may say so, she had become a little high in herself recently. There was a goat also who, not content with eating a gatepost and a wire fence, consumed several of my trees and half the produce of my garden. I never knew an animal with such a prodigious appetite. No sooner had I some rare and valuable herbs planted, than they disappeared into her stomach. I'm fond of animals myself, but I do think that if one keeps livestock, one should keep them under control. Don't you agree with me?'

Fursey nodded bleakly.

'Oh Tibbikins,' said the sexton turning towards the hearth, 'perhaps you would like to take Albert into the other room and offer him a bowl of blood.'

Albert had no tail, but he wagged his hindquarters to show his appreciation as he shuffled out of the room in the wake of the brindled cat.

From *The Unfortunate Fursey* by Mervyn Wall

The Cat as Aphrodisiac

If the liver of a black cat was ground into a fine powder and infused into a potion it served as a powerful aphrodisiac. The one who drank the potion would instantly fall passionately in love with the one who proffered it. The tale was told of the pretty Nora who wooed the young squire with a potent brew of strong tea laced with the ground liver of a cat. The squire inevitably fell head over heels in love with the coquettish Nora and made a proposal of marriage to her, but he was saved from a fate worse than death when some of his relatives set upon him with hazel sticks in the most vigorous manner possible. He was dragged from the bosom of his betrothed on the eve of their wedding night. He soon recovered, however, for the power of the hazel sticks had overcome the influence of Nora's sorcery – and if the squire complained of a sore head for a few weeks, well at least he had been spared the indignity of spending the rest of his life with one who enjoyed killing cats and pulverising their livers.

From *Irish Superstitions and Legends of Birds and Animals*,
ed. Patrick V. O'Sullivan

The Governor

General Gordon described an Indian superstition that earned military honour for a whole tribe of regimental cats.

My staff duties at Poona brought me into contact with two regimental commanding officers who laboured hard to make mountains out of molehills, and to bring into ridicule the institution of trial by court-martial. They were both martinets of a severe type, and had no sense of the sympathetic or amusing side of things. One of them commanded a regiment of British infantry, and on returning from leave of absence to England, he decreed the cessation of wearing beards, a custom which had been permitted during and after the Mutiny campaign.

In the other case the officer commanded a regiment of native infantry, and it had been discovered that for twenty-five years past an oral addition to the written standing orders of the native guard at Government House, near Poona, had been communicated regularly from one guard to another, on relief, to the effect that any cat passing out of the front door after dark was to be regarded as His Excellency the Governor, and to be saluted accordingly. The meaning of this was that Sir Robert Grant, Governor of Bombay, had died there in

1838, and on the evening of the day of his death a cat was seen to leave the house by the front door and walk up and down a particular path, as had been the Governor's habit to do, after sunset. A Hindu sentry had observed this, and he mentioned it to others of his faith, who made it a subject of superstitious conjecture, the result being that one of the priestly class explained the mystery of the dogma of the transmigration of the soul from one body to another, and interpreted the circumstances to mean that the spirit of the deceased Governor had entered into one of the house pets. It was difficult to fix on a particular one, and it was therefore decided that every cat passing out of the main entrance after dark was to be regarded as the tabernacle of Governor Grant's soul, and to be treated with due respect and the proper honours. This decision was accepted without question by all the native attendants and others belonging to Government House. The whole guard, from sepoy to subadar, fully acquiesced in it, and an oral addition was made to the standing orders that the sentry at the front door would 'present arms' to any cat passing out there after dark. The notion was essentially Hindu, yet the Mahomedans and native Christians and Jews (native Jews are to be found in the Bombay army) devoutly assented to it. Dread of the supernatural overcame all religious objections, and every one scrupulously bowed to the heathen decree.

> From *A Varied Life: A Record of Military and Civil Service, of Sport
> and of Travel in India, Central Asia and Persia, 1849–1902*
> by General Sir Thomas Edward Gordon

Absent Cats

Dostoievsky

Our cat had gone
When we returned from holiday.
A week forgetting him,
Browning our pallor miles away,

And he was gone. Walked out on us.
His alert, delicate contempt had suggested Dostoievsky,
And so I'd called him:
The name satisfied my intellectual vanity.

The kids called him Dusty
And profligated the love of youth
On him. He ignored them, preferring
To snap wasps with his red mouth,

Eating them, stings and all. He was like that –
A baroque destroyer, researching
A library of garbage with taloned eloquence,
Minutely secret as a professor.

When we came back from the seaside
He was gone. No goodbye,
Merely an absent wish
And something to remember him by –

A pillow's worth of feathers
And two dead birds on the living-room floor,
Guts spilling from the half-open corpses like
Underclothing from a dowager's boudoir drawer.

Among the intestine clots
A million maggots wagged,
Bulbous whitey things, wriggling, squirming, gorging
In half-gore carcasses stiff like crags.

The children missed him,
Dusty, they searched and called.
He didn't come. This indifference
Was once for all.

I'd only called him Dostoeivsky
Out of intellectual pride;
When Dusty went,
The children cried.

Robert Leach

Blooding Smut

William attempts to derive some entertainment from Aunt Florence's prize cat, with unfortunate consequences.

He soon left the little town behind him and strode on towards the open country. He walked till he found himself near a farm. There was a large, fascinating-looking barn in a field near it, and William distinctly saw a rat in the act of disappearing beneath its supports. He went nearer to investigate. Beneath the supports of the barn was a perfect warren of rat-holes. It would be a paradise for rat-hunting. William had often vaguely thought of finding a ferret and training it to hunt rats, putting it into the rat-holes one by one to bring a rat out of each. It was a fascinating idea, and he had often looked for a ferret in order to try it. He hunted for a ferret for the rest of the morning, but had to set off homeward as usual without having found one. It was as he was on his homeward way that another idea struck him, an idea so obvious that he wondered why he had never thought of it before.

Why not train a cat to go down rat-holes and catch rats just as a ferret catches rabbits? He felt that he could hardly wait a second before putting the idea to the test. The rats were there, the rat-holes were there, and – Smut was there. He hurried homeward, trying to hide his eagerness as he reached the house and to assume the expression of an invalid who has nevertheless benefited from a nice brisk walk.

'How do you feel now, my boy?' said Aunt Florence.

William assured her that his side felt much better – so much better, in fact, that he thought he'd go for another nice long walk that afternoon.

'I have to go to a meeting this afternoon,' said Aunt Florence; 'a lecture on Central Asia by a returned missionary. I'd thought that perhaps you'd like to accompany me.'

William hastily said that he thought that wouldn't do his side any good and that what he needed was another nice long walk.

Fortunately for William's plan Aunt Florence set off for her meeting directly after lunch, leaving him in possession of the house. It was the work of a few moments to find the basket in which Smut was conveyed to and from the local cat shows, to ram him into it, and set off briskly for the open country and the rat-infested barn. No one was in sight, and William at once began his task of training Smut. Smut, however, was not in a trainable mood. Though quite accustomed to his cat basket, he was not accustomed to the cavalier fashion in which he had been crammed into it without the usual lining of soft down cushions. And he was not accustomed to being swung backward and forward as William had thoughtlessly swung the basket during his walk to the farm. He emerged bristling with outraged dignity. He was not soothed or reassured by being unceremoniously thrust head first down a rat-hole to the accompaniment of: 'Go on, Smut, boy! Fetch it out!' There was no doubt at all that Smut was too large for the rat-holes, but William did not see why he should not be trained to accommodate himself to them by a little muscular compression. With this object in view he rammed the head of the unfortunate animal into several of the largest holes, cheering it on in its new task as he did so: 'That's right, Smut! Jolly good, old boy! Fetch 'em out, then! Fetch 'em out!'

Smut, goaded to madness by this ignominious treatment, half suffocated, completely coated with mud, managed at last to free himself by an agile twist and fled from the scene like the proverbial greased lightning. William pursued him unavailingly for some distance calling: 'Come on, Smut boy! Come on, then! Good boy! Milk, Smut, milk!'

Smut refused to listen to his cajolements, but the farm dogs came to see what it was all about, and William helplessly watched his aunt's cat streaking away over a ploughed field in the opposite direction from its home with four or five farm dogs in hot pursuit.

From *William the Gangster* by Richmal Crompton

A Catless Young Woman

In the summer of 1906 Gwen John went to visit her lover, Auguste Rodin, at his villa in Meudon. Naturally, the cat came too.

She found a 'room' among the bushes outside the fence, unpacked her cat and her sketch-book and started to draw the villa. Tiger was ecstatic. 'It was a pleasure to see the little figure in the country,' she told Rodin, 'beaming with happiness, her tail straight as she ran.' Soon a woman came into the garden, followed by two dogs, and sat on the bench. She was elderly and dressed in grey, and Gwen John felt sure she was Rose Beuret, the peasant woman who had shared Rodin's life and borne him a son, but had never been his wife. To Gwen John she was a friend for while Rodin was at Meudon with the thorny Rose no other woman dared approach him.

When darkness fell Gwen took the tram home. To her horror, when it stopped at St Cloud, Tiger shot from her shawl and out through the door. Some 'red dogs' in the street gave chase and soon the cat had disappeared. Frantically Gwen John ran up and down the village calling her name. She asked everyone she saw, 'Have you seen my cat?' Some of them laughed at her, imitating her pronunciation and several men offered her an arm and said *they* would find her a cat if she would come this way. Three evil-looking girls sitting outside a house with their 'mother' started pretending to see the cat when it wasn't there, and the old woman who called Gwen John a *poupée* turned out to be the owner of the local brothel.

Between the houses and the river there was a piece of waste ground. Frantic to get away from the jeering prostitutes and their patrons, Gwen John wandered there among the clumps of nettles and piles of rubbish. The ground was rough and several times she stumbled into holes. Sometimes she thought she heard the distant cry of a cat, but it was always too far away. She decided to spend what was left of the night on the ground.

For nine days Gwen John went native. 'I am living like Robinson Crusoe under a tree,' she told Rodin. She laid an elaborate grid of meat parcels over the whole area each night and lay down to wait. Her dreams were punctuated by the squeaks of rats and toads, for 'only loathsome creatures inhabit this place'. She woke stiff each morning and found the grass drenched. The meat parcels would be gone, but she knew it was not Tiger who had taken them, for she would have 'unwrapped the paper, not torn it'.

Then she launched a campaign of which a general might have been proud. She offered a reward of twenty francs for the finder of the cat (the money to be paid by Rodin) and she asked Rodin to send her a permit to search every garden in St Cloud and Meudon. This searching of gardens was not popular. One wealthy widow by the river at St Cloud refused to open her premises to a hatless young woman (Gwen John afterwards insisted she was wearing a *small* hat) and promised to investigate the garden herself. Gwen came back that night uninvited and searched it. Once when trespassing at night she was chased by a big dog. Playing for time she threw it the parcel of meat she was carrying and flung herself over the garden fence only to find herself suspended by her skirt on the far side. By undoing the skirt she managed to release herself, but was left standing in the street naked from the waist down.

After six days she lost hope. The men of St Cloud had taxed their brains for original ways for a cat to die and were gratified by the English lady's reactions to their suggestions. *La chatte* might be shut in a house, she might have died of hunger, or boredom, might have been eaten by a dog, a rabbit or a tramp, she might have eaten a frog, she might have gone down a railway tunnel or down a well. She might even have swum the Seine and got to Boulogne.

Gwen John was by now dishevelled and desperate. She went into Paris to keep a modelling engagement with Constance Lloyd, an old friend from the Slade, but turned white and had to stop after an hour. Worse still, there was an unkind letter from Rodin waiting. He had been angry with her for losing the cat and was angrier with her for sleeping out. After reading the letter she knew that Rodin no longer loved her because she was a stupid person who could not even take care of a cat. 'All is finished for me,' she wrote to him. 'I would like to live longer but I will not be pretty and happy for you without my cat.'

She walked that night by the Seine and sat on the high parapet of the Pont d'Alma. The black water sparkled under the lights of the barges. Suddenly she looked round and saw a crowd behind her. Too embarrassed to move, she looked back at the water and hoped they'd go away. 'Why are you sitting there, young woman?' someone called.

'She's a foreigner.'

'Yes, English.'

'Are you alone in Paris?'

Still Gwen John did not reply.

'Poor thing.'

Now she saw a hand beside her on the parapet. It was a *gendarme*. 'Keen on fishing?' Everyone laughed and Gwen John at last found the courage to escape.

Her room looked forlorn after six days' neglect. Tiger was no longer curled on the wicker chair. She began to prepare the room for death. She did not want Rodin to find anything out of order when she was gone. She dusted and polished and changed the flowers. Perhaps she thought of the death scene in the last chapter of *The Idiot*. And then a message came from Meudon. A cat that looked white from the front and tabby from the side had been seen near the Villa des Brillants.

Gwen John took the train to Val Fleuri and hurried up the hill to her 'room' among the bushes. Secretly she had always thought Tiger would return to the place where they had spent the day together. Once more she arranged meat on paper plates among the surrounding bushes. A kind peasant woman living with her husband and child near Rodin's villa said, 'As sure as I carry this pot you will see your cat in eight days.' She insisted on making up a bed for Gwen John in her garden but once she was asleep Gwen John slipped away to sleep in her 'room'. The grass rustled, the owls hooted and the mice 'played the flute and the piccolo'. For three days and nights she lay in the undergrowth, naked by day, and turned brown. And then before dawn on the morning of 17 July Tiger came. Gwen John had just risen, stiff from the wet ground, to take a look at a Greek torso. When she returned to the 'room' a white figure was standing there with big unhappy eyes. It was Tiger. In a moment the cat was purring in her owner's arms. Gwen John ran to the peasant's house to proclaim the good news and get food for the famished animal. But it was still only four a.m. and he and his wife were asleep. By climbing on to an outhouse roof Gwen John could see them in bed through the bedroom window. There was nothing to do but settle down once more and wait. The exhausted cat lay quietly across her stomach. When the peasants woke she broke the news. 'How happy we are, Mademoiselle,' they cried. 'How beautiful the little *chatte* is,' although in fact, as Gwen John remarked, she was not beautiful at all but thin and dirty.

From *Gwen John, 1876–1939* by Susan Chitty

Old Cats

Old Cats

Those who love cats which do not even purr,
Or which are thin and tired and very old,
Bend down to them in the street and stroke their fur
And rub their ears and smooth their breast, and hold
Their paws, and gaze into their eyes of gold.

Francis Scarfe

Cheerio My Deario

(By Archy the Cockroach)

well boss i met
mehitabel the cat
trying to dig a
frozen lamb chop
out of a snow
drift the other day

a heluva comedown
that is for me archy
she says a few
brief centuries
ago one of old
king
tut
ankh
amens favourite
queens and today
the village scavenger
but wotthehell
archy wotthehell

its cheerio
my deario that
pulls a lady through

see here mehitabel
i said i thought
you told me that
it was cleopatra
you used to be
before you
transmigrated into
the carcase of a cat
where do you get
this tut
ankh
amen stuff
question mark

i was several
ladies my little
insect says she
being cleopatra was
only an incident
in my career
and i was always getting
the rough end of it
always being
misunderstood by some
strait laced
prune faced bunch
of prissy mouthed
sisters of uncharity
the things that
have been said
about me archy
exclamation point

and all simply because i was a
live dame
the palaces i have

been kicked out of
in my time
exclamation point

but wotthehell
little archy wot
thehell
its cheerio
my deario
that pulls a
lady through
exclamation point

framed archy always
framed that is the
story of all my lives
no chance for a dame
with the anvil chorus
if she shows a little
motion it seems to
me only yesterday
that the luxor local
number one of
the ladies axe
association got me in
dutch with king tut and
he slipped me the
sarcophagus always my
luck yesterday an empress
and today too
emaciated to interest
a vivisectionist but
toujours gai archy
toujours gai and always
a lady in spite of hell
and transmigration
once a queen
always a queen
archy
period

                    one of her
                    feet was frozen
                    but on the other three
                    she began to caper and
                    dance singing its
                    cheerio my deario
                    that pulls a lady
                    through her morals may
                    have been mislaid somewhere
                    in the centuries boss but
                    i admire her spirit
                                archy

                                        Don Marquis

A Cat

She had a name among the children;
But no one loved though some one owned
Her, locked her out of doors at bedtime,
And had her kittens duly drowned.

In spring, nevertheless, this cat
Ate blackbirds, thrushes, nightingales,
And birds of bright voice, and plume, and flight,
As well as scraps from neighbours' pails.

I loathed and hated her for this;
One speckle on a thrush's breast
Was worth a million such; and yet
She lived long till God gave her rest.

                                        Edward Thomas

Ageing

He blinks upon the hearth-rug
And yawns in deep content,
Accepting all the comforts
That Providence has sent.

Louder he purrs, and louder,
In one glad hymn of praise,
For all the night's adventures,
For quiet, restful days.

Life will go on for ever,
With all that cat can wish;
Warmth, and the glad procession
Of fish, and milk and fish.

Only – the thought disturbs him –
He's noticed once or twice,
The times are somehow breeding
A nimbler race of mice.

Alexander Gray

Esther's Tomcat

Daylong this tomcat lies stretched flat
As an old rough mat, no mouth and no eyes.
Continual wars and wives are what
Have tattered his ears and battered his head.

Like a bundle of old rope and iron
Sleeps till blue dusk. Then reappear
His eyes, green as ringstones: he yawns wide red,
Fangs fine as a lady's needle and bright.

A tomcat sprang at a mounted knight,
Locked round his neck like a trap of hooks
While the knight rode fighting its clawing and bite.
After hundreds of years the stain's there

On the stone where he fell, dead of the tom:
That was at Barnborough. The tomcat still
Grallochs odd dogs on the quiet,
Will take the head clean off your simple pullet,

Is unkillable. From the dog's fury,
From gunshot fired point-blank he brings
His skin whole, and whole
From owlish moons of bekittenings

Among ashcans. He leaps and lightly
Walks upon sleep, his mind on the moon.
Nightly over the round world of men,
Over the roofs go his eyes and outcry.

From *Lupercal* by Ted Hughes

The White Cat of Trenarren

(for Beryl Cloke)

He was a mighty hunter in his youth
At Polmear all day on the mound, on the pounce
For anything moving, rabbit or bird or mouse –
    My cat and I grow old together.

After a day's hunting he'd come into the house
Delicate ears stuck all with fleas.
At Trenarren I've heard him sigh with pleasure
After a summer's day in the long-grown leas –
    My cat and I grow old together.

When I was a child I played all day,
With only a little cat for companion,
At solitary games of my own invention
Under the table or up in the green bay –
    My cat and I grow old together.

When I was a boy I wandered the roads
Up to the downs by gaunt Carn Grey,
Wrapt in a dream at end of day,
All round me the moor, below me the bay –
   My cat and I grow old together.

Now we are too often apart, yet
Turning out of Central Park into the Plaza,
Or walking Michigan Avenue against the lake-wind,
I see a little white shade in the shrubbery
Of far-off Trenarren, never far from my mind –
   My cat and I grow old together.

When I come home from too much travelling,
Cautiously he comes out of his lair to my call,
Receives me at first with a shy reproach
At long absence to him incomprehensible –
   My cat and I grow old together.

Incapable of much or long resentment,
He scratches at my door to be let out
In early morning in the ash moonlight,
Or red dawn breaking through Mother Bond's spinney –
   My cat and I grow old together.

No more frisking as of old,
Or chasing his shadow over the lawn,
But a dignified old person, tickling
His nose against twig or flower in the border,
Until evening falls and bed-time's in order,
Unable to keep eyes open any longer
He waits for me to carry him upstairs
To nestle all night snug at foot of bed –
   My cat and I grow old together.

Careful of his licked and polished appearance,
Ears like shell-whorls pink and transparent,
White plume waving proudly over the paths,
Against a background of sea and blue hydrangeas –
   My cat and I grow old together.

                                  A. L. Rowse

Requiescat

Lines on the Death of a Cat

It is so important that my grief be not absurd.
Some part of me is under earth with the cat:
The black-and-white, the woman-looking cat –
(Children sob for dogs, dead aunts only frighten them)
This is the stammering sincerity of the humbled.

It is so important that you should not laugh –
Some life that loved me is sordidly ceased.
Me out of a world of betters this free warm thing
Sought me and me at every instant. Who now
Seeks so? None. I pray you do not smile:
For o it is so important my grief be not absurd.

John Gallen

The Early Purges

I was six when I first saw kittens drown.
Dan Taggart pitched them, 'the scraggy wee shits',
Into a bucket; a frail metal sound,

Soft paws scraping like mad. But their tiny din
Was soon soused. They were slung on the snout
Of the pump and the water pumped in.

'Sure isn't it better for them now?' Dan said.
Like wet gloves they bobbed and shone till he sluiced
Them out on the dunghill, glossy and dead.

Suddenly frightened, for days I sadly hung
Round the yard, watching the three sogged remains
Turn mealy and crisp as old summer dung

Until I forgot them. But the fear came back
When Dan trapped big rats, snared rabbits, shot crows
Or, with a sickening tug, pulled old hens' necks.

Still, living displaces false sentiments
And now, when shrill pups are prodded to drown
I just shrug, 'Bloody pups'. It makes sense:

'Prevention of cruelty' talk cuts ice in town
Where they consider death unnatural,
But on well-run farms pests have to be kept down.

From *Death of a Naturalist* by Seamus Heaney

A Writer's Cat

The sea throws up fishes and ideas;
Two children dressed as penguins walk by its edge in a
carnival parade.
I remember the day a favourite cat died.
At dawn I carried him into the garden and laid him on a bed
of mint,
Still breathing.
The eyes I had known for almost thirteen years followed me
about.
When the post arrived, he gave a short purr:

It had been his habit since a kitten.
It was his last link with my world of manuscripts and books.
Our parting would be soon.

Later when I wrapped him in an old cardigan
I thought of Anatole France and St Maël's baptism of the
penguins
And how St Catherine had said:
'Give them souls – but tiny ones.'

I will settle for that
For my cat.

Neville Braybrook

The Big Sleep

15 December 1950

Our little black cat had to be put to sleep yesterday morning. We feel pretty broken up about it. She was almost 20 years old. We saw it coming, of course, but hoped she might pick up strength. But when she got too weak to stand up and practically stopped eating, there was nothing else to do. They have a wonderful way of doing it now. They inject nembutal into a vein in the foreleg and the animal just isn't there any more. She falls asleep in ten seconds. Pity they can't do it to people.

A letter from Raymond Chandler to H. N. Swanson in
The World of Raymond Chandler, ed. Miriam Gross

Peacefully, at Home

We have lost our dear old cat Tom, the black and white one, in his 16th year – peacefully at his home in West Oxfordshire at the end of January. He had been getting very fragile and thin (and very trying too!) but we didn't have to take him to the vet. He just quietly expired on a copy of *The Times* one Saturday morning. When he became cold the fleas left his body – I suppose that was how one knew he had really gone. I'd never seen that happen before. We still have Minerva, our brindled tortoiseshell.

Part of a letter from Barbara Pym to Philip Larkin, 6 March 1976,
From *A Very Private Life*, Barbara Pym, Hazen Holt and Hilary Pym eds.

N.B. Minerva lived to an even riper old age, largely on a preferred diet of fried tomato skins and custard.

Killing Willie

Ernest Hemingway had so many cats that he had to have a separate house built to accommodate them, but he still mourned the death of a favourite, as Mary Walsh Hemingway remembers.

As I came down from the tower after sunning on February 20 [1953], I found our cat Willie hunching himself forward along the terrace, all tilted to starboard. Willie was smiling and purring and his gray-and-black striped coat looked still shiny from his morning lick-bath. But his right forepaw was doubled under. He was crawling on the knee. Then I saw with horror that his back hip was broken, a bit of bone protruding through the fur. 'Willie, Willie, wait,' I moaned, stroking his head. He was heading for the Cat House, our cats' sanctum. I ran to Ernest in his room and panted, 'Something terrible has happened to Willie. He's all broken apart.' Ernest came back unbelieving from wherever he was in his manuscript. We went out and there was Willie near the Cat House door, purring, no blood showing. Tears were making rivulets down my cheeks as Ernest examined him.

'You think he's hurt internally? Could we make splints for him?'

'Don't handle him. Don't let him see you cry. Splints no good.'

'A plaster cast?' René had joined us, and Roberto.

'Get me the .22,' Ernest said.

'No. No. No. Why can't we try a plaster cast? Why can't we get a vet? Why does this have to be so quick?' I was blubbering.

'He's too smashed up. He'll begin to feel it soon.'

I ran to my refuge, my bed.

The happenings of that day gave us no chance to try to assimilate our grief. While René held Willie gently in his arms and Ernest shot him in the head, a Cadillac stopped at the front steps, having ignored the signs on the gate, and a young man and his white-coated attendant emerged. Before anybody could stop them they were inside the house, the attendant saying their clinic for the mentally deranged had given them permission to come to Cuba to visit Ernest, as I heard it through the door as I dressed for lunch. The young man spoke cruel phrases – 'An interesting time to arrive . . . Hemingway crying because he has shot a cat . . . He loves cats . . . so he shoots them.' I waited for the sounds of a shot and a body collapsing but heard only conversation and the front screen door announcing their departure.

When the boys had been children, Willie had been Patrick's and Gregory's favourite cat and had elected himself a non-cat people's chum except when the lure of bird hunting overtook him. To strangers he presented a conservative banker's mien, aloof and businesslike. But with friends he allowed himself to be picked up, cradled, his stomach stroked, or he would dance across the floor.

From *How It Was* by Mary Walsh Hemingway

Poem for Pekoe

Our lives were only half gone
when she had used up

all her nine. Time came
upon her like a sledgehammer:

her insides dropped, she
waddled like a duck,

her belly ballooned,
not with child – she'd

never kittened, early on
was 'fixed.' Her belly

carried cancer and stones,
her muscles too flaccid

ever to tighten again.
Her bowels moved wherever,

she who had been so
extremely fastidious.

The vet said she had
only days, not months.

But the alertness!
The grandmotherly face!

We hoped. Then she couldn't
eat. You tried everything.

She became a wire sculpture.
Still we couldn't stand

to 'put to sleep'
a life that'd been family

for fourteen years – traveling
to Austria, France, Italy,

uncomplaining in her carrying
case. I was away

the day you had to
have them do it.

When I called I said,
'What's new?' – then heard.

And though our two new cats
are handsome, I cannot

stroke them long. They
never stay in my lap

as if to say they know.

                                        Robert Phillips

Bunch – A Cat

I opened a book
And on the white glossed page
 Are the two brown pad prints
   You made.

  Down the garden path
  I watch the delicate tread
Of your feathered feet round the little bright pools
   And your questioning head;

       I see your body sweep
    Up the trunk and along the green boughs
       Of the apple trees,
     Then a clawed pad dip to thrust
At the hand that gently shakes a branch beneath
      And your beating, swaying brush.
    And still with shivering desire you creep
Where angry sparrows shrill battle in the peas,
     Where the fledgling thrushes hide,
Or the bold chaffinch tempts with frantic cheep and chide
    From his nesting mate in the elder tree.
A hundred times in vain you poise, you leap;
      Crestfallen, stand denied.
     Yet too often a broken body hangs
     Limp, in your tiger fangs.
Or you stalk, ever near and nearer,
White butterflies that flit in the sun
From sweet alyssum to fragrant phlox,
From crimson snap-dragons to lofty hollyhocks;
    And the warm dusk June nights every one
You lie deep hid in the mowing grass
Till the little white moths float crazily by
    And you follow running, leaping high.

      After milk is lapped
   By the winter fireside, on the rug,
And the dangling hare's foot tempts to no game
     On my knees you settle snug,
     Warm bunch of sweet-smelling fur,
And with rushing wind, clock tick, rustle of flame
    Drowses your sing-song purr.

You'll not come again
In your dear imperious way
To drum at the window pane
    On a rainy day;
  Never bite, clutch, kick
The hand a small rough tongue would after lick;
    No wind shall stir
   That soft luxuriance, your tawny fur;

In your Spring, in your body's pride,
Jet, amber, red-brown coated, agate-eyed,
  We found you in your form,
  Curled in your wonted bed
    Asleep and warm,
     But dead.

Claude Colleer Abbott

The Acquiescent Cat

John Middleton Murry's daughter Katherine remembers one little unloved cat with guilt, but its passing proved a key to her own unhappy relationship with her stepmother.

Once, a few years ago, I had a little female cat. For some reason I did not love this cat as I have always loved the others. She got on my nerves. She was too fawning, she had none of that proud independence I associate with the feline race. Sometimes I even hated that cat. She became ill and still I hated her. I nursed her forcibly, opening her jaws to make her take her medicine, but I did not love her. I was torn between hatred and remorse and pity. It was a vile, sick feeling and the more I hated her the more she came and rubbed herself against my legs, miaowing. She hardly grew at all but in the spring her belly swung between her paws with new life.

Then she became ill again and disappeared. The gardener next door found her in an outhouse, dead. He called to me over the hedge and gave her to me, and I went and fetched a spade, took the animal on a sack into the wood and dug a hole. The sun filtered through the young green leaves, little beechnuts and acorns were thrusting out tender shoots, the birds were singing pure. I stared at the little cat lying on the sack, my heart filled with regret and pity. 'Why couldn't I love you?' I murmured, touching the soft fur. And as I put it into the hole a long shuddering sigh came from its body, the sigh of the unloved, a terrible reproach for all the dispossessed of this earth. I laid it very gently, and very gently covered it up with the soil that was bursting with life, and heavily made my way back up the path.

How could I, normally a fairly kind sort of person, have felt such an elemental passion of hatred for a creature so innocent?

It was a terrible question.

And in a flash, for the first time, I understood Betty. I was like the little cat, fawning, wanting, insisting on affection that she did not want to give me. I was there, a presence, a permanent accusation, speechlessly demanding a mother's love, the love that so many of us take for granted, are even irritated by or worse, this was my profoundest, unconscious need. With what eagerness I fetched and carried, with what docility I watched and learned to cook and do all those domestic things she was so good at; how ingratiatingly I slaved and skivvied for her, instead of doing my homework.

Thus, I thought, I would earn her love. By doing all I could. Mute so as not to anger the gorgon, careful not to encourage my father's expression of his love for me lest that very gorgon unleash its jealous fury. No glance, no flicker of an eyelash would betray the inner me. Poetry I loved, but since she associated it with my father, his books, his world that drove her into uncontrollable rages, I would read in secret, hiding in the greenhouse behind the boxes of tomato plants and mustard and cress, in the warmth of the little oil-stove.

> Many a green isle
> Needs must be . . .

But I am now convinced that, like the little cat, the more I tried, the more I desired her love, the more she spurned me. She needed someone to fight her, not to acquiesce.

From *Beloved Quixote* by Katherine Middleton Murry

Cat

Not all cats manage to inspire abiding love in their owners but most contrive, in one way or another, to be unforgettable.

Cat arrived one day on the doorstep, only about four inches long, and his face lopsided from a kick. Since no cat has ever been turned away from any doorstep beyond which I or any member of my family lives, he was taken in and fed and, knowing a good thing when he saw one, announced that he was going to remain (he did this by crawling under the stove and flatly refusing to come out for three days). Unfortunately, the kick had permanently disfigured him, and his face never grew straight again. This did not seem to worry him at all, though he looked bizarre, as a great length of pink tongue always hung, unretractably, from the corner of his mouth. One day, sleeping in the sun over the porch, he rolled off and fell to the ground, landing on his head and biting off the surplus tongue. To our astonishment, all he did was to unroll a fresh length, which protruded as far as before, though the end of it was now concave in shape.

Cat, incidentally, later on fell from a windowledge two storeys up, and sur-
vived even that, though I think he was never quite right in the head thereafter.
Later still, he developed some problem with his jaw, as well he might, and was
in great pain; we suggested having him put to sleep, but the vet would not hear
of it, briskly saying that all he needed was to have his teeth out. Out they came,
and he was as fit as ten immediately, though the fact that the two canine teeth
had been left, combined with his by now very irregularly shaped face, made
him look like a feline Dracula. He never seemed to have any trouble eating,
though he never learnt the trick of doing so with his paw like the one in the
television advertisement. Cat died of a fit.

From 'The Life and Times of Smoky Dostoievski' by Bernard Levin

Sonnet: Cat Logic

Cat sentimentality is a human thing. Cats
are indifferent, their minds can't comprehend
the concept 'I shall die', they just go on living.
Death is more foreign to their thought than
to us the idea of a lime-green lobster. That's
why holding these warm containers of purring fur
is poignant, that they just don't *know*.
Life is in them, like the brandy in the bottle.

One morning a cat wakes up, and doesn't feel
disposed to eat or wash or walk. It doesn't panic
or scream: 'My last hour has come!' It
simply fades. Cats never go grey at the edges
like us, they don't even look old. Peter Pans,
insouciant. No wonder people identify with cats.

Gavin Ewart

An Unusual Cat Poem

My cat is dead
But I have decided not to make a big tragedy out of it.

From *Serious Concerns* by Wendy Cope

Never Again

Growing up on a farm in Rhodesia, a young Doris Lessing encountered love and bitter loss.

After a certain age – and for some of us that can be very young – there are no new people, beasts, dreams, faces, events: it has all happened before, they have appeared before, masked differently, wearing different clothes, another nationality, another colour; but the same, the same, and everything is an echo and a repetition; and there is no grief even that it is not a recurrence of something long out of memory that expresses itself in unbelievable anguish, days of tears, loneliness, knowledge of betrayal – and all for a small, thin, dying cat.

I was sick that winter. It was inconvenient because my big room was due to be whitewashed. I was put in the little room at the end of the house. The house, nearly but not quite on the crown of the hill, always seemed as if it might slide off into the maize fields below. This tiny room, not more than a slice off the end of the house, had a door, always open, and windows, always open, in spite of the windy cold of a July whose skies were an interminable light clear blue. The sky, full of sunshine; the fields, sunlit. But cold, very cold. The cat, a bluish-grey Persian, arrived purring on my bed, and settled down to share my sickness, my food, my pillow, my sleep. When I woke in the mornings, my face turned to half-frozen linen; the outside of the fur blanket on the bed was cold; the smell of fresh whitewash from next door was cold and antiseptic; the wind lifting and laying the dust outside the door was cold – but in the crook of my arm, a light purring warmth, the cat, my friend.

At the back of the house a wooden tub was let into the earth, outside the bathroom, to catch the bathwater. No pipes carrying water to taps on that farm: water was fetched by ox-drawn cart when it was needed, from the well a couple of miles off. Through the months of the dry season the only water for the garden was the dirty bathwater. The cat fell into this tub when it was full of hot water. She screamed, was pulled out into a chill wind, washed in permanganate, for the tub was filthy and held leaves and dust as well as soapy water, was dried, and put into my bed to warm. But she sneezed and wheezed and then grew burning hot with fever. She had pneumonia. We dosed her with what there was in the house, but that was before antibiotics, and so she died. For a week she lay in my arms purring, purring, in a rough trembling hoarse little voice that became weaker, then was silent; licked my hand; opened enormous green eyes when I called her name and besought her to live; closed them, died, and was thrown into the deep shaft – over a hundred feet deep it was – which had gone dry, because the underground water streams had changed their course one year and left what we had believed was a reliable well a dry, cracked, rocky shaft that was soon half filled with rubbish, tin cans and corpses.

That was it. Never again. And for years I matched cats in friends' houses, cats in shops, cats on farms, cats in the street, cats on walls, cats in memory, with that gentle blue-grey purring creature which for me was the cat, the Cat, never to be replaced.

From Particularly Cats by Doris Lessing

The Death of a Cat

Since then, those months ago, these rooms miss something,
A link, a spark, and the street down there reproves
My negligence, particularly the gap
For the new block which, though the pile of timber
Is cleared on which he was laid to die, remains
A gap, a catch in the throat, a missing number.

You were away when I lost him, he had been absent
Six nights, two dead, which I had not learnt until
You returned and asked and found how he had come back
To a closed door having scoured the void of Athens
For who knows what and at length, more than unwell
Came back and less than himself, his life in tatters.

Since when I dislike that gap in the street and that obdurate
Dumb door of iron and glass and I resent
This bland blank room like a doctor's consulting room
With its too many exits, all of glass and frosted,
Through which he lurked and fizzed, a warm retort,
Fourd room for his bag of capers, his bubbling flasket.

For he was our puck, our miniature lar, he fluttered
Our dovecot of visiting cards, he flicked them askew,
The joker among them who made a full house. As you said,
He was a fine cat. Though how strang to have, as you said
   later,
Such a personal sense of loss. And looking aside
You said, but unconvincingly: What does it matter?

Extract from 'The Death of a Cat' by Louis MacNeice
From The Collected Poems of Louis MacNeice, ed. E. R. Dobbs

ACKNOWLEDGEMENTS

First, my thanks are due to Laura Brady, who assisted in the research for this volume and whose tireless archival excavations for feline references in prose, verse, letters and lives has turned up many delights and curiosities. Thanks also to Martin Carpenter, whose reading fell under whiskery influences during the compilation of the work. I am indebted to Beatrice Doran, librarian at the Royal College of Surgeons in Ireland, who generously put her own remarkable collection of cat anthologies at my disposal and to many other helpful librarians, in particular Maire Kennedy at the Gilbert Library in Pearse Street, Eilis ni Dhuibhne at the National Library of Ireland and Jan Chapman, Far Eastern Curator of the Chester Beatty Library. Friends and literary acquaintances too numerous to mention have chipped in with lit. kits but especially helpful have been Noeleen Dowling, Alan Wilkes, Francis King, Niall McMonagle, Michael Holroyd, Umberto Eco, Professor Joel Conarroe, Clive Fisher, Christopher Hawtree and Paul Ryan. A particular thanks is due to those authors, publishers, agents and executors who endeavoured to make extracts available at affordable prices; and to Hilary Frost who undertook the momentous task of clearing permissions and especially to Roger Cazalet, my editor, for endless patience, encouragement and support. A debt of gratitude is also due to all the compilers of previous cat anthologies whose diligence and humour have afforded much inspiration; I hope this volume will do the same for someone else. A kind of thanks is due to Gertie, my cat, under whose baleful eye this companion was compiled and who acted as a censor, reminding me that pretension and sentiment are inappropriate to her species, as indeed is gratitude, so I shall just leave out something for her to steal and call it quits.

INDEX